The Role of Modern Accounting Practices in Businesses, Financial Stability, and Sustainable Development

Ibrahim Mert

The Role of Modern Accounting Practices in Businesses, Financial Stability, and Sustainable Development

During Digital Era and Artificial Intelligence Applications

PETER LANG

Lausanne • Berlin • Bruxelles • Chennai • New York • Oxford

Library of Congress Cataloging-in-Publication Data
A CIP catalog record for this book has been applied for at the Library of Congress.

Bibliographic Information published by the Deutsche Nationalbibliothek
The Deutsche Nationalbibliothek lists this publication in the Deutsche Nationalbibliografie; detailed bibliographic data is available online at http://dnb.d-nb.de.

ISBN 978-3-631-89425-5 (Print)
E-ISBN 978-3-631-89433-0 (E-PDF)
E-ISBN 978-3-631-89434-7 (EPUB)
DOI 10.3726/b20454

Published by
Peter Lang GmbH, Berlin, Deutschland

info@peterlang.com - www.peterlang.com

This publication has been peer reviewed.

To my little worth the world children, Deniz Ali and Ayse Dilan,
the time was allocated for this book, instead of feeling their childhood.

Preface

After COVID-19, the methods of the business and the associated process have been changed. The pandemic has brought new challenges for the employers and business owners. The economies of the states have also suffered. Modern business methods have been changed overall. Accounting plays a key role in the monitoring and management of businesses. Accounting helps business owners and managers in organizing valuable transactions and keeping information about the cash flows, credits, balance, and overall financial position of the business. Maintaining the record of the financial transactions, providing the information about the credits, loans, cash flows, preparation of the financial reports for the internal and external users, forecasting the feasibility of the business in future, auditing, and helping the businesses in surviving the tough situations, the accountants without any doubt play a significant role in the businesses. The accounting profession has also served the needs of the governments of the states. The roles and the responsibilities of the accountants may vary in the project and product-based companies; however, the purpose of the job is the same. In the first chapter of the book, a comprehensive detail on the role of accountants in the project and product-based companies have been provided. The role of the accountant in the process and success of the new product development is also explained in detail in the first chapter of the book. A case study highlighting the role of the management accountants in the success of the company and business has been presented.

Financial reporting done by accountants have got a significant impact on the decision-making process of the management, investors, and shareholders. The financial reports serve the needs of both internal and external users. The interest, information required, and the parameters needed vary for the internal and external users. In the second chapter of the book, a detailed description related to the needs and interests of both internal and external users have been provided. The characteristics of the financial reports prepared for the internal and external users have been briefly described. Cash flow-based statements, income statements, and the accrual and historic convention in the accounting have been explained. Accounting standards requirements and the legislative requirements related to the financial statements have been briefly described in the second chapter of the book.

Financial stability can be defined as the ability to expedite and strengthen economic processes, manage risks and nullify shocks. Financial stability is considered a continuous field, varying over time and consistent with the various combinations of the integral elements of finance. An attempt has been made to describe financial stability clearly from different perspectives is made in the third chapter of the book. The concept of the financial crisis and the need for the standardization and implementation of the financial stability policy has been described. The credit crisis that initially occurred in London, and then Europe has also suffered from this crisis has been explained. The Great Depression of 1929–39 has been mentioned. This was the worst economic crisis of the 20th century. It was believed that the major cause of The Great Depression was the Wall Street crash of 1929 and bad policy decisions by the US government at that time. This crisis lasted for 10 years causing a great deal of poverty, unemployment, income loss on a very large scale. Past experiences have shown that financial crisis or financial downfall cause a great economic and financial imbalance in the society which not only affects the financial institution but also cover every aspect of life. If the banking system is collapsed then every party involved in transaction or banking activities will suffer. A Lot of factors contribute to these crises like an unstable macroeconomic environment, significant distortion in the economy. The major sources of financial instability have been mentioned. The macroeconomic sources of vulnerability such as instability, inflation, liberalization, and design failure of macroeconomic policies have been explained. For the complete description of financial stability, it is necessary to understand the characteristics of both financial stability and financial instability. The features of financial stability have been mentioned and described in the text. One of the most important features of financial stability is that financial stability should not be so demanding that it classifies any change as evidence of instability because as we know small to large losses can occur financially. Financial structures need to adapt to the variation in the economy. If any entity tries to stop that kind of change, then it may result in a great imbalance. The key principles for the definition of financial stability have also been mentioned. The development of financial stability can't be measured and quantized as a unit. Unlike price stability, there is not a single unit that can be used to measure financial stability. This shows that financial stability is multi-dimensional with a variety of variables. Since the implementation of financial stability is very crucial, all preventive measures should be taken to ensure that system doesn't move toward instability. In this regard, various preventive measures have been discussed. Accounting plays a vital role in the achievement of financial stability. The economy is very much dependent on financial statements. Financial institutions and organizations make their planning and a lot of decisions based on these statements. There are two types of accounting approach, one is the principle-based accounting standard and the other is the rule-based accounting approach. Both have their practical applications and pros and cons. The most common practice is the principle-based approach but some countries use the rule-based approach also. Accounting standards must be designed in such a way that they generate financial statements that give a detailed explanation of the economic substance of activities. Criterion 1 to 9 have been discussed, and the role of accounting in the achievement of financial stability has been discussed. The financial stability within the context of the IFRS standards has been discussed.

Bankruptcy is a legal process in which a person, organization or business gets relief in case they are unable to pay their debts to creditors. They get relief from a portion of their debt or maybe all of it depending upon various situations. The bankruptcy and insolvency, and types of insolvency have also been discussed. The differences to distinguish between insolvency and bankruptcy have been discussed. Several types of bankruptcy are identified in the form of chapters. They vary from the liquidation of assets to payment plans and many other options. Chapters 7, 11, 12, and 13 have been discussed. The advantages and disadvantages of filing for bankruptcy have been discussed. For a detailed understanding related to bankruptcy, it is necessary to understand the historical details under which the concept of bankruptcy has been realized. Bankruptcy in the Ancient World and the middle-ages have been discussed. And the Roman law of Bankruptcy has also been defined.

Keeping in view the recent changes in the climate, and the scarcity of resources, the concept of sustainable development was realized, and the proper planning related to the implementation came into the effect. The concept of sustainable development can be defined in simpler terms as the development made by human society in such a way that capacity and resources for the development of future generations remain available. International organizations particularly UNESCO, World Bank, and UN itself are emphasizing the practical implementation of the goals of sustainable development. Sustainable development, directly and indirectly, affects the method and workflow of all human activities. UNESCO has highlighted four main dimensions of sustainable development, which are, society, environment, culture or norms, and economics. For sustainable development, the progress and growth parameters are needed to be achieved in all of the four dimensions. Since all of these four dimensions are closely associated with each other. It is important to understand that environmental degradation directly impacts the economic as well as the infrastructural development. The concepts of sustainable development and sustainable economic development have been explained in detail.

In the seventeenth session of the United Nations General Assembly, a resolution named "Transforming our world: the 2030 Agenda for Sustainable Development" was adopted on 25th September 2015. In the agenda, 17 sustainable development goals and 169 targets were declared. More emphasis in this book has been laid on the description of economic and sustainable economic development. Since the accounting profession has been a key contributor in the field of development economics, and the accountants play a key role and hold an important responsibility in the society, the role of the accountants in achieving the goals and targets of sustainable development has been explored and described. IFAC has identified eight goals which the accounting profession and the professionals can focus on and contribute significantly to the implementation of the new sustainable development agenda of united nations 2030. In this text, the eight goals and targets that were defined by the IFAC have been explained, and the measures that the accounting profession and the professionals have taken in the achievement of these goals have been highlighted. The contribution of the profession in quality education, gender equality, and the incorporation of decency in the work pattern has been described.

The reliance on the use and implementation of communication and information technologies has increased significantly. With innovations happening in every domain of life, the utilization of advanced information technologies is of utmost importance for the smooth flow of operations. Digitalization has changed the workflows of processes in almost all professions and industries. The incorporation digital and modern computer-based methods have resulted in the achievement of accurate and reliable results, and the efficiency of the processes has increased manifolds. The usage of information technology in accounting has already delivered desirable and fruitful results. The impact of information technology on the accounting profession and practices has been explained. The benefits of computerized accounting systems have been described. Modern computer-based tools used in accounting practices have increased the efficiency of the process, reduced human effort, and resulted in the minimization of the chances of error. To improve the understanding of how to better manage the operations and transfer of data, modern technologies like artificial intelligence, machine learning, big data, data analytics and data science, etc., are utilized in accounting and finance domains. A detailed description of the modern tools in the accounting profession has been provided. The role and benefits associated with the usage of ERP (Efficient Resource Planning) and CRM (Customer Relationship Management) have been explained. The accounting profession requires intensive decision making. The uncertainty and risk associated with the decisions can be minimized using the techniques of Artificial Intelligence and Machine Learning. The usage of Cognitive Computing models such as IBM Watson has opened new pathways in the process of augmented thinking. Artificial intelligence can be directly used in accounting. Various tools and techniques for auditing and assurance have been developed, since the auditing, auditing tasks, and the environment involves a lot of risk and uncertainty, and complexity as well. In general, the usage of Artificial Intelligence, machine learning for expert accounting systems and task automation has been explained. By using modern methods such as cognitive computing based on AI, the complexity involved in accounting practices can be handled easily.

In general, the role of accounting in businesses, and the achievement of financial stability has been explained. Moreover, the role of accounting in achieving the goals of sustainable development has been explained. The overall contribution of accounting to the economic development in specific and the general sustainable development of the society, in general, has been highlighted. A review of the literature has also been done to study the contributions and findings of the previous research. The modern methods and computer-based tools that are currently employed in accounting and also have the potential of modifying or changing the workflows of accounting practices have been described in detail. The use and implementation of financial and accounting terminologies have been highlighted in detail. The concepts of financial stability, bankruptcy, and insolvency have also been explained to highlight the role of accounting in each of these. The aspects of the financial reporting, and types of financial reports have been described briefly. The role of the financial statements has been highlighted.

Foreword

In this book, the role of modern accounting practices in issues such as ensuring financial stability and sustainable growth in different businesses is examined in detail. The subject of the book is examined under the titles such as financial reporting, the role of accounting practices in ensuring financial stability and financial stability, the consequences such as bankruptcy that may arise as a result of failure to provide financial stability, and the contribution of accounting practices in sustainable growth, and the subject is clarified with a case study.

In our age, when digital applications such as artificial intelligence have become daily necessities, it was unthinkable for accounting to stay away from these realities. In this book, recent applications such as artificial intelligence, big data and smart contracts are examined in terms of their effects on financial reports. Ibrahim also mentioned this interaction in his book, giving examples from digital applications and presenting the contributions of these applications to the accounting and financial audit processes. In the explanation of the subject with its financial dimensions, including the application and sample tables and graphics explaining the subject under each title contributed to the explanation of the subjects. I believe that these approaches will provide important contributions to students, researchers and practitioners.

I believe that the book will contribute to master's and doctoral students, researchers and practitioners, thanks to its theoretical and exemplary application model.

Istanbul, September 2022

Assoc. Prof. Dr. Huseyin MERT
huseyin.mert@okan.edu.tr

Acknowledgement

It is a great happiness for me to get this book to be published by one of the most distinguished publishing company, Peter Lang. Other than publishing my doctorate thesis by Springer Nature, this will be my first book published.

It was almost a four-year length to conclude and make this book ready for publication. Since starting to write this book, my children are four years older now. For this reason, I first of all thank to my lovely children Deniz Ali and Ayse Dilan because I saved lots of hours from sharing life with them. I also thank to my wife, Gulay, because she has more responsibilities during these four years.

I would also thank Esra Bahsi, Senior Commissioning Editor in Peter Lang, because of enlightening me about future steps of publishing process.

I also need to thank Kalyani Kanekal, Editorial Assistant in Peter Lang, for her contributions on final process and procedures.

Other than above mentioned names, I thank the persons who contributed for preparing this book.

Table of Contents

List of Abbreviations

ABC	Activity Based Costing
ACCA	Association of Chartered Certified Accountants
AFS	Available for Sale
AI	Artificial Intelligence
BCBS	Basel Committee on Banking Supervision
BIS	Bank for International Settlements
BOQ	Bill of Quantities
BSC	Banking Supervision Committee
BSE	Bombay Stock Exchange
BTB	Balanced Target Books
CEBR	Center of Economics and Business Research
CEO	Chief Executive Officer
CFO	Chief Financial Officer
CGMA	Chartered Global Management Accountant
CIMA	Chartered Institute of Management Accountants
CIO	Chief Information Officer
CPA	Certified Public Accountant
CRM	Customer Relationship Management
CSA	Community Supported Agriculture
CSR	Corporate Social Response
DSS	Decision Support Systems
ECB	European Central Bank
ECL	Expected Credit Loss
ERP	Efficient Resource Planning
ERP	Enterprise Resource Planning
ESCB	European System of Central Banks
ESG	Economic, Social, and Governance
EU	European Union
EAD	Exposure at Default
FASB	Financial Accounting Standards Board
FSB	Financial Stability Board
GAAP	Generally Accepted Accounting Principle
GCP	Google Cloud Platform
GDP	Global Domestic Products
GE	General Electric

GRI	Global Reporting Initiative
HR	Human Resources
IAS	International Accounting Standards
IASB	International Accounting Standards Board
ICIA	Institute of Chartered Accountants of India
IFAC	International Federation of Accountants
IFRS	International Financial Reporting Standards
IISD	International Institute for Sustainable Development
IMF	International Monetary Fund
IRS	International Reporting Standards
ISAR	International Standards of Accounting and Reporting
ISSB	International Sustainability Standards Board
IT	Information Technology
JQI	Joint Quality Initiative
LGF	Loss Given Default
ML	Machine Learning
MMS	Modern Manufacturing Systems
MSME	Micro, Small and Medium-sized Enterprises
NGO	Non-Government Organizations
NPD	New Product Development
NPD&D	New Product Development and Design
OPEC	Organization of the Petroleum Exporting Countries
PD	Probability of Default
PwC	PricewaterhouseCoopers
QbD	Quality by Design
RTGS	Real Time Gross settlement
SGD	Signed
SMB	Small and Medium Businesses
SMEGA	Small and Medium-sized Enterprises Guidance
STEM	Science, Technology, Engineering, and Mathematics
TCD	Technical Concept Description
UNCTAD	United Nations Conference on Trade and Development
UNESCO	United Nations Educational, Scientific and Cultural Organization
US	United States
USD	United States Dollar
XGBoost	Extreme Gradient Boosting

1 Introduction

The accounting profession plays a diverse role in society to ensure the efficient utilization of economic resources. Keeping in view the sustainable development goals and changes in the businesses in the fourth era of industrialization. The traditional role of the accountant from bookkeeping has been evolved to more diverse and more impactful. Accountants around the globe provide their services and implement useful cost control strategies in product and project-based firms. The role of the accountants in strategic decisions related to the new product development is important for the success of the product. In the first chapter, the role of the accountant and accounting profession has been explained in detail. A case study related to the premium auto group has also been added to demonstrate the role of management accountants in the decision-making process.

One of the key responsibilities of accountants working in businesses and industries is to generate financial statements. The financial statements serve the needs of internal and external users. There are some regulatory requirements related to the financial statements. Based on the financial statements, the investors decide about the investment decisions whether it would be the value for the resource to invest in this company or not. The financial statements should be able to provide information that is used in the calculation of the financial ratios. The financial ratios can be used to evaluate the performance of the firms. In Chapter 3, the financial statement of BMW has been presented to practically show the parameters included in the financial statements. A case study has also been included to make the readers aware of the information presented in the financial statements.

Financial stability is defined as the ability to expedite and strengthen economic processes, manage risks and nullify shocks. Processes to achieve financial stability must ensure that all transactions and financial activity must satisfy the monetary economy. Financial stability is associated with the careful utilization of resources and intelligent investment decisions. In Chapter 4, the financial crisis of different times has been discussed. The Credit Crisis of 1772, The Great Depression of 1929, The Asian Crisis of 1997, and the Global financial crisis of 2007–2008 has been discussed in detail. Instability, Inflation, Liberalization, and Design failures of the Macroeconomic policies are the Macroeconomic sources of vulnerability. These sources have been discussed in detail in Chapter 4. The preventive measures related to financial instability have also been discussed in Chapter 4.

In Chapter 5, the role of the accountant in achieving financial stability has been described. The financial reports provide accurate and meaningful information about the performance of the businesses and firms. Through efficient usage and analysis of the financial statements and reports, accountants can assess the risks, and formulate the methods to minimize the impacts of spillovers and avoid stressful situations. The ECB (European Central Bank) and Basel Committee on Banking Supervision coordinated with each other and came to a decision point about amendments of IAS39 regarding the importance of financial stability. The Banking Supervision Committee (BSC) of the European System of Central Banks (ESCB) thoroughly studied and analyzed that accounting standards are worthy to establish and maintain financial stability. The IFRS Accounting Standards related to financial stability have been discussed in Chapter 5. The financial stability board is an international organization that analyzes, monitor and make recommendations about maintaining financial stability internationally. Several countries are part of this board. The boards design practical measures for ensuring financial stability at the international level. At the end of the chapter, a case study has been included to demonstrate the role of long-term organizational investors on financial stability. Another case study related to the role of financial inclusion, governance quality, and its impact on financial stability has also been added.

In Chapter 6 different aspects of Bankruptcy and Insolvency have been explored. Several types of bankruptcy that are identified in the form of chapters, and explanation of different bankruptcy filing codes have been explained for the readers. A summary of the bankruptcy prediction and bankruptcy probability has been provided in the chapter to provide awareness about the different techniques and models used for bankruptcy prediction. A condition in which a person or company's total liabilities exceeds total assets than they become insolvent. Difference between bankruptcy and insolvency has been explained as well.

Sustainable development is a concept that is associated with the careful utilization of resources in such a way that these resources including the opportunity remains available for the future generations. Sustainable development can be defined in multiple ways. As per the definition of sustainable development from Oxford Languages, **"conductance of economic activities without the depletion of natural resources"**. In the seventeenth session of the United Nations General Assembly, a resolution named "Transforming our world: the 2030 Agenda for Sustainable Development" was adopted on 25th September 2015 (United Nations, 2015). The detailed agenda of the sustainable development 2030 was published and is also available at the website of the United Nations sustainable development goals. In the agenda, 17 sustainable development goals and 169 targets were declared (United Nations, 2015). There are three main dimensions of sustainable development. These dimensions are economic, social, and environmental. The sustainable developmental practices need to be incorporated in all of these dimensions simultaneously. The concept of sustainable economic development has been discussed in detail in Chapter 7. After the approval and adoption of the sustainable development agenda in 2015 and 2016 respectively, IFAC has identified eight goals that the accounting profession and the professionals can focus on and contribute significantly to the implementation of the new sustainable development agenda of United Nations 2030. Some of these goals have been discussed in Chapter 7.

In the current era, a lot of focus of the development and productivity is on the information technology sector. Accounting practices and business methods are changed by the use of devices like computers, servers and personal devices like mobile. Transactions are done within a second because of the centralized banking system, whereas previously it would take hours or sometimes days because of lack of development. The role of information technology in the field of accounting has been discussed in detail in Chapter 8. The role that the technologies such as Artificial Intelligence, Machine Learning, and cloud computing are and can play to automate and integrate accounting tasks has been discussed in detail.

2 The Role of Accounting in Different Businesses

Abstract: The role of the accountant may be different in different sectors, but the purpose is the efficient and transparent utilization of the resources. Accountants play a very important role in the process of the product development in general and especially the new product development. The cost and price control strategy proposed by the accountants determine the success of product as well as ensure that product compete excellently in the market. A case study has also been included in this chapter to demonstrate the role of the management accountant in the supporting the strategic decisions of the successful company. The management accountant has got more diverse role in the society. Accountants working in the project and product-based companies employ different strategies to ensure the success of the business. The Accounting profession is directly associated with the economic development. Accountants not only play a positive role in supporting businesses but also help the government in making regulations related to the taxation, business transparency, and auditing.

Keywords: Role of Accounting, Function of Accounting, Effect of Accounting, Impact of Accounting.

The paradigms of global economics have changed due to the fast-paced technological development. The major change is associated with the pandemic of COVID-19. Various small to medium scale businesses have collapsed. The world has seen a major downsizing. The hospitality industry has suffered a lot. Over the period of six months, it is estimated that more than 60 million Americans have applied for unemployment insurance (Borden et al., 2020). The ways of doing work have changed. The market trends have also changed, and variations in these trends are abrupt, complex, and drastic. A significant portion of the modern workforce consists of remote workers, the number of remote workers working in different companies have increased significantly since the spread of COVID-19. Employers, as well as employees, have learned the pros and cons of remote working, the businesses have changed their working and marketing methodologies. The nature of the capital and wealth has also changed. Moreover, the term "flexibility", has changed the working hours, place and methods.

The accounting systems developed across the world have a purpose to record financial transactions, and these recordings should be made in such a way that the management could make decisions to ensure the financial growth and prosperity of the company in future. The uncertainty of the financial markets and the increasingly complex relations of the variables that define the financial value of the capitals are making it difficult for businesses to attain financial stability. An accounting system can be generally referred to as the system that systematically measures, analyze and process, and transmit financial information regarding an economic agency (Lim, 2013).

The purpose of studying accounting systems, elements, and subtopics of the accounting system, is to understand the functioning and capabilities of the system and to analyze the methods that the system offers in achieving financial stability in the current situation of economic uncertainty. The accounting system operating in any firm can't be separated from the social as well as the process and operations taking place in and around the organizations (Mellemvik et al., 1988). Mellemvik et al., performed a comprehensive study about the reasons and the ways the accounting system is important for the local firms, agencies and organizations (Mellemvik et al., 1988). The functionality of the accounting system has been studied using the broader perspective (Mellemvik et al., 1988). From a general and classical point of view, the accounting system is based on the broad and diversified definitions and explanation of costing systems, management in accounting, budgeting techniques and financial accounting (Mellemvik et al., 1988). The social accounting system and consideration of the social factors in the accounting system will give a detailed understanding of the economic changes taking place at the level of the society, and how each group is involved in making economic contributions. As stone describes the social accounting system as a methodology of practically explaining and describing the economic activities in the system in the form of transactions between the established accounts, these activities should be recorded as a double-entry rule (Stone, 1951).

2.1 Why Do We Need an Accounting System?

One of the foremost and important questions related to an accounting system that usually arises in the mind of the general public and even in the minds of the people belonging to the operations and engineering background is why we need an accounting system? The answer can be simple if overall industry and businesses are considered. However, the fact that is established over the past few years is that almost every business requires an accounting system and accountants not only for keeping records of the financial activity, and for the long-term prosperity of the business. But the role that the accounting system plays in society is different for different entities. For some types of businesses, the accounting system provides more fruitful benefits compared to others.

This is the reason that in the past a huge amount of research has been done for identifying the role of accounting in society, medium and small enterprises, in social systems, and the socialists' states.

Ainsworth and Deines have provided a simpler yet very relatable and understandable concept of the business as, the business is mainly the exchange of services or items between the agencies that are beneficial for both agencies, and the business should be based on the fair-trade function (Ainsworth and Deines, 2017). The purpose of the business is to get a mutual benefit. Although intentionally or unintentionally, sometimes a party is more benefited by a business deal compared to another party. The business is based on the rule of supply and demand. Consumer demand is the main parameter involved in the business that motivates the business dealers to produce or arrange the goods that the customers are demanding. The variation of supply and demand defines the trends of the market. The study of supply and demand is a complex one, the idea of the customers' demands, market trends, and the need requires the understanding of customers' needs. The experts of marketing are required to identify the demands of the customers and market. Similarly, the business on any scale requires functionalities of different nature. If the company is product-based, then the production team would be responsible to produce the product in a timely and efficient manner. Financial experts in the company would be able to identify the amount of capital required for the production. The accounting professionals would be able to guide about the financial data available from the past sales, record every economic activity that occurred during the production, marketing and distribution. Therefore, a multi-functional approach is required to run a business successfully.

Accounting helps business owners and managers in organizing valuable transactions and keeping information about the cash flows, credits, balance, and overall financial position of the business. Based on this information, the future of the company can be predicted, and the decisions that can ensure prosperity for the business can also be ensured. These parameters are important irrespective of the size of the business. Apart from maintaining the record of the financial transactions, which is the major job the accountants do, a well-qualified accounting department in any business can help in the prediction of the cash flows, managing the budget, and forecasting the revenues. The prediction of the finances is the critical part of the job the accountants do to aid the management in taking financially sound and more feasible business decisions.

For the detailed understanding of the question of why we need accounting, the knowledge of the business operations is essential for understanding which business operations require the knowledge of accounting, and how accounting helps in integrating these business operations with each other. The understanding of the business operations and the changes in these operations over the period will give useful insight into the way accounting as a discipline is evolved. One of the fore most changes that have changed the business operations is technology. Technology has changed the methods of business operations. Marketing, for instance, has changed completely. The form of wealth and income has changed. So, in order to keep pace with the modern world, accounting has also developed and evolved from traditional bookkeeping to predicting the future moves for businesses.

2.2 Role of Accounting for Project-Based Companies

The role of accounting in a product-based company can be different from a project-based company. The project-based company relies on the different business ventures by offering the services in a different form. Some businesses provide academic to the clients, some types of firms offer human resource services, some firms are associated with the construction of medium and large-sized products, and some of the companies provide engineering solutions for the clients it would be beneficial to define the project first before going into the details of the accounting methods applied to the project. As Bragg has defined two main distinguishing features of the project, which are, the uniqueness of output, and the proper initiation and ending of the project (Bragg, 2014). This means that the project is intended to produce an output activity or a specific product. It would be a one-time job, and will not carry on. As the example in the book is provided, it is not as continuous as production or assembly line. It must be mentioned that the project can involve the manufacturing of a specific number of units, or the construction of several houses or buildings, once the construction or manufacturing is complete, the project ends. The second distinguishing feature of the project is that the activity has a start and ending date as stated in the contract of the project award. The project is not a continuous process. The ending or start date may get delayed due to certain circumstances, but the project must have an end. The company and the business are dependent upon the frequency, nature, and size of the projects. Sometimes it is difficult to survive in the cases when the overall economic conditions of the geography in which the company is situated. The main variables that the accountants deal with while working for project-based companies are revenue, billings, and cost including cost analysis. The financial transactions of the project are managed mainly. The concept of accounting principles is applied more rigorously as compared to other economic scenarios.

There are many phases of the project. Normally there is a bidding period. The bill of quantities (BOQ) and technical requirements are published by the project awarding agencies. The bill of quantities and bill of materials are the two main documents that define the scope, price, and size of the project. Mostly the project awarding body has to evaluate the financial as well as the technical bid for the evaluation of the profile, capabilities, and the approach to a specific project of the applicant company. In designing the financial bid, the accountants work along with the engineering or technical team to prepare the lowest possible, feasible, and yet profitable bids. The cost of the labor, material, outsourcing services, and other miscellaneous expenditures is calculated. The accountants evaluate the financial feasibility of the project. The tax in different forms associated with products, General Sales Tax etc. are also calculated. The estimation of the tools, inventory that is already the property of the company and can be utilized in the project is also evaluated by the accountants.

In general, the benefits and the cost of the projects are estimated by the accountants. the evaluation of the most profitable projects, and the projects that has resulted in the financial as well as the capital loss to the company are also needed to be evaluated to improvise the working for the future. The evaluation is also done before bidding that is it feasible and profitable for the company to invest time, material, resources, and engage man power for a particular project. The shipping cost of the material is also estimated. In case the company is awarded a project, the financial requirements of the main contractor, consultant, and managing the payment of the sub-contractors are included in the responsibilities of the accountants. Project based practices of accounting play an effective role in the management of the project by keeping track of the financial transactions and the progress of the project as well. The accountants play a critical role in the successful completion and handing over the project. The handing over phase also includes necessary tests, assurance that the requirements of the project have been met, and written statements of the client that all the requirements and tasks associated to the project have been completed. During the handing over period, the experts of the company help in initiation and running of the project for the client so that project awarding organization may not face any difficulty while running the project. After the fourth industrial revolution, the nature of the complexity of the projects across the globe has increased significantly. Project now involves extensive work of variable nature, sometimes multiple funding agencies are involved, and multiple contractors are working. Managing the resources, keeping track of the performance of the project as well as the individual contractors are the complex tasks that requires accountants to adopt the modern practices and tools as well. In the recent past, various projects carried out by the firms in Middle East were unique and first of their kind. For a company, it is always difficult to operate and manage the accounts in a foreign land. Such projects require the team of highly qualified and experienced accountants as well as trained managers.

2.2.1 Construction Accounting

For the projects related to construction and buildings, the construction-accounting plays its role for the proper estimation, allocation, as well as the management of the resources. The construction projects are different from other projects due to their complex nature and requirement. The costs involved in the construction projects are different from those of the regular business. These costs include the mobilization, shipping, delivery, packing, and even lifting up the materials from the project site upon the completion of the project. The construction companies employ the percentage completion approach, the revenue calculation is based on the estimated profit offered by the contract, and how much percentage of the project has been completed. It is also a common practice in the field of construction and building to left the unfinished contract. During these crucial moments, it is necessary to estimate the true cost of the project, utilize the cost accounting methods for the calculation of the profit and loss of the unfinished project. The regular business account for the sale of a business offers one to five categories of the products and sales, while the construction companies offer services and products of a wider range consisting of labor work, consultation, engineering equipment and estimation, designing, and the material. While offering a range of products and services, it is difficult to keep track of the costs, the expenses, and the exact break down of the profit.

The construction business usually involves direct and indirect costs as well. It is difficult for the accountants working in the construction company to calculate the direct and indirect costs coming from different sources. The project-based accounting concepts are practically applied to the construction accounting industries. The cost of the material itself, the currency, and shipping costs vary almost every day. For the construction accountants it requires experience and the ability of judgment to estimate the costs, calculate the profit, and consider for the losses keeping in view all these variations. The inaccurate calculations have resulted companies to face a huge loss in the construction projects.

There always exists an inconsistency with the projects in the construction market. Some of the seasons or can be termed as cycles are productive in which companies are doing multiple projects, while in some cases, there is a complete absence of the projects. Due to unpredictable circumstances, the contractors and construction companies are not able to maintain or retain a sizeable inventory and tools. As a consequence, the productivity of the company related to projects is not at full capacity at some instances, therefore a proper planning is required for the management of budget and to ensure the company faces minimal loss in any of the unpredictable circumstances.

The construction projects have a different payment method as mentioned above, the payment is made as per the milestone and progress of the project, and it is still delayed most of the time. Sometimes the payment is withheld due to multiple reasons. In such cases the management of the cash and cash flows requires accurate and precise tracking and handling. For Many business transactions general ledger serves the purpose, since the construction business and contractor-ship itself is different from the general business operations, therefore the job costing method is used for keeping a record of the financial transactions. For the construction projects, the job costing and general ledger both are utilized. The general ledger is used to keep the records of the company's finances, while the job costing is used to evaluate and record the financial activity at the project level. Job costing is based on the accumulation of individual cost of the material, labor, shipping, unloading, and overhead costs.

Another concept that is mentionable here as the part of the discussion is revenue recognition. Revenue recognition is a part of GAAP (Generally Accepted Accounting Principle) that is used to identify when the revenue and expenses are recognizable. This concept is applied due to the over delays in the payment. As mentioned above, the payment method in contractor construction is based on the completion of tasks. Billing is done, and the bills are checked and verified by the client, and finally payment is made. Due to these delays, accountants use the method of the income recognition. The traditional and fundamental methods that the contractors used are the cash method, contract completion method, and the percentage completion method. The delays in the payments causes difficulty for the contractors and the construction companies. As per ASC-606 guidelines, the contractor side accountants can now decide when to keep an entry for the revenue reorganization, either single point or overtime, it depends in the transferring the control. As it is stated and translated that the revenue is recognizable when the company is able to satisfy the performance obligation by transferring the good or service as promised (stated in the contract documents), that is the time period when the client is able to take control over the good and service. There are also some special methods that are used for billing in the construction related projects. One of them is fixed price billing method. Fixed price billing is based on the declaration and acceptance of the contract on the basis of the total estimated price of the project. This type of billing is further classified into two types, that are fixed hard price bid and the negotiable fixed price bid (Foundation Software, 2023). The hard type bid is based on the fact and statement that the project should be completed on the basis of this price under any circumstances. This can cause difficulty and loss for the construction company or the contractor, as the conditions of the project may change, the prices can be altered, and even the condition on the site is changed sometimes.

Keeping in view all the above-mentioned complications and difficulties associated with construction business, the accountants play a critical role in the proper management of the project, but also ensure that the company's financial situation is stable enough to survive and all the taxes are being paid. The role of accountants in the construction industry is significantly important not only for the projects but also for the companies as well

2.2.2 Details of the Project-Based Accounting

The project-based accounting practices should not be merged with the general accounting policies and protocols used in the business. Generally, the normal business transactions are mixed and dealt with the project related transactions, this is the reason that the breakdown of the transactions and categorization is not possible. As some of the details about the role of the project accountants' have been mentioned in the discussion above, more project specific role and accounting practices would be discussed here.

In some of the countries, it has been observed that the project accountants of the companies travel to the project sites, and aid directly aid the staff members and engineers in billing, and preparing the cost related documentations. The delivery challans, quotations, purchase orders, and approvals have to be compiled to form a complete billing document. This signifies the role that the accountants play directly in making a progress towards the completion of the project.

More specific duties of the project accountants gave been mentioned in the book published by Bragg (Bragg, 2014). The foremost job is the building of the project account for the project (Bragg, 2014). This aids in the systematic management of the project related accounting tasks, as a separate project account also helps in maintain the documents separately. The accounting department or the project accountant shall maintain the project related records, documents, contract, and a log of all the amendments that have been agreed upon. Authorization, access, and the security of the project related documents is being the important parameters that are fundamental to company's benefits and integrity. It should be assured that only the relevant staff and organizational members have got the access to project related documents, especially the account related documents.

The procedure for provision of access to the project account and the project related documents should be clearly defined and the higher management of the company should be taken in confidence related to the access and security policy associated with the project.

The account department should be in close and regular coordination with the company's own project manager. Daily updates, meeting memos, and progress should be first documented in rough form, and then the organized and structured summary of the progress should be documented, and if possible, the progress should be recorded in the graphical form as well. This step assures that the reporting is precise, organized, and meaningful. The progress documented in organized form will be presentable not only to the senior management but also to the client as well. The organization and presentation aspects of reporting reflects the capabilities and potential of the company, which directly and indirectly improves the reputation of the company. As mentioned previously, the authorization of transfer of funds into and from the project account as well as the documents should also be clearly defined (Bragg, 2014). One of the primary mistakes that the accountants do is the non-closure of the project account after the completion of the project. As soon as the project is completed and handed= over to the client the project should be immediately closed. The management if the account and the project account related documents is the fundamental responsibility of the project accountant. If possible, the management should appoint a qualified accountant and the duties shall remain exclusive to the project only, in this way the focus of the person should be entirely upon the improvement of costing, billing, and taxation related matters. For the proper management of the project-account and related financial matters, special planning and experience is required.

The invoices are one of the main indicators of the financial payment that has been agreed upon between the seller and buyer for the exchange of the product. The accountant also has the responsibility to review, study, give approval for the invoices supplied by the suppliers. The comparison of the quotations from the suppliers, and the price quoted for the project at the bidding state gives an overview about the fact that either company is obtaining supply profit, or is it facing the loss. In many countries, the labor works at per hour rate or hourly rate. The timesheets provide an indication for the actual working hours of the workers, this helps in defining the wages, as well as it allows the project managers to schedule and allot the work on hourly basis as well. The overhead charges related to the project should be calculated. The account total expenses and assets related to the project should be carefully reviewed.

Invoice is a document of commercial nature provided by the selling agency to the buying entity associated with the transaction sale. Often printed on the letter head of the seller. It indicates the product, amount of the product, quantities, mutually agreed upon prices.

Variance is an important parameter used to measure the spread of the numbers in data set (Hayes, 2021). The variance is an important statistical measurement parameter employed by the investors, and specifically by share traders and market analysts to evaluate volatility and market security (Hayes, 2021). Investors also use variance to determine the risk that is associated with an investment for determining that the investment is successful or not. One of the most suitable and proper use of the variance is the comparative performance analysis of the assets in the project for the proper allocation. The accountant should also determine the variances associated with the project.

As mentioned above, the accountants directly help in creation of the project bills. The project bills should be created timely, and after approval it should be presented within the timeframe to the client. The project expenses that have been incurred on the site or office or in any other manner other than bills should be evaluated. The write off approval should be done for the project related billings that cannot be billed. Sometimes, these types of the expenses accumulate to such large amount, that it becomes burden on the company. Timely evaluation can also aid in the reduction of the expenses that are not necessary. The success of the project and earning maximum profit is very much related to the financial management, asset management, resource allocation, and accurate categorization and recording of the financial transaction. The expenses, costs, billings, wages, and overheads need to be classified properly for the project.

2.2.2.1 Reporting for the Management

Volatility is the statistical evaluation or assessment parameter used for determining the dispersion of the return for market or security index (Hayes, 2021)

The report submitted to the management related to the project progress is necessary, so that any major change if required in the working mode of the workers, or payments, or any other alteration required should be implemented in timely manner. The accountants present the reports on the profitability of the project to the management. Many of the project require the material supply and services as well. Since the companies usually have the experience in dealing with such supply materials, as the firm has already used these materials in different other projects. Therefore, they know the potential buyers who can supply the material for reasonable cost. In this way the company earns profit on both supply and services as well. Proper reporting on the profitability can increase the possibility for the maximization of profit earning.

The variance reports collected by the accountant for the project should also be presented to the management so that the management is aware of the performance of the assets allocated to the project. There are many tasks and services that the company offers during the project and are not billed to client. The company can earn a lot of profit for such services in mega-projects especially. The project accountant has the detailed understanding of the services and materials that are currently being billed. The accountant should present proper reports to the management about the presence of the opportunities that can generate additional bills to the clients.

Most of the time many companies are handling different parts of the projects. And there are some services that the company has got experience in provision of these services, and the client has not allocated any agency to do the job. The accountant should highlight these opportunities to the management so that they can propose an increase in the scope of the project and bill as well. for example, of the company has the project for the construction of a building for a specific client, and the client hasn't yet decided to allocate any firm for finishing and painting the interior of the building, company can propose the service to the client if it seems profitable. For these opportunities, the costs, profits, and other expenses should be evaluated first.

One of the primary mistakes that is done by the companies handling the project is the inability to realize the nature as well as control the project fund. Therefore, it is always recommended that the project amount should be compared with the progress. The accountant should present the reports to the manager about the availability of the remaining fund for the completion of the project.

As mentioned above, one of the main duties of the project accountant is to evaluate the taxes related to the project it, document it, and help the company in submission of the tax. The tax payable by the company yearly as a business owner, and tax related to the projects that the company is doing. The governmental tax reports that have to be submitted on the yearly basis should be prepared by the project accountant. As the accounting department is fully aware of the company's financial position as well as the transactions, and the accountants also know the tax legalities, therefore the accountants are the most suitable persons in the company to record and submit tax related documents.

If the yearly or quarterly internal or external audit of the company is scheduled, the accountants should also make preparation for that as well. as stated by Bragg in his book, the accountants help the project-based company in Record management, expense monitoring, customer billings, reporting to management as well as the outside reporting.

It would be an interesting discussion to discuss the position of the project accountant in the hierarchy of the organization (Bragg, 2014). As Bragg has discussed and it also observed keeping in view the projects, the position or role of the project accountant is the extension of the role of the cost accountant. As the project involves multiple roles as defined above, and the responsibilities of the project accountant are broader and more extensive than the cost accountant. Bragg has proposed that depending on the magnitude of the company, size of the team, financial condition of the company, and the projects that the company is dealing with, it is more suitable that the project accounting department reports directly to the company controller, either he or she has got the position of CEO (Chief Executive Officer) or CFO (Chief Financial Officer). Assuming that company has hired multiple project accountants for the different projects that the company is dealing with, Bragg has presented an organizational chart for the demonstration of position and role of the project accountant (Bragg, 2014). Figure 2.1 posted below shows the organizational chart (Bragg, 2014).

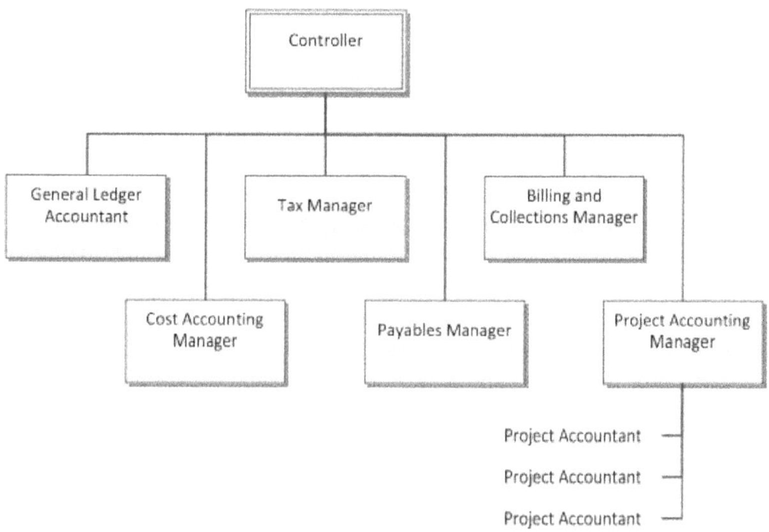

Figure 2.1 Default organizational chart including different project accountants. (Image source: Bragg, 2014).

The roles that the accountant plays in a project-based company and for the projects mentioned above are more likely to stand applicable for the generic projects. The role can be slightly different for the projects having different nature and complexity. For example, the accountants might have to play a slightly different role or use different strategies for the company working on off-shore oil rig project that includes drilling for three to four months. However, the basic functionalities and core duties of the accountant remains the same irrespective of the nature and complexity of the project.

It is recommended that the accounting departments should present the reports to the higher management and should report directly to the company's primary running officer to avoid the influence of the managers and other staff members. And it is also necessary for the main company running entity to know the status of the progress of the project and the amount of the capital allocated to each of the project.

2.3 Role of Accounting for Product-Based Companies

This section is dedicated to the role of accounting in aiding the product-based businesses. As mentioned previously, the dynamics of the product-based businesses are different from project-based business. As mentioned previously, the product sale is closely associated with the supply and demand principle. The product-based companies are associated with the product development. There are many stages of the product development. The management accounting plays a direct and more specific role in success of the product-based business.

Accounting not only plays role in the product development, but also plays a significant role in the successful running of the product-based business. For the detailed understanding of the role of accounting in product development and product-based businesses it is therefore necessary to study the stages of the product development. Hertenstein et al. have shared two types of the cycles that are used for the product development (Hertenstein and Platt, 1998). One of them is old cycle. Figure posted below shows the stages of the product development using old style (Hertenstein and Platt, 1998). The researchers have indicated that 75 to 90 percent of the costs of the products are illustrated on Figure 2.2.

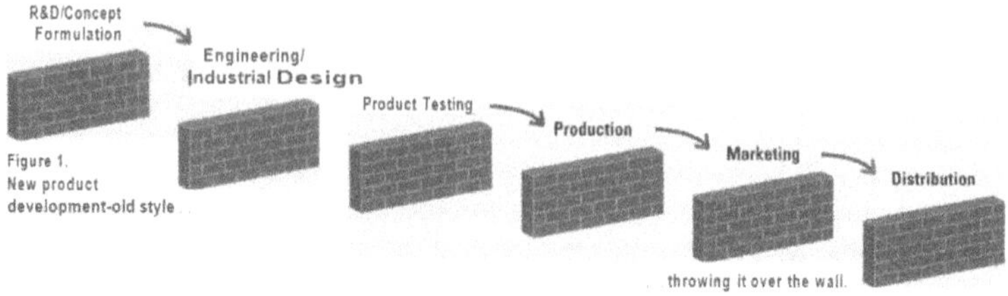

Figure 2.2 Stages of the product development using old style. (Image source: The picture has been taken from the publication of Hertenstein and Platt (1998)).

The first step as mentioned in the figure is the research and development or the concept formulation. The research and development phase can involve many stages. It can involve the prototype development and testing, design failures, testing of different designs, and the research on the basic concepts the research phase could have involved the extensive market research from the need and demand point of view as well. the questions like "is the product needed in the market", "in what ways the product is different from the similar ones being sold in the market" etc. will help in the finalization of optimum design. The second step is based on the manufacturing of the industrial design in which company either manufactures the product itself or outsource it completely, and even some parts of the products are outsourced. The out sourcing is common, for example the car manufacturers often outsource the interior and seat cushioning parts to other manufacturers. The third stage depicted in the figure is the product testing. Tests are conducted by the company and some independent testing agencies are hired to perform tests to insure the transparency. Finally, the stages of production and marketing arrives. In which the product is produced and marketed using advertisements and other techniques. After that stage, the product is distributed using various channels. Some production companies give their distribution to other agencies as well. the concept of throwing over the wall is very interesting as discussed by the authors (Hertenstein and Platt, 1998). This means that the product was used to transferred from one department to another department (Hertenstein and Platt, 1998). There was no proper coordination between the departments. The ideas and experiences of the people of one department were not able to be exchanged with the people belonging to other departments. Despite of the fact that all the departments had a direct impact on the product's success in the market.

The approach defined above is called a sequential approach. The sequential approach cannot be used in the current era. The sequential approach has also resulted in captivating the creativity in the industries. The flaws related to the product have rarely been discussed between the departments in the meetings and sessions. From the product development point of view, the approach was outdated. However, the product related businesses and industries have gradually learned the importance of the integrated workforce environment. As mentioned above the current complexity and advancement, an integrated and combined input of people belonging to different educational backgrounds is required related to the product. The cross-functional product design is not only important for the companies but it will surely improve the lives of the people who are going to use the product. The product can be withering a car, a cloth, an electronic gadget, a plane, and any cooking item etc. The product designed keeping in view the input of the people from all the departments, customers' feedback, and the need of the society will have the unique features that will provide an outstanding start at its launch in the market. The modern practice of the product development has been shown in the Figure 2.3 posted below (Hertenstein and Platt, 1998).

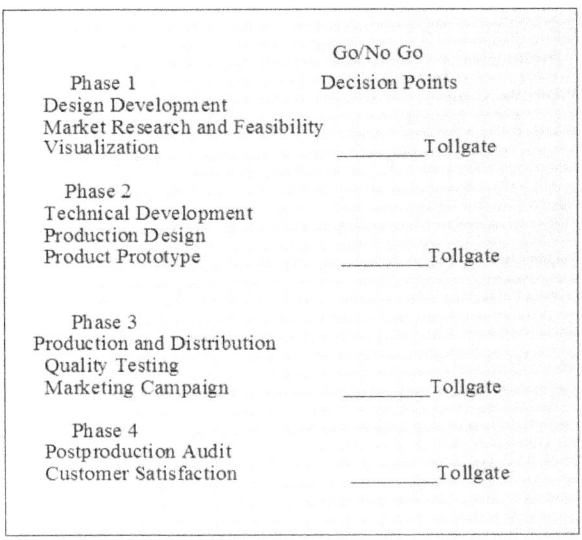

Figure 2.3 Product development cycle using an integrated, cross department, and cross-functional approach. (Image source: Hertenstein and Platt 1998).

As seen from the Figure 2.3, the phase 1 is related to the design development, design research, market research, feasibility, and use of the visualization techniques to properly understand the results as well as to predict the future of the product. The four processes have been included in the first phase of the product development and requires the collaboration of experts belonging form different departments. The "toll gate" process highlighted in the figure refers to the process that involves the team members and management to assess different features and characteristics related to the product, and they collectively decide whether the product qualifies all the requirements and goals that have been previously defined for this phase, so that it can be moved forward to the next phase. This approach results in the development of strong collaboration and a well working relationship between team members, departments, and the management. This also gives the staff members a realization that the management is also actively contributing and concerned with the success of the product.

The model presented above demands the role of the accounting from the first phase. the design development will require the experts related to the project, if the product is electronic based, then electronic and electrical engineers are included. Similarly, of the market research and feasibility, the technical experts will work along with the accountant to develop a feasibility related to the product, it will include the technical feasibility as well as the financial feasibility. The market research also includes the consideration of "need" factor, data acquisition related to the product, data related to the raw materials, sales data, and the information related to the similar products. The accountant can actively participate and utilize this opportunity to control the cost of the project (Hertenstein and Platt, 1998). The cost control is an important aspect in the early phase of the development of the product. As a member of combined team in which management and staff are working together for the finalization of the product, the accounting person will be well aware of the company's resources that have been allocated for the product, in this way it will be ensured form the start that the expenses are in control and within the defined budget range. The visualization can be defined as the techniques used to present and analyze the data acquired by market research and apply it to the design development. The visualization is also referred to the fore sighting the future of the product based on the experience, history, and market trends. The role of the management accountant in this approach will be as the decision supporters, who can understand and implement the relationship between the financial functionalities along with the design requirements and market needs as well. if the team considers that the product is not feasible for the next phase, then the working may start again to change the design development, and look more extensively towards the design parameters again to make the product feasible for the business, market, consumer, while ensuring the quality. By the interaction between the team members, management accountants

The next phase includes the processes such as technical development, finalization of the product design, and product prototype. The technical development requires the combination of skills of different people. The finalization of the production design is a critical step that is related to defining the characteristics of the product. The economic and aesthetic aspect of the product is also important. The experts that deal with the ergonomics of the products define the comfort level if requires or visualize the interaction of that product with the human beings. The features definitions directly impact the cost of the product. The management accountants can directly contribute to evaluate the costs and the functionality is better that the purchase managers who are working along with production teams (Hertenstein and Platt, 1998). The management accountants are qualified not only to evaluate the cost of the products but also consider the factors that contribute to the cost increment, the complexity of the cost functions, and fundamental relationship between manufacturing process and costs as well (Hertenstein and Platt, 1998). It must be mentioned that cost information is the inculcated in the product design, and as soon as the product reaches the manufacturing line it is difficult to further reduce the costs (Davila and Wouters, 2006). Although there are methods that can be used to change the workflow of the manufacturing processes, however, it becomes difficult to control the cost at that level. Therefore, it is recommended that management accountants should carefully review the costs in the design phase, as the most aspects of the cost driving factors are under consideration at this phase, including the product raw material. The product manufacturing operations are dependent on the product design. Manufacturing process of the product is virtually guided by the design.

The optimality of the production design is the function of objectives, costs, functionality, aesthetics, safety, and requirements. The management accountant provides valuable input related to the design that can ease the production process. The expense analysis of the production procedure, the relationship between the expenses production, production design, and methods are the discussions that involve the accountants, engineers or experts, and the management to discuss the most suitable method of production that is cost-effective as well as easy to continue in future, and is most suitable for meeting the production design requirements.

Management accounting is a discipline in which accountants identify, measure, analyze, interpret the financial knowledge and information to the management of the company for the achievement of organizational goals.

Another important aspect of the production cycle is the development of the product prototype. The cost and expense of the prototyping is calculated and defined by the accountants and the engineers or experts. The number of prototypes needed to develop for the testing is also defined by mutual agreement. It must be mentioned that experts not necessarily mean and limited to engineers only if the product is a clothing or garment item, then textile experts and designers are the part of the team. After the decision of the quantity and expense of prototyping, the prototype is then developed and this ends the second phase of the product development cycle. As mentioned above, at the end of this phase, the team decides that has the prototype met the requirements of the design defined above, does the prototype justifies the cost and expense decided earlier, and is the prototype suitable for testing and should we move to the next phase or not. The continuous analysis at the end of each step may prolong the production process, but it meets the features and requirements of the Quality by Design (QbD). The errors, mistakes, and the flaws are not passed or forwarded to the next phase, and continuous assessment ensures that the quality standards' requirement related to product are being fulfilled.

The third phase involves the more practical and applicable usage of management accounting. The production of the products from raw materials to finished form is a complete process. The modern manufacturing systems (MMS) are the new methods to produce the products using smart approach and with the help of automated machine and robots. The complexity and intricacy requirement of the products are very difficult to meet using traditional manufacturing methods, and the old methods are also time taking and inefficient. The management accountants carefully analyze the production scheme, observe the processes form a perspective that could increase the overhead costs, note down the working hours of the labors, and other aspects of the production. In this way the costs incurred on the production including the running hours of the machines, electricity cost, requirement for the maintenance of machines etc. are calculated by the accountants. The quality testing is an important phase for the evaluation of the product itself. The quality testing involves the assessment of the product against the standards developed by international organizations for that particular product. The commercial aspect of the third phase of new product lifecycle is the marketing campaign. The accountants calculate the cost required for the optimal marketing. Optimal marketing can be referred to as the way of promoting and advertising the product in such a way that the minimal cost is incurred and the maximum amount of customer market is approached. The accountants formulate the marketing budget, and the sales and marketing team promotes the product by properly advertising the products at various platforms.

The last phase of the new product development (NPD) is the post production audit of the product and the evaluation and incorporation of the customer satisfaction. Post production audit is done by the company accountants or external group of the accountants to verify the expenditure that has been incurred on the production of the product is genuine and is truly occurred on the production of the product itself. This is a sort of evaluation that the cost defined for the production during the early phases of NPD is being justified and correct. If there are any additional expenditures incurred other than the estimated ones, then how the expenses have deviated from the planned ones. This allows the production team to evaluate the process once again if there is any miscalculation, under or over estimation.

The customer satisfaction is the also the one of the best evaluation parameters for the product. The sales of the products are directly linked to the remarks that have been provided by the customers on different platforms. In the present era of social media and digital marketing, customers usually review the comments and ratings of the previous customers related to the product. The digital marketing and SEO strategies are employed by the companies to boost the sales, and the firms use social media for remaining closer and connected to their customers. The best example of social media usage and customer connection are the practices employed by GE (General Electric) and Nike. However, the detail of these methods is beyond the scope of discussion of this text.

2.3.1 Role of Management Accountants in Cost Handling for NPD (New Product Development)

The emphasis in the discussion made above has been laid on the role of the accountants that they play in the development of new product. one of the key responsibilities is the cost estimation, control, and evaluation. The cost modeling is a complicated task that requires the deep understanding of the market, knowledge about the raw materials, and realization of the role of the cost driving factors. However, as mentioned above, the role of the accountant is broader than just the cost evaluator. But in this section the discussion will be precisely on the methods of cost control and evaluation done by the account management experts as they work along or parallel with the production teams.

2.3.1.1 Target Costing Method

Target costing is an expanded technique that is used to control the cost during the stage of the production design. The method is highly suitable for the products and items in which the price is a key contributive factor that serves as a basis for the competition. In target costing the company decides and plans about the price points, product cost, and the profit margins as well associated with the product that it wants to develop. The company even decides to shut down the plans of the product design if it is not able to meet the target cost. This is much relatable to the production cycle defined above, in which the team doesn't move to the next step, if the requirements are not being met. In such type of product markets, there is less room for the price definition, and the profit margins earned are low. The companies mostly rely on the quantity of the sold units of the products to increase the overall profit. The profit earnings are also based on the manufacturer's ability to maintain the functionality in the best possible way that the price points require keeping the lowest possible cost (Davila and Wouters, 2006). The raw materials of the product and the prices of the market play a fundamental role in defining the target cost that the production teams have to achieve using the optimized production and developmental process (Davila and Wouters, 2006). As mentioned above the target costing is suitable for the markets where the cost is the main aspect of the product and cost interpretation is easier (Davila and Wouters, 2006).

2.3.1.2 Other Cost Management Techniques

Davila and Wouters have suggested other techniques that can be used to control the costs during the product development level. These researchers have classified the cost management strategies into two types, one of them is applicable for the products that are the part of product development project, and the second types of the techniques are applicable for the products those have a series or categorized as product family (Davila and Wouters, 2004).

At the new product development or project level product development the strategy that the researcher has described is to provide more information about the cost to grab the attention of the technical staff that this factor is a defining feature for the success of the product. The suggestion provided is related to asking and proposing the designers and managers to reduce the cost of the process and manufacturing as well.

Rabino and Wright have highlighted the changes that have been occurred in the field of manufacturing and technology, and production, that have forced the management accountants working in the production and technology to review the costing methods (Rabino and Wright, 1993). The traditional manufacturing and production system relied heavily on the input of the labor itself, the labor was operating machines, controlling the floor process, labor was involved in the packaging, and the manpower was used for loading the raw-materials. The traditional cost modeling and accounting systems that have considered the labor as the major components that contribute to the major portion of the cost in the production systems are not accurately applicable to the current system of production, and when applied to current manufacturing systems, the outcome is the distortion of the cost values, and deviation of the costs from the realistic grounds (Rabino and Wright, 1993). The traditional approaches are not able to identify the outcomes of the operations due to inaccurate identification of the cost relationships, and result in the unfair assessment and performance evaluation of the modern manufacturing systems. The shorter lead times and product cycles have also made it challenging for the management accountants to estimate the costs accurately.

The researchers have also compiled the changes that have been occurred in the manufacturing systems and the impact of these changes on the traditional cost accounting systems. Table 2.1 shows the changes (Rabino and Wright, 1993).

Table 2.1 The Impact of Changes in the Manufacturing and Production Technologies on the Traditional Cost Accounting Systems (Table Source: The table has been taken from the original online publication of Rabino and Wright published in 1993)

Change	Impact on the production system	Impact on the traditional cost accounting model
Movement toward flexible manufacturing systems	Reduction in labor inputs	Traditional cost systems focus on Labor as a means to allocate indirect costs
	Achieving cost efficiencies at lower production levels (e.g., small batches can be produced economically)	Traditional cost systems fail to capture cost efficiencies and consider related costs (e.g., setup, design, quality)
	Lower total costs and smaller production runs	
	A large variety of products can be offered at a lower average total cost	Need to evaluate product profitability and achievement of strategies

Rabino and Wright have also mentioned the detailed short comings of the traditional costing systems that fundamental cost accounting system is based on the fact that the product cost should be reflected in terms of the manufacturing cost, while the other costs such as the marketing and distribution, and advertisement costs are considered to be the costs of the periods (Rabino and Wright, 1993). The costs of the research and development, software usage, distribution, and designing have raised significantly over the past few years, and one of the major shortcomings of the traditional costing system is that these systems normally do not consider these costs. As Rabino and Wright have mentioned that the modern manufacturing involves a major portion and a step that is based on the software development or the software usage, the product is designed on the software, simulations are performed on the software, computer models that are later provided to the machines for manufacturing are also constructed using software. Moreover, many product-based companies tend to develop their own software along with the project, such as an electronic or semiconductor industry provides software along with the hardware as a complete product. therefore, the inclusion of the software usage or development costs must be considered in order to make the costing accurate.

One of the two shortcomings that Rabino and Wright have mentioned about the traditional cost accounting systems that result in the creation of inaccurate and distorted costs are as follows (Rabino and Wright, 1993).

- The traditional system of cost accounting considers the volume of production as a measure for the assessment and allocation of the overheard costs
- The traditional system only considers the production costs.

The shortcoming measures related to these cost accounting systems have been mentioned above. The modern production process's output and other associated parameters cannot be correctly estimated using the concept of volume of production. The modern production world works on different processes, uses advanced methods, tracks the productivity using different methods, and involves intensive research and development procedures. For the correct costing method, an unorthodox and modern approach of assessment is required.

2.3.1.2.1 Activity Based Costing

Keeping in view the current modifications in the workflow and technology associated with the production and manufacturing industry, various adaptations to the cost accounting methods have been proposed to cater for the changes that have been occurred.one of such systems is termed as Activity Based Costing (ABC). The intention of introducing such system is to obtain more detailed, and accurate costing information related to the products and related operations. The activity-based costing system considers the broad and diversified factors that result in bringing the variety in the costs associated with the products, such factors are termed as cost drivers (Rabino and Wright, 1993). The cost drivers not only consider the costs based on the production volume but also operational cots as well (Rabino and Wright, 1993). In activity-based costing system, the overheads and indirect costs are assigned or designated to the products and services. The activities that are required to produce the product have a cost, and this makes more sense when the manufacturing design, and other aspects related to product development are considered. Allotting activities involved in the complete product development a cost is the core of the activity-based costing system. Overheads which are fixed are converted into activities which are termed as cost pools.

As the activity-based costing system also considers the operational parameters related to the product development, the production system arrangement, product work flow, distribution channels, and product raw material procurement can be related to the operational functionality of the firm, and these parameters when considered will reflect the utilization of the product resources. The costs related to the manufacturing, sales, distribution, and organization would be considered in the product cost, therefore this costing method would be able to reflect and display the complete sources required to produce a product.

2.3.1.2.2 Parallel Costing Methods

Another approach that is mentioned in the literature and that seems very useful is to utilize the parallel costing method. The approach is based on the usage of parallel costing team. Instead of merging the cost accountant into the developmental teams, the costing team works in parallel but outside the main product development team. The approach is different from the ones described earlier, as these approaches required the active involvement of the accountants in the product development team. The method allows the accountants and the development team to work independently, and the accountants do not implement the cost considerations into the process of engineering for saving time, however, they use the main working of the engineering team to optimize the cost functionality.

The timing of announcement of the results and working of the cost teams is important. Sometimes, the part of the product is redesigned before launching it to reduce the cost, and save the raw material for upcoming product versions. But most of the times the cost reduction strategies are implemented after the launch of the main product into the market. So, these teams work continuously to reduce the costs of the product and processes but do not hinder the process of product development.

Continuous cost reduction efforts are necessary as it save the production firm from difficult financial situations. And the engineering team is always busy with the technical part of the job, monitoring the pre-defined workflow, meeting the production targets, and making design improvements. The aspect of the cost reduction although a major goal of the team doesn't fit in along with the technical part of the job. The accountants working in parallel can reduce the burden for the attainment of the common goal, that is, to produce a high functionality product with minimal possible cost.

Hertenstein and Platt have mentioned the case of Yokogawa Electric, a manufacturer of industrial testing equipment, the headquarters of the company is situated in Japan near Tokyo (Hertenstein and Platt, 2000). Due to the financial difficulties the company needed to reconsider the design for the improvement of financial outcome parameters. The product designers have significantly reduced the costs of manufacturing and assembly by redesigning the covers and knobs. So, the manufacturing operation was changes and the cost of raw material was also saved by reconsidering the design (Hertenstein and Platt, 2000). However, for the purpose of the cost reduction the team of cost accountants working in parallel with the product development team should have a strong knowledge of the product's raw materials and manufacturing operations as well.

The parallel team strategy in the product development is not only restricted to the costing teams. Arditti and Levy has mentioned various scenarios of the history in which the various development teams working on a single product have resulted in excellent performance outcomes (Arditti and Levy, 1980)

2.3.1.2.3 Application of Modularity in Cost Management

As a part of discussion of cost management and reduction, it is important to discuss the role of the product design and other practices that are applicable to reduce the cost of the products not only during the regular product development but especially from the point of view of new product development (NPD). Most of the cost management practices are associate with the product design itself. The accountants working in a technology environment guide the designers and operation specialists how they can change their practices to properly manage the cost. The cost specialists also provide valuable feedback to the decision makers about the investment of resource percentage of the company into the new product development. Either the resource company is intending to spend on new product would be feasible for the firm keeping in view the strategic goals and objectives of the company.

As mentioned previously, most of the cost management strategies are associate with the product design. The concept of modularity is not a new concept when the product design and the variable of cost is under discussion. Modularity can be defined as the segregation of a complete system into subparts which can be regarded as logical entities (Siddique et al., 1998). From management and cost reduction point of view, these sub-systems can be treated as independent systems if they do not belong to the major competitive parameters of the product. A more detailed design and cost optimization is possible when individual modules of the product are considered. When the product design is divided into modules, the cost becomes an important variable in the completion list (Davila and Wouters, 2006). Moreover, the modular system also allows the accountants to analyze the costs of raw materials and manufacturing operations adopted to develop a certain product module. This individual consideration can lead to more intensive optimization of each module of the product. The modules can also be categorized as per functionality. it is also possible that a part of the product is not more relevant to the functionality of the product, yet a huge amount of resource is being used for development of that part.

Moreover, there are many functional benefits operational benefits of the modularity that are more or less relevant to the costs. These benefits include the usage of common and established supplier for the raw material and accessories, less inventory, easy to handle jobs, fast production process, and less technical drawings etc. (Guo and Gershenson, 2007).

As far as the relationship between cost reduction is considered, Guo an Gershenson, have compiled significant statements from the literature, in which the researchers have stated that the modular product design reduces the cost of the products (Guo and Gershenson, 2007). However, Guo and Gershenson have performed a detailed study including the experiments for finding out the relationship between modularity and cost, and they have stated that there exists no significant relationship between the life cycle modularity and life cycle cost, until there are considerably huge modularity modifications (Guo and Gershenson, 2007). The modularity may even do not contribute in the cost reduction of the product; however, it can be clearly observed that it significantly makes the cost management effective and easy. And there are many technical benefits of modularity, some of which have been mentioned above.

2.3.2 Role of Management Accounting in New Product Development Strategies

As Rabino and Wright have mentioned that one aspect of the cost accounting and management system is to modify the behavior of the organization particularly product development teams to pay more attention to costs and then on the next stage cost control (Rabino and Wright, 1993). This behavioral method is extension of the activity-based costing system (Rabino and Wright, 1993).

Quality by Design (QbD) concept was first introduced by Joseph M Juran who was an engineer and management consultant. The concept states in simpler terms that the quality should be incorporated into the product from start and the most of the quality related problems are traced back to the stage when product was planned.

The approach can be useful if the management accountants are the part of the product development team. In this system performance measures are set by the company, and then cost factors or cost drivers are modified to achieve the performance measures. The performance and financial measures are similar in some aspects. As a simple explanation, the product should be able to perform best while it should also be cost-effective as well. as majority of the experts have indicated that the product cost and operational cost of the processes are the main financial measures for evaluating the performance of industrial design (Hertenstein and Platt, 2000). Therefore, by allowing the management accountants to be the part and process of the product development, the process of product development will be more cost focused and the team will be able to utilize the experience of the management accountant in controlling the cost of the process associated with the product development.

Hertenstein and Platt have mentioned, that the most of the experts associated with the new product development have said that for determining the product cost, first a target cost is defined, and the product cost is determined on the basis of the target cost. So, in other words, the cost drivers have to be modified to meet the target cost. For controlling the cost drivers, the services of the management accountant and cost accountant would be highly useful. Moreover, the accountants working in the technology or product manufacturing companies with time acquire the understanding and knowledge of the technical aspects of the product as well.

In the field of production and manufacturing, the development of new products is an essential process that is necessary for the survival of companies. With time, there is a realization in the society about the growing needs and requirements that customers demand in their products. Moreover, almost every product in the market needs improvement and optimization up to some extent. Software companies release latest version of their products every year or on quarterly basis with bugs removed and new functionalities addition. Car manufacturers launch new models every year with improved functionalities and new features. Therefore, new product development (NPD) is a continuous procedure that almost every industry does. New product development affects the physical and financial growth of the companies. Some industries are more actively involved in the new product development keeping in view the needs of the customers.

There exists a huge potential for the growth of the industries related to bio-products and automotive. However, investors tend to be afraid of investing in the NPD sector. The major fear is due to the uncertainties associated with it. As mentioned in the report published by CIMA (Chartered Institute of Management

Accountants) in 2011, the financial management of the NPD and design related uncertainties and randomness are due to the major changes that have been occurred since 2000 (cite). The changes and transformation in the field of technology and new product development and design (NPD&D) is a continuous process that will increase its pace in the upcoming years, and this change is being reflected in the increasing complexity of the product requirements. The main question that has been answered in the research performed by the researchers for CIMA is that how the management accountants' stance on the changes that is are taking place in the new product design and development and how these accountants are going to respond the changes that have been occurred in the process of NPD (Nixon et al., 2011). The case-study has been included in this section of the book to practically demonstrate the role of the management accounting in strategic decisions of the new product development firm. The case study was sponsored by CIMA, the main focus was the premium auto-group sector. A huge percentage of sale is invested in the globally on the industrial research and development. The reason that CIMA has selected the automotive industry for the case study is that it involves an extensive new product development, and the automotive market is highly competitive in terms of research and development, and this industry utilizes all those advanced tools that have changed the frameworks of manufacturing. Therefore, from modern perspective, and from the point of view of change in the field of technology and production, it would be very suitable to study the role of accounting management in establishing the communication and connection necessary for the efficient working of multi-disciplinary teams and fulfilling the needs of the diverse range of customers. The role of multi-disciplinary teams in product development has already been explained in detail.

The well-established, experienced, and outstanding in terms of performance automotive company was chosen for the case study, and the company has not disclosed its name for the confidentiality purposes. The basic objective of the case study in clear terms is to study the changes in the technology, and the variations in the product range and management changes in the process of new product development and design process. As a consequence of these changes what role can management accountants play in the decisions and strategies of the new product development companies. The report states that the competition in the market and ongoing efforts of intensive research and development has enabled the companies in the premium sector to utilize the price led costing method for new product development and design (Nixon et al., 2011). Here the role of the management accountants starts, as these companies have to design annual planning round (APR). This approach was adopted by the company which was selected for the case study. In price led costing method the price that the customers can pay defines the allowable cost. Marketing teams normally determine the price that the customers are willing to pay. Since the case study involved the premium auto group sector, the more value the company is putting in the products in terms of features, design, luxury, and comfort, the more price the customers would be willing to pay. But it is not simple now as it is stated, the competition and the changes in the technology strategies have made this challenging. In annual planning round companies review the progress in achievement of strategic objectives, and estimate the resources required for the achievement of these goals. The product manufacturers estimate the total expense available for upcoming product versions, updates, and changes in the current product designs. The expense calculation and feasibility involve the management accountants. The researchers found out that the company's plan for the class, performance, and the profit margin criteria is clear (Nixon et al., 2011). The previously mentioned three parameters were backed up by clear and detailed description of definitions and criteria in every design parameter. Marketing experts as well as the industrial designers were involved in defining the class in every segment. Class, purity, and specifically used term "pedigree" consists of all the parameters of interior and exterior design, and also the service support (Nixon et al., 2011). Performance in this case consisted of excellent validation with the standard, and the design engineers were mainly responsible for it. The design engineers measure performance for each type the customer group. In this way the performance requirements for different customer types are known. The performance requirement for automotive customers varies as per the type of the customers. The design engineers get idea about the variety of the customers' demand in terms of performance parameters. Performance parameters are also determined via marketing. The feedback of the premium and executive customers is valuable. Performance and class (pedigree) forms the main source of technical concept description (TCD). One of the most relevant findings that is relatable to the topic under discussion is that the CIMA reports states that majority of the cost, value incorporation of the engineering, and the risk calculation related to the design and engineering and the technical workflow are handled under the strategy and target setting category. Twenty engineers determine the variables and parameters that fall under the category of strategy and target setting, and these engineers report to a single management accountant directly. This strategy and target setting department ensures the creation of balanced target books in the planning and strategic stage of the product development (Nixon et al., 2011). Moreover, the technical concept description including pedigree and performance parameters are balanced using balanced target book approach, the profit design criteria of the company along with the price and customer ownership cost is incorporated.

The success of the company in the current competitive environment is due to the multiple factors. The team structure of the company is matrix based. The responsibilities are assigned as matrix type formation. The management accountant serves the dual roles and is responsible for the managing the finances and administrative aspects of strategy and targeting. This dual responsibility, and the authority shows the importance of management accountant in the firm. The main reason of giving importance to management accounting is due to the fact that the market competition demands more than the engineering excellence, the strategic and financial strategies of the firm have an impact on the overall standing of the firm in the market. The management accounting considers the important aspects that have valuable impact on the company's overall performance in the market, from cost management to customer's satisfaction, each and every aspect of the financial and managerial nature is considered by the management accountants. The study revealed that the new product development process in the company which was selected for the study is a team work involving the extensive coordination and exchange of thoughts among the diversified and different functional bodies, module heads, and the complete team involved in the new product development and design process. This approach is the same as mentioned previously that the modern product development strategies involve the strong integration and coordination of multi-disciplinary teams. And if a proper channel of communication and exchange of the ideas is established in the company, the communication and knowledge exchange process become more systematic and efficient. The study if the company's planning and manufacturing process reveals that the estimated workflow and the time required to establish a new particular motor vehicle producing system requires four to years, and the life expectancy of that system is 15–20 years (Nixon et al., 2011). The customer ownership life comprises of 20–25 years (Nixon et al., 2011). This long-term planning requires the strong planning and management of the plans. The increased customer ownership exhibits the strong and trusted after sales services (Nixon et al., 2011). This long-term planning and execution require the detailed and accurate estimation of all the variables involved. The forecasting of the cost increment on the basis.

In order to explore the role of accounting management in supporting the modern process of product development, the case study also involves the observation and understanding of the process of new product development and design itself. The way the new product meets the demands of customers and how it performs in the competitive market depends on the process itself. The organized, structured, and well-planned process of the product development results in the creation of the product that is designed, evaluated, and rectified at each stage of the production. As two types of the product cycle were discussed in the text above, the recommended product cycle involves the evaluation of the product at each stage, and the next stage is not initiated until the requirements of the previous stages are not met.

Now a days, many companies have developed certain phases/stages of the new product development, and these stages are specific to the type of the industrial sector and the experience of the company. Companies review the stages of the new product development cycle, and the accountants guide the management about modification of the phases depending upon the efficiency of each stage and the resources that are reserved for each stage. There might exist certain phases of the product development, in which a lot of time and resource is consumed, and yet it is not relevant to the production process.

The automobile industry that was selected for the study had an excellent process of the new product development and design due to very well-defined arrangement and highly structured workflow. The process is based on the tasks and results of each of the 14 stages of process into the 5 phases that can be possibly a part of new product development project (Nixon et al., 2011). These five phases are, strategic and conceptual development, approval of the concept, design and validation, volume ramping, and entry into the market (Nixon et al., 2011). The first phase of the process is very important, that is the strategy and conceptual development. At the starting of the planning or strategy definition, the financial and the market goals should be incorporated. A team of product development headed by the management accountant will definitely ensure that in this phase, the planning and strategy for the achievement of financial benefit, resource management, revenue results, and the sales, are aligned with the long-term financial goals of the organization. The reason that the process of the company is outclass is that the 14 stages do not run sequentially, however, the processes run in parallel with each other. The parallel structure of the execution saves a lot of time (Nixon et al., 2011). Moreover, the hurdles, obstacles, and the important factors on which the success depends are considered in every phase (Nixon et al., 2011). The lateness and the delay factor as well as the "delivery" task is considered in early stages, of the product development due to the reason that the team working on the project of the new product development doesn't changes (Nixon et al., 2011). The consistency in terms of working persons for the product development allows the team members to understand the weaknesses of the product from the earlier stages, and in the next version the team ensures that the same mistakes are not repeated.

The balanced target books for the project demonstrate the parallel working approach used in the company (Nixon et al., 2011). Figure 2.4 presented below shows the Balanced Target Books (BTB) for the projects that company uses (Nixon et al., 2011).

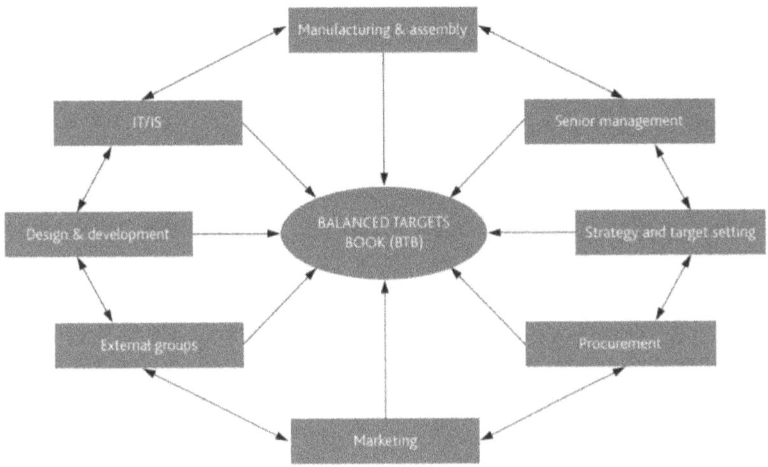

Figure 2.4 BTB approach used by the company for new product development. (Image source CIMA).

The BTB approach and method is agreed upon by the multiple reiterations which are done in the top bottom approach. The agreeability is achieved among all the project participants in the 4th stage (feasibility) of the strategy and concept description phase (Nixon et al., 2011). From the management perspective, the overall approach reflects the complete participation and collaboration of the entities involved on the process of product development (Nixon et al., 2011). However, the report of the case study also describes the highly structured, disciplined, and controlled approach related to the product development, and the methods do not involve the artistry, inventiveness, and uncertainty which are normally the part of the product development method (Nixon et al., 2011). The uncertainty in the product development can leads to the instability and drastic changes which are very difficult to survive for the new startup-based companies. The creativity and the fresh ideas are very necessary for the innovation in the product development. Particularly for the design perspective, the creativity is essentially required to introduce the changes in the old products that are relevant to the functionality, attractive to the customers, and more specifically meet the customer's requirements.

The initial BTB consists of financial and non-financial targets which are in phase with the general pedigree, performance, and profit design parameters. The targets are set for the two vehicle designs which are competitive in nature (Nixon et al., 2011). The categorization of the targets is a unique and useful approach, in which the importance is given to financial and managerial aspects of the product, rather than just focusing on the engineering. The success of the product is based on the timely achievement of financial and non-financial targets.

The financial targets are classified into four categories. These financial targets are return on sales and the investment, cost incurred on the design and development of the product, manufacturing and assembly cost, and finally the total ownership cost (Nixon et al., 2011). The more specific financial targets include, fuel consumption, milage, price, resale value of the vehicle, maintenance costs etc. (Nixon et al., 2011). The financial targets are one of the most important competitive dimensions in the modern production industry. Figure 2.5 posted below shows the connection of the non-financial targets with the balanced target books (Nixon et al., 2011).

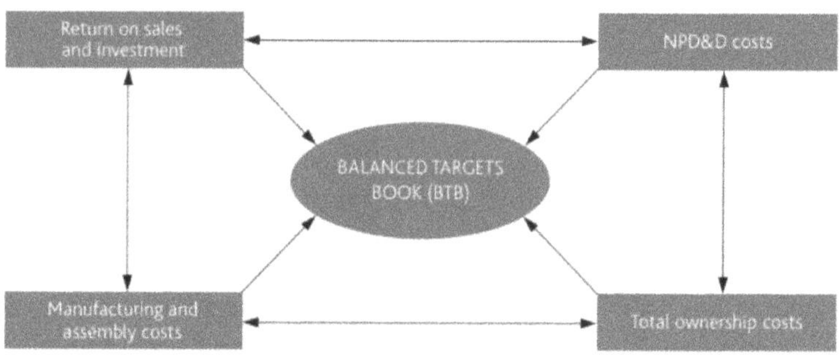

Figure 2.5 Financial targets and balanced target books of an automotive industry (Nixon et al., 2011). (Image source: CIMA).

The cost analysis of the firms cost management system suggests that the company adopts conventional and fundamental cost management approach that is based on the statement that the future costs are controlled through today's design (Nixon et al., 2011). The approach is very narrow and tapered, and is late with the phase of the new product design and development process (Nixon et al., 2011). But for the firm under study, the approach might be working due to the fact that there is a large planning required for the new product, and the time difference between the strategy and market launching phase is large, as mentioned above. The design related decisions have long implication on the standing of the product in the market. But the unpredictability and the financial fluctuations in the market are very rapid, and it would be really challenging to incorporate the cost-based changes in the any of the phase, if the international prices of the raw materials and other assets involved in the product development change drastically. This is the reason that the case study report states that the approach of cost management is late as per the pace of the new product development (Nixon et al., 2011).

As mentioned previously, the company has a well-defined structure that is used to integrate the process with the business method, phases with the new product development process, and the 14 stages with the five phases (Nixon et al., 2011). The activities in the stages are created in such a way that they support the vertical communication in the stages, and the horizontal flow of the information in 14 stages of the new product development processes that can last for 4.5 years (Nixon et al., 2011). The purpose of this vertical and horizontal communication is to incorporate the competitive and new product development objectives effectively into the operations (Nixon et al., 2011).

2.3.2.1 Managing Uncertainty and Implementing Strategies in the Company

Company has also maintained the financial and non-financial data in a very orderly and structured arrangement. CIMA has analyzed the empirical data of the company and based on analysis the experts have identified six elements that support each other to manage the unpredictability, uncertainty, and implementation strategy (Nixon et al., 2011). These six elements have been explained below (Nixon et al., 2011):

1. Structure of the Organization and Workflow
   The formation of the product strategy formulation team, project team, people working on modules and engineering team is comprehensive, and demonstrates the active involvement and participation in the new product development (Nixon et al., 2011). Vertical communication is appreciated and recommended in part with the matrix type responsibility, and participation of all the representative groups is ensured (Nixon et al., 2011).
2. Role of Accounting in different Sectors
   The management of the finances and the accounting aspect is represented and demonstrated at each level of the process and influences the functionality of each member including senior management, product strategy team,

engineering team, and in the product modules by strategy and target setting committee (Nixon et al., 2011).

3. Information System

The company's information system that also involves the management accounting and balanced target book activities and tasks and is specifically built to support the competitiveness and new product formulation strategies. In the current era where the intellectual capital holds a major share of company's capital, it is critical that the information system collects and analyze the most relevant and updated information. It must be mentioned that the content and the workflow of the information system of the company supports the retroactive, simultaneous, and anticipated usage of every pedigree, performance, and the financial checks of every target balanced book (Nixon et al., 2011).

The company's information system lies under the responsibility of the financial directory, who is functionally responsible to the company's chief information officer (Nixon et al., 2011). It must be mentioned that the activities and tasks under the high-end functionalities support integration strongly. The integration of the tasks and activities can be seen in the functionalities of the risk management and assessment, investment assessment, assessment and measurement of the performance, and the cost and value management (Nixon et al., 2011). As seen in the Figure 2.6 presented below, these tasks are conducted simultaneously for the effective control and planning purposes (Nixon et al., 2011)

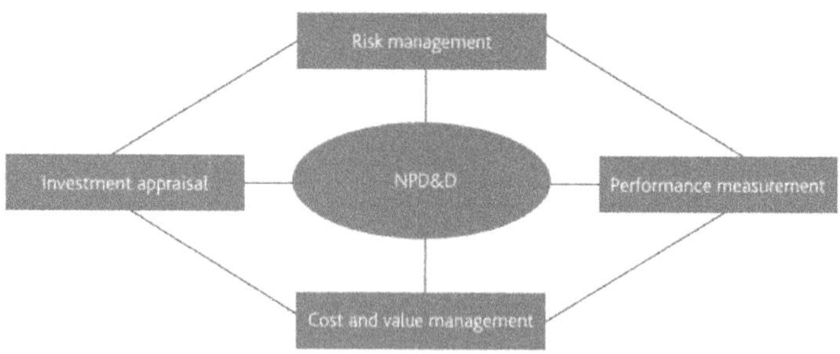

Figure 2.6 Simultaneous financial management of new product design process (Nixon et al., 2011).

4. Management
   The Top-down recursive style of management of new product development processes, and strategy and concept development exhibit the uncertainty and unpredictability that is inherent in many phases as the innovation is included (Nixon et al., 2011). This uncertainty and implementation gaps in the strategy are reduced with the help of loop-based processes that synchronize the company's strategic goals with the operations (Nixon et al., 2011). In this way it is ensured that the strategic planning that involves uncertainty as a result of innovation doesn't distort the focus on the company's major strategic goals in any way.
5. Effective Planning and Control Method
   The financial and non-financial targets that were defined earlier in the strategy and concept definition phase are then used effectively in planning and controlling all the tasks and activities new product development phase (Nixon et al., 2011). A special attention and emphasis is given to the realistic and effective planning for avoiding the cost that is incurred due to the lateness, delays, errors and incorrect estimations. Fundamental historic control checks are used, and variance analysis methods are employed to avoid unrealistic forecasting, and for the purpose of learning and understanding as well (Nixon et al., 2011). It is critical to avoid the over-optimized approach in the planning, as based on the initial planning, the moves for the next 4–5 years are decided. The incorrect or inaccurate planning can lead to the damage that is sometimes very difficult to be recovered. The parameters that are used for the planning should be relevant, updated, and accurate.
6. Unofficial Information system
   The organized and semi-organized modules of the official information system of the company are supported by a well-developed informal information system. The elements of this information system consist of groups and communities of the loyal customers, suppliers, automotive dealers, and other sources that are associated with the automobile industry. This informal information system provides the strategy development team the market trends, the requirements, technology trends, and other information that is necessary to compete in the market. A well understanding of the market trends is required in order to produce products that can compete in the current financial markets.
7. Company's culture
   As far as the behavior or methods are concerned, the involvement of multi-disciplinary teams working on the projects play a major part in the activities conducted in the company. The company's culture is based on the values and

concepts and is displayed in the artefacts in the manifestation of the company, and the culture is celebrated in terms of history and values associated with the brand and the emphasize the company has laid on the performance and pedigree (Nixon et al., 2011). Most of the employees working in the company are serving for longtime, and they are proud of their achievements in terms of vehicles they have helped to produce (Nixon et al., 2011). Team is also proud of the rich history of the company. Throughout the history of the company, the concept that the engineering and design performance alone cannot automatically ensure the financial sustainability of the company, and no new project of product development goes beyond the first phase until the criteria related to the performance, pedigree, and profit are well established, strong, and are specific in nature.

Throughout the detailed analysis of the company's working procedure, philosophy, and business model, one thing is very clear, that the company has well acknowledged that the engineering alone cannot ensure the financial growth and sustainability of the company. The operations, planning, design, services, every functionality has a link with the accounting management. The well-organized structure of tasks and activities have helped the company to achieve the performance, outclass, and profit as per defined criteria in products. The integration of the activities, communication, and participation of the representative groups have resulted in minimizing the effects of uncertainty. The weaknesses in the cost management structure are compensated by the structure and order implemented in almost everything. Huge value is given to financial targets, and it is ensured at every cost that the balancing of the target books is achieved.

2.4 Role of Accounting in Different Sectors

The financial stability of public sector entities is crucial for the economic growth of the businesses situated within the vicinity of the state as well as for the prosperity of people. The financial stability of the public sector entity can be described as the ability of managing and maintaining the short- and long-term financial capacity while maintaining a certain level of services (Caruana et al., 2019). The accounting frameworks can play a broader role in maintaining and ensuring the financial stability of the public sector entities, because the accounting frame works are broader in nature. The accounting plays a critical role in the management and monitoring of the national statements, and the financial transparency is ensured across the institutions as well as in the context of the tax collection from the industries and business. Accounting profession plays a direct role in the budgeting at the national level.

Accounting plays a critical role in the supply chain management and the increase the capacity of supply chain management by reducing the cost and improving the execution (Setyawati, 2018). Husin and Ibrahim have highlighted the role of accounting services on the performance of small and medium enterprises in manufacturing sector of East Coast region of Malaysia (Husin and Ibrahim, 2014).

Melnyk et al. have highlighted the accounting trends in the modern world (Melnyk et al., 2020). According to the survey conducted by the Chartered Institute of Management Accountants (CIMA) and University of Bath, the financial professionals across the world are adapting and embracing the more strategic role for the company's management (Melnyk et al., 2020). The accounting plays a broader role in the society and contributes to the GDP and human growth. A result of the study conducted by the Center of Economics and Business Research (CEBR) of International Federation of Accountants (IFAC) has been posted which proves the close relation of the share of the accountants in the total employed population of world and increase in GDP (Melnyk et al., 2020).

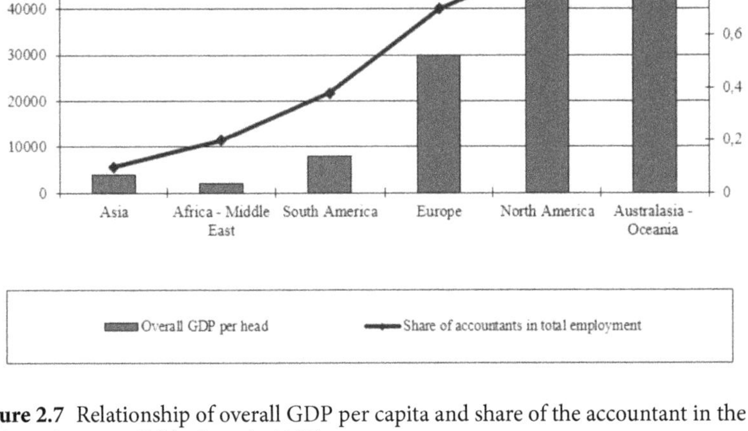

Figure 2.7 Relationship of overall GDP per capita and share of the accountant in the total employment (Melnyk et al., 2020).

Karagiorgos et al have performed a study in which role of the administrative accounting and contribution to the small business have been highlighted (Karagiorgos et al., 2020). The researchers have highlighted that the cost accounting practices added together with the knowledge and skills which the particular SME owner should have will allow better collaborations with the experts (Karagiorgos et al., 2020).

Cescon et al have provided a detailed description of the strategic choices, strategic decisions, and the role of the strategic management accounting in the large manufacturing firms (Cescon et al., 2018). Researchers have also highlighted the strategic management accounting techniques with special focus on the manufacturing firms (Karagiorgos et al., 2020). Figure 2.8 presented below shows the techniques.

SMA technique categories	SMA techniques
Strategic costing	Attribute costing
	Target costing
	Life cycle costing
	Quality costing
	Value chain costing
Strategic decision-making	Strategic pricing
	Brand valuation
Competitor accounting	Competitor position monitoring
	Competitor cost assessment
	Competitor appraisal based on published financial statements
Strategic performance measurement	Balanced scorecard
	Risk analysis/management

Figure 2.8 Categories of the strategic management accounting (Karagiorgos et al., 2020).

Burchell et al have written a paper in 1980, and highlighted the role of Accounting in organizations and the society, the paper is heavily cited due to the description and the explanation provided (Burchell et al., 1980). Accounting has acquired and will acquire more prominent role in the functioning and management of the industrial societies (Burchell et al., 1980). Burchell et al have also discussed the complexities of the accounting profession (Burchell et al., 1980).

The platform organizations comprise many modern businesses such as Uber, Airbnb, and other services such as Ebay. Kornberger et al. have described the evaluative infrastructure and methods that describe the accounting practices for such platform-based organization (Kornberger et al., 2017).

From the state institutions to platform industries, accounting profession plays its role in the management, budgeting, reporting, and imparting transparency. The accounting profession is helping the society to efficiently manage and spend almost all kind of resources.

2.5 Conclusion

The role of accountant in the business is very fundamental, and the success of the businesses without any doubt relies on the accounting practices. From auditing to aiding the management in the strategic decisions, accountants ensure that the business are aligned with the strategic goals, and business contribute effectively to its creators and the society as well. The role of the accountant may be different in different sectors, but the purpose is the efficient and transparent utilization of the resources. Accountants play a very important role in the process of the product development in general and especially the new product development. The cost and price control strategy proposed by the accountants determine the success of product as well as ensure that product compete excellently in the market. A case study has also been included in this chapter to demonstrate the role of the management accountant in the supporting the strategic decisions of the successful company. The management accountant has got more diverse role in the society. Accountants working in the project and product-based companies employ different strategies to ensure the success of the business. The Accounting profession is directly associated with the economic development. Accountants not only play a positive role in supporting businesses but also help the government in making regulations related to the taxation, business transparency, and auditing. The accountants working in the governmental organization ensure that governmental projects executed along with the partnership of private contractors are executed within the frame of the financial targets define initially. Accountants are also involved in the budgeting process of the companies and the governments as well. The accountants also provide the valuable feedback and are involve in the designing the insurances, schemes, and loans to the businesses and individuals. The accountants play a diverse role in the society to ensure the economic prosperity and efficient allocation of wealth and resources.

3 Financial Reporting

Abstract: The financial statements provided to the internal and external users are sometimes framed as per the needs and the interests of the management as well. There are some of the regulatory requirements that compel the companies across the world to release the financial statements. The good financial statements are the ones which provide the data for the calculation of the financial ratios. The financial ratios are the true and accurate picture of the success and the future of the business. The investment opportunities, loans, and the AIS provided by different agencies are based on the performance shown by the companies on the financial statements. The Governments also release the balance sheets to show the financial activity. The financial reporting is one of the key areas that needs attention, and it will augment the process of achievement of the sustainable development goals. There are different types of the financial statements, some of which are the cash flow statements, income statement, and the balance sheet. The Accounting standards also have the requirements related to the financial statements. Financial Reporting is a domain in which the accountants directly contribute to.

Keywords: Financial Statements, Financial Reporting, Reporting Methodologies, Balance Sheet, Income Statement, Cash Flow Statement, Statement of Changes in Equity.

The concepts of accounting and maintaining finances along with their records go back a long time in history. As the process of transactions in the form of buying and selling of basic materials from life necessities to exquisite goods has been around for a significant amount of time, keeping the records of all the financial transactions became a common practice in all businesses. Finance means the management and record keeping of all the business transactions that includes investment, debts, budgets, saving, and lending along with the forecast of the planning related to the business dealings that may occur in the future.

In today's modern world, finance and accounting has become significantly vast. Every aspect of business managed and properly looked after by professionals who keep a track of every single dealing and transaction along with the cash flow. The purpose and the idea behind the process of financial management and accounting along with the analysis of the financial state is to keep the organization informed about its financial standing and to provide valuable information about the situation of current finances. This information is significantly valuable in making critical future decisions that would drive an organization towards the better and more profitable approach in the future.

Financial Statements:

Financial statements are one of the key elements related to the finance and accounting of an enterprise. Financial statements are a means of keeping a formal record of all the financial activities, the performance, strength, financial effects of business transactions, and liquidity of a company.

Analysis and assessment of the financial standing and performance of an entity or an enterprise is critically significant to make decisions that would be most profitable for the enterprise. The analysis and assessment of financial statements is process of comparing and evaluating certain parts of the balance sheets from the past, present or the future to make critical decisions about the enterprise (Hasanaj and Kuqi, 2019). The analysis of financial statements is an important aspect and key process in the financial analysis which is a significantly crucial tool that interprets reports used and provided by the investors, creditors, executives, and others.

Financial Statements: Twelve Basic Principles:

Financial statement preparation and analysis is a complex task, but accountants and financial experts rely on twelve basic principles to draft-up financial statements. These rules are not necessarily strict guidelines one should follow while drafting financial statements, but they significantly help in making the process easier and the financial statements drafted cover-up all the necessary elements. Following are the 12 basic principles:

1. Accounting entity
2. Concern going
3. Measurement
4. Unit of measure
5. Historical cost
6. Materiality
7. Judgments and estimations
8. Consistency
9. Conservatism
10. Periodicity
11. Substance over form
12. Accrual basis of presentation

These rules and assumptions define and explain what financial reporting and financial statements are about.

1. **Accounting Entity:** Accounting entity means that the financial statements are prepared for a business unit which is the accounting entity. The principal idea behind an accounting entity states that there is a separate fictional person

or a company other than the business entity itself for which the books and the information is written.

2. **Concern going:** The preparation of the financial statements is aided by one of the assumptions taken into consideration by the financial experts and accountants that the enterprise or the entity is going to be around for a significantly long period of time unless there is evidence to the contrary. In most scenarios, this assumption is not always true, but still helps in drafting the financial statements to keep in account the financial standing of an entity. In any event, the accountant or the financial expert responsible for drafting financial statements and reviews concludes based on the analysis that the entity is going to be bankrupt, a "qualified opinion" should be issued stating the bankruptcy and its effects on the entity.
3. **Measurement:** Finance and accounting

3.1 Classification of the Users and the Accountant's Role

One of the functionalities that accountants perform is sort of communication. Accountancy is also a skill that is based on the communication of the financial information about a business to the shareholders and the managers (Elliott and Elliott, 2009). In previous chapters the role that accountants play in passing relevant information to the management about the businesses (project and product type) has been explained in detail. In this section of the text, the information that the accountants provide will be discussed in detail. The information and communication that the accountants generate and provide to the management is in the form of financial statements (Elliott and Elliott, 2009). Financial statements show and demonstrate in monetary terms the economic resources available under the control of management (Elliott and Elliott, 2009). Once the information is generated and passed on, the management and accountants can decide in better way about the management of these available economic resources. As mentioned previously, the skill is based on generating the relevant information that is beneficial and useful for the management and shareholders (Elliott and Elliott, 2009).

In simpler terms, the purpose of the financial statements is to provide the information about the outcomes of the operations, the financial standing of the business and the firm, and most importantly the cash flows of an organizations. The hierarchical understanding of the organizations is necessary to understand so that the readers can know about the audience of information, and the purpose. The simple questions such as who needs this information, why this information is required, and is this information generated annually, quarterly or even more frequently.

Elliot have provided a good description in the book written about the people who need this information (Elliott and Elliott, 2009). Shareholders require the financial information periodically, to know that the managers assigned for the businesses are utilizing the economic resources that have been put under their control (Elliott and Elliott, 2009). The information provided by the accountants to the shareholders helps them in evaluating the performance of managers (Elliott and Elliott, 2009). The information is important, because the performance of the managers will demonstrate the utilization of the resources, the shareholders can get the answers form the information that has there been a growth in the business, are the resources properly utilized, is there any loss in the economic resources etc. (Elliott and Elliott, 2009). The shareholders need the information to predict the future performance and standing of the business as well. Elliot suggests that in 2009 it is not necessary for the companies to make the future forecast financial statements. The information required by shareholders and managers have different purposes.

In the financial reporting context, the shareholders can be viewed as an external user. The information and knowledge reported to shareholders is limited as compared to the managers in a sense that higher level information about the costs and administration costs are provided to the shareholders, and profit loss statements. But the method of composition of these statements or analysis how the numbers have been calculated is not shown. Despite of the fact that the shareholders own the company, the amount of the information they are entitled to is limited. The limitation to the financial information of the shareholders is based on the legal implications, such as listing regulations, and market regulations etc. Elliot has provided an example in this case to explain why and how the limited financial details are provided to the shareholders, although the shareholders want to know the detailed information about the forecasted values of the future cashflows to predict and analyze the dividends, but the directors will not give the information to shareholders, as the directors think that providing this information might benefit the competitors or they may face criticism from the directors if the forecasted values are not as per the expectation (Elliott and Elliott, 2009). Also, the quality of the information is the concerning part on the basis of which the information is not fully provided. The estimation costs of long-term projects or bidding costs, and other details related to the costs of the future projects that company would do, there always exists the chances of error and miscalculations related to such estimations (Elliott and Elliott, 2009).

The financial information presented to shareholders is often used by the loan providers and creditors, and the information provided by the company is in the form of the general-purpose reports (Elliott and Elliott, 2009). Often the companies tend to prepare general purposes documents that can be used to provide financial information to multiple parties such as shareholders, loan providers, and the government as well. Sometimes it is difficult for the companies or the businesses to fulfill the informational needs of the users. But the reporting of financial information is beneficial for the company itself, as the managers and other entities included in the higher management can get aware of the company's performance so that the future strategy can be made. The timescale of the information might be different for different types of the users (Elliott and Elliott, 2009). Shareholders want the detailed information consisting of the past performance or the profit values and costings of three to four years, while the creditors or loan providers need the information about the most recent financial performance measures.

The primary focus of the financial reporting should be the shareholders, because the government gives importance to the shareholders, because they have done the economic investment into the company, and their resources serve the basic needs of the company (Elliott and Elliott, 2009). Despite of the technical, performance, or legislative reasons, that the limited amount of the financial information is provided to the shareholders, yet it is important for the company to compile correct, comprehensive, and beneficial financial statements for the performance evaluation. Moreover, the financial statements compiled in detail can also be useful for the company to apply for loans or other financial planning such as insurances for the employees as well.

Managers can be treated as internal users, who are fully aware of the financial performance and situation of the company. The internal users have the access to the detailed financial statements, and they have got the information about the extent of variation of the financial statements from the estimated or budgeted values and the future budgeted values. Moreover, they are aware of the profits and loss statements. The internal users of the financial statements can be the partners, sole traders, and company managers and directors (Elliott and Elliott, 2009). As there are no legal restrictions that restricts or limits the access of internal users to the company's financial statements. The limitation that can restrict the access of the internal users to the financial statements is the company's own policies. If there is any policy formulated that states that the managers or directors have access to only a particular amount of financial information, then this implication can limit or restrict the access of internal users to the financial statements. However, this scenario has been rarely observed. The companies mostly adopt the moderate approach, and the financial information is provided on need-to-know basis (Elliott and Elliott, 2009). The directors have full access to the company's complete financial statements. And it must be mentioned that employees do not normally have the access to any of the information that can enable them to justify the demands for the increment of financial benefits (Elliott and Elliott, 2009). Keeping in view the above discussion, it is clear that the financial statements are designed keeping in view the type and need of the user, and the company's so-called interest is always prioritized,

Based on the information and reporting as mentioned above, the users can be categorized as internal and external users (Elliott and Elliott, 2009). Elliot has categorized the financial reports as internal and external reports as well (Elliott and Elliott, 2009). The accountants working for the companies are responsible for the compilation of financial statements. The capability of the accountant working in the firm is reflected in the financial reports as well. keeping in view the nature of reporting, Elliot has categorized the competency of the accountants for the internal and external reporting, however, here the combined skill required for the internal and external reporting have been presented keeping in view the Elliot's explanation. In literature, the competency and the skills required by the accountants to work on these financial statements have been mentioned. The accountant should possess following skills (Elliott and Elliott, 2009):

- Technically sound understanding of the listings, market, and legal regulations, so that the accountant can ensure the financial statements are in agreement with these regulations (Elliott and Elliott, 2009).
- The commercial understanding and awareness are required to ensure that the financial statements present the elements of the business and commercial transactions into which the company is involved (Elliott and Elliott, 2009).
- Fully aware of the financial standing of the company including assets, and the announced and unannounced economic resources.
- The accountant should be able to fully understand the need and the requirement of the user. Based on the requirement, the financial statements should be formulated, and the accountant should also be able to explain the implication and impact of the financial statements to the user in a way that is understandable. The explanation and the description should be able to provide the confidence to the user.
- Accountant should be able to measure the related parameters objectively.
- Accountant should also be able to understand and realize the importance of time-scale. The timescale should be presented along with the financial

information so that user should be able to take decisions within time. The examples of importance of time-scale have been explained above.

- The accountant should be able to formulate and produce the financial statements that are verifiable. The reports that are intended for the internal users must contain the complete description of the transactions that have actually occurred in the past or recent past.
- The factor of the reliability should be depicted in the work of the accountants especially in the context of the internal reports that are intended for the internal users. The reliability in the current description means that the reports that the accountant make should be free from the biasness as much as possible.
- The accountant should be able to compile the reports that represent the complete picture of the material items.
- The accountant should ensure that the information presented to the user is the fair and true representation of the financial transactions and the financial events that have been occurred in the past.

Keeping in view the above defined skills the accountant can formulate, gather, and analyze the financial information as per the need and type of the user. As mentioned above, for the external users, accountants formulate the general-purpose reports that are required for decision making and are in agreement with the legislations ensuring the reliability. For the internal users, the decision-making information is provided by engaging with the user and establishing which particular financial information is required in which time frame to support the relevancy of the information with the decision-making process (Elliott and Elliott, 2009).

The financial analysis requires the ratios extracted from the financial statements to standardize the financial information to make a comprehensive comparison of the internal and external performance (Arnold et al., 2018). The internal and external performance factors are then analyzed in detail. The financial statements are quite useful in analyzing the financial situations for academic researchers for the research purposes, investors to make accurate and correct financial decisions, and regulatory authorities to monitor the transparency in the businesses (Arnold et al., 2018). Financial Accounting Standards Board (FASB) determines the qualities of the financial statements in the concept no 2 statement of the financial statements, and also provided the main qualitative attributes related to the usage, relevancy, and reliability of these financial statements (Arnold et al., 2018). As per the statements of the FASB, the relevancy of these statements should be evaluated in terms of the ability of making a difference in the decision-making process and possessiveness of a predictive value and characteristic (Arnold et al., 2018).

3.2 Reporting Methodology for the Internal Users

Elliot has suggested that the financial decision model should be used to study the user/accountant interface for establishing the specification of the financial information (Elliott and Elliott, 2009). The accountant user interface is required and this interface is established in steps (Elliott and Elliott, 2009). Figure 3.1 presented below shows the general accounting and financial decision model that would be helpful in establishing the interface (Elliott and Elliott, 2009).

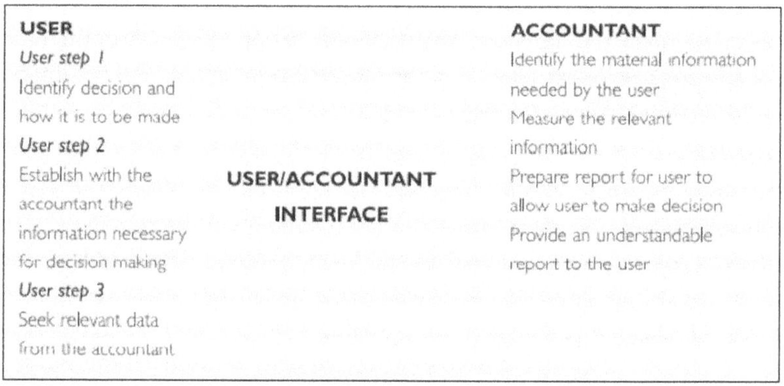

Figure 3.1 Financial decision model presented by Elliot (Elliott and Elliott, 2009).

The model presented in the figure above consists of the steps that will ultimately lead to the development of the interface (Elliott and Elliott, 2009). In the first step the accountant ensures that the appraisal-based method is followed for the decision-making process (Elliott and Elliott, 2009). The user and the accountant in the first step decide the methods for the decision making. The finalization of the method to make decision is based on the user's requirements, accountants only guide the user about the pros and cons of the methods based on their knowledge and experience. The accountant in the first step determines on his end the material information that is need by the user. In the first step both accountant and the user can decide the meeting strategies, working platforms, collaboration platforms and duration of meetings etc. that can aid the complete process.

In the second step, user highlights and specifies the financial information that is needed for the decision-making process (Elliott and Elliott, 2009). The accountant should establish and measure the relevant information that is need by the user for decision (Elliott and Elliott, 2009).

In third step user looks for and demand the relevant information form the accountant. While the accountant makes reports for the user, and it is ensured that the user understands the impact of the financial information also keeping in view the level of understanding and the knowledge of the user (Elliott and Elliott, 2009). It must be mentioned that the accountant should not consider his/her job done with the printing and presenting the report, accountant should ensure that the user understands the financial information with the clarity and the information has actually helped in the decision-making process. Elliot have specifically mentioned that the current model is based on the assumption that the financial information presented is as per the needs and the requirements of the single user rather than the user groups.

The term material has a specific meaning in terms of accounting. The information is declared material in the field of accounting, if the absence of the information would have any on the users of the financial statements. The items and goods are considered material if they have any impact on the profits.

The interest of the internal users can be different, and so will be the decisions that are required to be made from the financial information. Based on the practical situations, it is more likely to occur that the user is going to use more than one appraisal methods due to the associated advantages and disadvantages associated with each method (Elliott and Elliott, 2009). Even if the accountant is preparing the financial information for single and same types of different users, the relevancy and requirement of each user should be identified first before the planning to make financial statements (Elliott and Elliott, 2009). It is possible that the accountant's prescribed method of assessment and the user's requirements may vary, but the accountant should report from the both perspectives so that the options available for the users are enhanced, and so is the understanding. The accountants that are working on the reports intended for the internal users, it is possible that the approach adopted by the accountant is receptive (Elliott and Elliott, 2009). The accountants normally determine the cashflows, as they are more relevant to the user, and the accountants normally measure it analyze it and report it (Elliott and Elliott, 2009). Figure presented below has been taken from the book published by Elliot, in which user wants to maximize the profit (Elliott and Elliott, 2009). The user accountant interface has been presented in the Figure 3.2

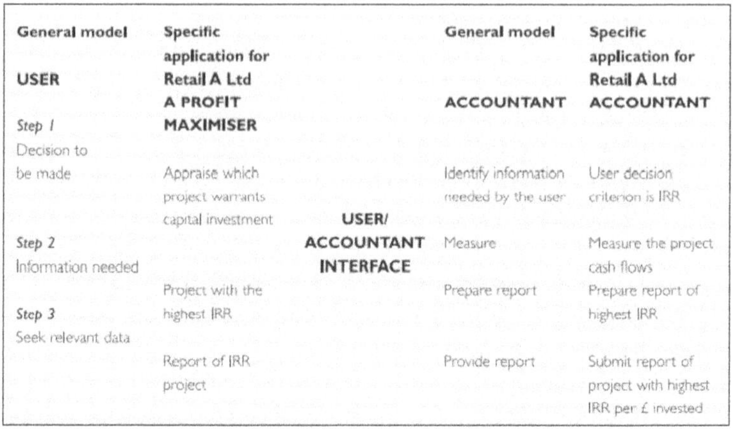

Figure 3.2 User Accountant interface for the profit maximization (Elliott and Elliott, 2009).

Before going any further, at this point it would be useful to define the cashflows. The term cash flow refers to the total amount of the cash or cash equivalent entities transferred within and without of the company. Received cash constitute the inflows, while the wealth or money spent is regarded as outflows. The company's value to the shareholders is determined on the basis of the ability of the firm to generate the positive cashflows. The cash flow statements or the statements of the cash flow refers to the reports that exhibit the cash generated within the specific period of time. Normally there are three section of the cash flow statements. These sections report the activities, and these activities are, operational, investment, and financing activities (Schmidt, 2023). The operating activities account for the main revenue generation that include all the activities other than investment or financing, and the cash flows associate with the present assets and liabilities (Schmidt, 2023). The investment activities account the cashflows that are associated with the obtaining and disposing the long-term assets and other investments that are not included in the cash equivalents (Schmidt, 2023). The main financing activities are related to the cashflows that are associated with the variations in the size and nature of the equity capital or entity borrowings such as bonds, dividends etc. (Schmidt, 2023).

IRR term used in the figure above refers to the internal rate of return, a parameter that is used in the financial assessment to estimate the profitability potential of the investment. Keeping in view the steps mentioned in the figure posted above, the first step is that the user has to make a decision related to the investment of the capital. As the scope of the decision is the profit maximization, the accountant has to determine which information is needed by the Retail A (sample company) that can help in taking the decision of the investment. As per the analysis and the user requirement, the accountant should be able to figure out that the criteria that would help the user to make the decision related to the capital investment is the IRR. It must be mentioned that the accountant in this case is fully aware of the need and requirement of the user and the functionality of the user as well that is the profit maximizer. From the accountant's functionality perspective, the second step is the measurement and preparation of the report. The accountant will then calculate and measure the cash flows of the projects and prepare the report on the basis of highest values of the Internal Rate of Return (IRR). In the last step, the internal user is seeking the relevant data to finalize the decision of the capital investment.

Relevant to the decision of the above-mentioned scenario, the concept of the agency costs that the share bear comes into effect. The financial report presented to the internal users including the managers and directors of the firm is based on the IRR value, however, the decision might not be based solely on the basis of IRR, but the project that the directors and managers think that ensure their employment security and financial benefits as well, can be selected (Elliott and Elliott, 2009). This results in the financial decision and investment that is not optimal in nature. The potential cash flow depreciation due to the sub-standardized decisions, and involvement in the long-term projects that do not possess the potential financial benefits result in the creation of the agency costs (Elliott and Elliott, 2009). The agency costs is the potential or opportunistic costs that is not availed due to the incorrect financial investment or any other reason (Elliott and Elliott, 2009). The cost is not recorded in the accounting reports and it does not appear on the financial statements as well. Neglecting the financial reports and statements, and making decisions on the basis of the personalized benefits or the employee benefits can result in the involvement of the company in a project that can cause a serious setback to the company. The accuracy and implementation of the financial reports should be ensured by the internal users to avail the potential financial benefits for the company in future. Moreover, there are many projects that involve more than one companies as explained above, and the involvement of multiple companies in the project make the success factors more complicated. Therefore, the managers and directors should demand more comprehensive and dynamic financial reporting from the accountant to consider every factor involved.

3.2.1 Cash Flow-Based Statements

As mentioned above, the statements of the cashflows are one of the important types of the financial statements. The types of the statements are categorized by the needs of the users. There are many benefits associated with the usage of the cash flow-based statements. The cash flow statements are one of the three essential financial statements that are generally required as per the Generally Accepted Accounting Principles (GAAP). Financial Accounting Standards Board (FASB) has made the cash flow-based statements an essential element of the financial reporting in 1987, and in 1988, companies have started reporting the cash flows on the quarterly and annual basis (Arnold et al., 2018).

In this section, a brief description of the historical context and usage of the cash flow statements have been provided. The cash flow statements include the information taken from the balance sheet and income statements in three categories for the calculation of cash flow (Arnold et al., 2018). The statement demands the classification of the cash statements and payments as per their association with the operating, investment and financing activities (Arnold et al., 2018). The main elements of the consideration and concentration of the cash flow statements are the liquidity, sustainability, and the durability (Arnold et al., 2018). Arnold et al. have done a comprehensive survey of the literature to analyze which type of the financial statements are currently used (Arnold et al., 2018). Cash flow statements can be utilized in providing the new dimension and direction as well to the directors, mangers, and investors by supplementing the information provided by the balance sheets and income statements. One of the distinguishing features of the cash flow statements is that these statements work on the principle of dividing the activities of the company into three categories that have been mentioned above to portray the financial condition of the company, and this information cannot be extracted from the balance sheets and income statements (Arnold et al., 2018).

The cash flow statements can be constructed using two methods these methods are:

- Direct method
- Indirect method

The statements of the cash flow based on the direct method utilize actual inflow and outflow of the cash from the operations of a company or firm. The indirect method of the formulating the cash flow statements is based on the presentation of the data that demonstrates how much a company has spent or earned during a certain time period, and the sources of these earnings and spending. The information is taken from the company's net income as mentioned on the income statement, and elements of the balance sheets are also used for determining the cash flows. In the conventional system, 90 percent of the cash flow statements are based on the indirect method (Arnold et al., 2018). Therefore, as mentioned above, the indirect method is based on the conversion of the accrual data in the form of cash in and out flows, and the cash flow statements include and combine the information from the income statement and balance sheet in three categories (attributed to the activity type) to highlight the variations in the cash and cash equivalents.

Cash flow statements can be effectively used to evaluate the company's position with reference to the liquidity and especially the prediction of the bankruptcy (Arnold et al., 2018). The detailed explanation of the bankruptcy will be provided in one of the upcoming chapters of the book. Financial rations can be utilized to effectively study the overall condition of the company with reference to the bankruptcy. Aziz and Lawson have performed a comprehensive study related to the cash flow's relevancy to the bankruptcy prediction (Aziz and Lawson, 1989). These researchers have concluded that the cash flow is an important variable that can be used in the prediction of bankruptcy (Aziz and Lawson, 1989). Financial distress can be indicated with the help of the financial ratios, and the analysis of the firm's cash flow can help in the earlier prediction of the demolishing financial situations, and the bankruptcy which will come into effect later, can be predicted earlier. In this way, cash flow can serve as a good indicator for the firms to start thinking about the financial operations at a stage where recovery is easily possible.

Arnold et al. have compiled and demonstrated the examples of the analytical techniques that use the elements from the statements of the cash flows (Arnold et al., 2018). The researchers have argued that the financial ratio analysis is the main tool that is employed for the financial analysis, and the impact of the common sizing of the financial data has also been explained (Arnold et al., 2018). The financial ratios are an effective parameter in the financial analysis, as these ratios allow the analysis and comparison of the data in relative terms rather than absolute terms, and the issue related to the sizing difference is eliminated (Arnold et al., 2018). The standardization allows the analysts to compare the parameters. As a result, the realistic and accurate financial analysis is performed. Absolute values are normalized by utilizing the ratios. Common sizing of the financial data is an example of usage of ratios. The common sized financial reports represent the values as percentage of common base number instead of absolute mathematical values. As a result, the common sized financial analysis allows the analysts to evaluate the companies having different sizes, and belonging to different market category, on a common ground. And fundamentally, a concept can be tested easily by applying it on different companies. The ratios that are based on the cash flow statements and can complement the traditional financial ratios have been discussed below (Arnold et al., 2018):

- Cash return on assets- the cash return on the assets is a measure of proportional total amount of cash spin off as a consequence of owning an asset group. Normally this parameter is used by the financial analysts to compare and analyze the performance of a business within the same industry. The ratio is highly useful for the evaluation of the performance of an asset in an industry.

$$Cash\,returns\,on\,assets = \frac{Operational\,cash\,flow}{Total\,Average\,Assets}$$

Normally while performing the calculations, the operational cash flows are derived from the cash flow statements, and the total average assets are derived from the balance sheets. It must be mentioned that all the assets written on the balance sheet are considered, not just the fixed assets. Higher value of the above-mentioned ratio represents the better performance and usage of the assets (Arnold et al., 2018). A considerable percentage of the cash return on the assets is required in an asset rich environment such as the production and manufacturing industry. In these business environments, the cash is required for maintaining and renovating an asset.

- Cash flow margin- another important variable that can be used in the financial analysis is the cash flow margin. The cash flow margin is a parameter that highlights the ability of a company to efficiently convert the sales into the cash. The parameter is important, as the purchase of an asset and the expense related to it is dealt with cash. Fundamentally it is a profitability ratio similar to the profit margin. The higher value of this ratio demonstrates the higher ability of a company or firm to transform its sales into the cash.

Cash flow margin – cash flow derived from the operating activities / sales.

Cash return ratio- cash return ratio is often used in the financial analysis. The parameters that are being explained in this section have a considerable significance, as these parameters tend to identify the financial condition of the company from different perspectives. Not only the survival factors or parameters are considered while performing a detailed financial analysis, the durability, growth perspective, and future prospective of the company is also considered.

The cash return ratio is calculated by dividing the cash flow derived from the operational activities with the average equity of the shareholders. This parameter is also a profitability ratio and is similar to the common stockholder's equity return. Cash return ratio exhibits the actual return on the equity in the future. Normally, the rising trend of cash return ratio is favorable for the business.

- Earnings quality ratio – The earnings quality ratio enables the analysts to understand the fact that either the earnings reported by the company on the financial reports are the result of the operational performance and competency, or either they are recorded from accounting adjustments. The Earnings quality ratios can be determined by dividing the cash flow derived from the operational activities by the net income. The higher value of earning quality ratio represent more sustainability in the earnings and as result an increased integrity or quality of the earnings (Arnold et al., 2018).

Dividend can be referred to as the cash, financial reward, or other form of financial benefit that the company provides to its shareholders.

- Dividend coverage ratio – The dividend coverage ratio is also known as dividend cover. The dividend cover is the financial parameter that determines the number of times that a company is able to pay the dividends to its shareholders. Dividend coverage ratio can be calculated by dividing the cash flow derived from the operational activities of a firm with the common dividends. Dividend coverage ratio can also be calculated by dividing the net income with the declared dividend. There different interpretation criteria associated with the dividend coverage ratio. If the value of the dividend coverage ratio is greater than 1, this demonstrates the fact that the earnings generated by the firm are sufficient for serving the shareholders with the dividends. The value of the ratio greater than 2 is generally considered good from the company's earning point of view. If a company has consistently the lower rates of the dividend cover ratio, that is less than 1.5, then it may be a concerning point for the shareholders. Constantly low values of the dividend cover ratio highlight the low profitability of the company in future, and the it is the warning that the firm will not be able to maintain the dividend payout level that is currently implemented. This ratio is technically similar to the reciprocal of the payout ratio The payout ratio is an important parameter for determining the sustainability of the dividends (Arnold et al., 2018).
- Cash Debt coverage ratio- the cash debt coverage ratio is calculated by dividing the operational cash flows with the average total liabilities. And the current

cash debt coverage ratio is the liquidity ratio that demonstrates the efficiency of a company in terms of the cash management (Tamplin, 2021). The ratio is useful in determining the relation of a firm's operating cash flow that was received within a time frame with the current liabilities that the company needs to clear (Tamplin, 2021). In simpler terms the current cash debt ratio determines the company's ability to of paying off its debts with the operational cash flow received within an accounting period. The current debt coverage ratio plays an important role for the potential investors to evaluate the solvency of a firm. The ratio provides the answers to two important questions that are relatable to cash management ability (Tamplin, 2021). These questions are, does the company generates enough operational cash flow that is sufficient for the business continuity, and secondly, is the operational cash flow sufficient enough to pay the decided dividends timely (Tamplin, 2021). As the ratio provides the information about the liquidity of the company, and the liquidity is more relevant and useful than generating profit for the continuation of the activities (Tamplin, 2021). The businesses are in danger or shuts down due to the crisis of the liquidity not by the low profit generation (Tamplin, 2021). So, the concluding remarks in this context can be written as the higher value of the debt coverage ratio exhibits the greater ability of the firm in carrying its debts (Arnold et al., 2018).

- Capital Intensity ratio – The capital intensity ratio can be calculated by dividing the capital expenditures by the sales. Capital intensity ratio is a parameter that provides valuable information about the company's financial condition. The measure is useful for the analysts to understand how effectively the firm is utilizing the capital or assets for the revenue generation. Technically the ratio tells the amount of capital or assets that a company needs to generate single dollar of revenue. The higher ratios values exhibit that the company is more actively reinvesting the sales into the capital assets (Arnold et al., 2018).
- Capital Expenditure Ratio – The capital expenditure ratio is calculated by dividing the capital expenditure with the net income (Arnold et al., 2018). Similar to the Capital intensity ratio, the higher value of the capital expenditure ratio shows the active reinvestment of the company's earnings in the productive assets (Arnold et al., 2018). The lower values of the ratio shows that the firm has the less resources available for spending on the property and equipment.

The purpose of explanation of these ratios that involve the cash flow is to highlight their worth as financial ratios that can aid in the financial analysis for understanding a more realistic and futuristic condition of the businesses. Arnold et al have compiled these ratios for 2013 and 2015 fiscal years for the companies like Apple, Home Depot, and Procter & Gamble (Arnold et al., 2018).

These ratios have been presented below for educational purposes.

Apple (AAPL)

Ratio	2016	2015	2014
CFO / Avg. Assets	0.2151	0.3112	0.2721
CFO / Sales	0.3053	0.3477	0.3267
CFO / Avg. Equity	0.5317	0.7039	0.5080
CFO / NI	1.4408	1.5220	1.5113
CFO / Dividends	5.4176	7.0293	5.3670
CFO / Avg. Liab.	0.3611	0.5577	0.5862
CapEx/Sales	0.0591	0.0481	0.0524
CapEx/NI	0.2787	0.2106	0.2422

Home Depot (HD)

Ratio	2016	2015	2014
CFO / Avg. Assets	0.2272	0.2049	0.1870
CFO / Sales	0.1059	0.0991	0.0968
CFO / Avg. Equity	1.1987	0.7546	0.5035
CFO / NI	1.3373	1.2990	1.4165
CFO / Dividends	3.0924	3.2577	3.4008
CFO / Avg. Liab.	0.2804	0.2812	0.2974
CapEx/Sales	0.0170	0.0173	0.0176
CapEx/NI	0.2144	0.2273	0.2579

Procter & Gamble (PG)

Ratio	2016	2015	2014
CFO / Avg. Assets	0.1203	0.1067	0.0985
CFO / Sales	0.2363	0.1915	0.1680
CFO / Avg. Equity	0.2551	0.2196	0.2013
CFO / NI	1.4556	2.0448	1.1844
CFO / Dividends	2.0757	2.0047	2.0197
CFO / Avg. Liab.	0.2277	0.2076	0.1927
CapEx/Sales	0.0508	0.0490	0.0463
CapEx/NI	0.3125	0.5230	0.3265

Figure 3.3 Financial ratios that utilize the components from the cash flow statements (Arnold et al., 2018). The picture has been taken from the original publication of the Arnold et al. for educational purposes.

Elliot mentioned in the book the method for formulating the financial statements on the cash flow basis with very simplified example, and after the explanation of the method, reasons have been explained that why this data is relevant (Elliott and Elliott, 2009). It is interesting to study the reason why the authors have declared the financial statements based on the cash flow basis relevant (Elliott and Elliott, 2009).

The first reason that was provided was that the data presented on the cash flow basis is objective (Elliott and Elliott, 2009). There is no judgmental factor involved while compiling these statements or selecting values that should be included in the financial statements. Because each value written on the cash flow financial statement can be traced to the actual financial transaction performed with an entity, and a receipt or written statement for such transactions are always available

The second reason provided was the consistency. This reason seems more applicable in case of the periodic financial statements, the case that Elliot has used while demonstrating the example (Elliott and Elliott, 2009). The statements include the same cash flows in the periodic financial statements, as the cash flows have been recorded form the initial investment period. The reality of the decision is revealed by studying the cashflow statements of the complete financial period starting from the initial capital investment (Elliott and Elliott, 2009).

The third reason is the predictive value. The same reason that has been mentioned above and issued by the Financial Accounting Standards Board (FASB) that the financial statements should be predictive. Elliot has stated these financial statements can also be used for the revision of initial forecast if required (Elliott and Elliott, 2009).

The last reason is very specific to the example presented by the authors (Elliott and Elliott, 2009). The way the cash flow statements have been compiled eliminates the need for the disclosure of accounting policies that are required for regulation of the accrual accounting methods and practices such as depreciation methods (Elliott and Elliott, 2009).

By doing the detailed analysis, the researchers have found that the major literature portion of the financial analysis is based on the usage of balance sheet and income statements (Arnold et al., 2018). Moreover, the statement of the cash flow has been rarely used in the ratio analysis while performing the financial analysis (Arnold et al., 2018). Moreover, the amount of the literature associated with the cash flow statements is limited as compared to the balance sheet and income statements.

3.3 Reporting Methodology for the External Users

The categorization and needs of the internal and external users have been discussed in detail in the explanation provided at the start of the chapter. External financial reporting is based in the provision of the periodic financial information to the external users that mainly consist of investors and shareholders. For external reporting, Elliot have mentioned some of the characteristic features that companies should adopt. And these characteristics have been defined relevant to the cash flow statements (Elliott and Elliott, 2009). The concept of stewardship has been mentioned in internal and external reporting (Elliott and Elliott, 2009). The role of the accounting stewardship becomes more relevant when the financial reports are prepared for the external users. The steward's responsibility in the financial reporting ensures that financial benefits of the stock and shareholders are preserved. The cash flow-based reporting is actually stewardship-oriented approach and it ensures the transparency in the management of the cash resources and accountability over the investment decisions (Elliott and Elliott, 2009).

As mentioned above the shareholders are mostly interested in the capacity of the company to pay dividends. The cash flows of the past and the present are the good indicators for the prediction of the future values of the cash flows and dividends that the company will pay to shareholders, however, the cash flows can be misleading in certain cases (Elliott and Elliott, 2009). Therefore, the income statement based on the accrual practices can serve as a better measure for predicting the future cash flows, and the investors and shareholders as well (Elliott and Elliott, 2009). The importance of the cash flow statements and adherence to these statements can be estimated by the report of the financial reporting council published in 2008 in which it was stated that the directors evaluate that the company is constantly a concern or not and as for this assessment, they may compile monthly forecast based on the cash flows and monthly budget up to the period when the next financial statement is planned, and the situation is worsened when these forecasts are associated or based on the list of assumptions (Elliott and Elliott, 2009).

3.3.1 Accounting Standards' Requirement for the External Users

In 2005 IASB stated that the financial reporting done for the external users should be based on the financial statements, and these statements should include the following statements (Elliott and Elliott, 2009):

- Statement of financial position
- Comprehensive and detailed income statement

- Equity changes statements
- Cash flow statements
- Notes based on the significant accounting policies, methods, and practices.

In 2007 IASB issued following requirements with reference to the complete financial statements (Elliott and Elliott, 2009). These requirements are as follow:

- Financial position statements published at the end of the period. This means that both pre and post year titles shall be used for the periods such pre 2008 and post 2008 (Elliott and Elliott, 2009).
- Comprehensive income statements at the end of the period
- Statement of variations in the equity for the entire period
- Cash flow statement for the entire period
- Notes based on the significant accounting policies, methods, and practices.

3.3.2 Income Statements

Income statements present a report that show how much revenue is generated by the company in a specific time period. The costs and expenses incurred on earning that revenue is also mentioned in the income statements. In simpler terms, the total earnings and losses that the company have faced in a specific time period is reported in the income statement. Earnings per share is also the part of the income statements. Earnings per share calculation reveals that how much financial benefit or money the shareholders will get in case the company has decided to distribute complete total earnings for that particular period. Historic cost convention and the Accrual accounting concepts are two of the main methods that can be used for the compilation of the income statements.

The usage of the income statement is highly variable. As from the legal point of view and regulatory convention, shareholders shall be provided by the income statement of that period. The income statement can be used to formulate the financial ratios, and these ratios are the main tools for the evaluation of the financial conditions of the company. The ratios can also be used internally for evaluation of the company's position, and the areas that need improvement can be highlighted. Therefore, the income statements can be used internally as well. The main contents of the financial statements that are generally included are, total comprehensive income, tax expense, profit, and losses, etc.

3.3.3 Accrual and Historic Cost Convention in Accounting

The accrual concept of the accounting is based on the recording of the transactions at the time of occurrence, irrespective of the time when the actual cash flows are received for the transactions. Using this concept, the customer's cash receipts and the payments to the creditors are represented as revenues and expenses respectively. The accrual method of accounting provides the information about the real financial condition of the company, but the method is more inconvenient to adopt for the small companies and businesses. The accrual concept of the accounting is a standard procedure and both GAAP and IFRS acknowledge it as a standard accounting practice.

The historical cost convention is the more useful method of measurement of the economic resources. Using this method, the transactions are represented at the financial statements on the amount that was recorded at the date of the transaction. The results of the agency agreement can be determined with the confidence using this method, because the data reported in this way is objective. The historic cost of an assets represents the original cost that was paid at the time of buying.

3.3.4 Balance Sheets

The balance sheet is an important financial statement that serves the needs of external users. Assets, liabilities, and equity of the shareholders at a specific time is reported via balance sheets. Investors can use the balance sheets to evaluate the rate of return, and the situation of the debt and equity of the company can also be evaluated. As mentioned previously, the practical financial analysis requires the usage of ratios. Many useful financial ratios can be estimated and calculated using the information provided by the balance sheets. Two of the important ratios that can be estimated using the balance sheets are debt to equity and acid test ratio. From the investors point of view, the clear picture is obtained by the analysis of the balance sheets and the questions that are always the part of discussion as well as the decision of the investors such as How much resources or monetary wealth the company owns, how much debt company the company owes and the amount of the resources that shareholders have invested in the company, are answered by the balance sheets. By analyzing the statistics and numbers, investors make the realization that either the company has properly utilized the resources that have been invested by the shareholders. And this determines the decision of the investor of making the investment. For the external users Balance sheet serves as one of the decision-making factors. The balance sheet revolves around the simplified sum of the variables as presented below

Asset = Liabilities + Shareholders Equity

The shareholders' equity is an important parameter that needs attention and it is also sometimes referred to as the capital worth of a firm. The shareholders' equity is the amount of wealth or money left in the case when the company sale all of the assets it possesses and pay off all the liabilities. The money belongs to the shareholders and the owners of the company.

Arya et al. have provided detailed explanation of estimation of the transactions using income statements and the balance sheets (Arya et al., 2000). Balance sheets provide useful information which help in decision making in different businesses. Businesses can be of varied nature, such as health care, engineering, transport etc. Handley have provided different reasons about the usefulness of the balance sheets in demonstrating the outcomes, expenditures, and costs in the healthcare system (Handley, 2005).

It must be mentioned that not only the companies or firms issue or publish the balance sheets, but also the governments publish it. Balance sheet presents the assets, liabilities, and the net position of the government. The financial reports of the United States Government can be found at the official website of the Bureau of Fiscal services, which is the government website (Bureau of the Fiscal Service). Balance sheet of the United States Government is also available at this website, and the components of the balance sheet have been clearly stated (Bureau of the Fiscal Service).

For the commercial banks, or private companies, accounting data is the means by which management accountants provide the information to the shareholders about the performance of the organization (Hawkins, 2003). The parameters like net worth and profit may be the performance parameters for the private or commercial banks (Hawkins, 2003). The interpretation of the financial statements for the central banks is more complicated task, as the performance goal is not to maximize the profit but the goals tend to be more social in nature, such as lower the rate of inflation, ensure the financial stability etc. (Hawkins, 2003). The balance sheets of the central banks provide a lot of information about the environment that directly or indirectly provide the monetary policy of the institution and relative measure of the central bank independence (Hawkins, 2003). To highlight the elements which compose the balance sheets of the banks, the central bank balance sheet has been presented below.

Central bank balance sheets

% to GDP, end-2002

	Liabilities							Assets					
	Currency	Banks' required deposits	Other bank deposits	Central bank securities	Government deposits	Other liabilities	Capital, reserves etc	Foreign assets	Loans to government	Government bonds	Claims on financial institutions	Claims on private sector	Other assets
Hong Kong	9.8	0.0	0.0	9.7	24.1	5.6	25.8	70.2	0.0	0.0	5.0	0.0	0.0
India[1]	11.6	2.6	0.1	0.0	0.0	1.0	5.0	12.0	0.6	6.0	0.3	0.0	1.4
Indonesia	6.0	2.3	0.0	0.0	6.9	20.5	2.0	18.1	17.2	0.0	1.0	0.5	0.9
Korea	4.1	2.5	3.2	14.1	1.9	2.9	1.4	23.1	0.2	0.9	5.0	0.1	0.8
Malaysia	7.6	4.2	15.4	3.4	3.9	2.5	8.4	36.7	0.0	0.0	0.8	2.2	5.6
Philippines[2]	5.8	2.7	0.0	0.0	2.5	15.2	4.5	21.1	2.0	4.5	0.6	0.0	2.2
Thailand	10.3	0.9	0.1	0.0	1.0	6.5	30.0	31.2	0.4	1.8	5.6	0.0	9.7
Brazil	3.8	6.0	0.0	5.1	6.7	15.3	0.4	11.7	0.0	20.5	0.0	1.7	3.4
Mexico	4.3	2.5	0.0	3.7	1.4	0.7	0.6	8.1	0.0	0.0	2.2	0.0	2.8
Peru	3.3	5.5	0.1	1.0	5.6	3.0	0.4	17.1	0.0	0.2	0.1	0.0	1.7
Czech rep[3]	10.1	23.5	0.0	0.0	0.5	2.4	-2.1	30.6	0.0	0.0	0.0	0.0	3.7
Hungary	7.7	2.2	3.9	8.4	0.5	2.7	0.2	16.9	6.0	1.0	0.1	0.0	1.6
Poland[2]	6.1	1.6	0.0	2.8	1.4	1.5	5.2	16.5	0.0	0.9	1.0	0.0	0.2
Israel	3.7	10.3	0.0	0.0	10.7	1.1	0.6	23.0	1.0	1.2	0.6	0.0	0.5
SouthAfrica	3.6	1.5	3.4	0.7	0.1	3.6	0.0	6.0	0.0	1.3	1.1	0.0	4.4
Turkey	2.8	3.3	1.6	0.0	1.5	19.2	1.0	15.9	0.0	10.5	0.1	0.0	2.9
Australia	4.6	0.0	0.1	0.0	1.3	1.7	0.8	5.6	0.0	2.8	0.1	0.0	0.1
Canada	3.6	0.0	0.1	0.0	0.1	0.0	0.0	0.1	0.0	3.5	0.0	0.0	0.2
Euro area	5.6	0.0	4.0	0.1	0.6	2.2	2.2	5.3	0.3	1.2	5.6	0.2	1.9
Switzerland	9.5	1.1	0.0	0.0	1.7	0.3	16.7	12.8	0.0	0.6	0.5	0.0	15.3

[1] June 2002. [2] November 2002. [3] April 2003.

Source: Central banks, BIS estimates.

Figure 3.4 Central Bank balance sheets (The image has been taken from the original publication of the John Hawkins for educational purposes).

There exists a clear differentiation between the Liabilities and Assets. The financial stability of the company can be well assessed by carefully analyzing the financial statements. A firm or company that is not able to meet the liabilities finally arrives at a point in which the economic activity is almost zero, and the negative equity balance occurs, or reaches the point of bankruptcy (Çolak, 2021). In the past, researchers have worked on the optimization aspects of thee balance sheets of the banks, since the optimization applied to the balance sheets have several advantages (Júdice and Zhu, 2021). Many factors have been integrated into the balance sheets such as regulations, risk constraints, and various types of risks (Júdice and Zhu, 2021). Júdice and Zhu have used linear program for the optimization of balance sheet using duality (Júdice and Zhu, 2021). Sekkel conducted a real time, out of sample, analysis for finding the predictive power of aggregate financial intermediaries for different financial activities (Sekkel, 2015). The researcher has stated that the balance sheets of the leveraged financial institutions do have the predictive power for forecasting the future economic activity, and the ability to predict the future economic activity increases during the period of financial crisis (Sekkel, 2015).

The strength in the balance sheets and lower spending favor higher consumption and investments (Makrelov et al., 2020). Kulikova has demonstrated a method of using the determinants of the balance sheets as an informational model for determining the financial position of a company or firm using the economic and mathematical modeling (Kulikova et al., 2015). The balance sheets and other financial statements of the BMW are publicly available on the internet. For understanding purposes, the Balance sheet of the BMW Group published at 31st December has been shown below (BMW, 2020).

BALANCE SHEET AT 31 DECEMBER

in € million	Notes	2020	2019
ASSETS			
Intangible assets	1	488	405
Property, plant and equipment	2	12,520	12,473
Investments	3	2,826	3,762
Tangible, intangible and investment assets		16,834	**16,640**
Inventories	4	5,746	5,994
Trade receivables	5	778	964
Receivables from subsidiaries	5	18,939	16,698
Other receivables and other assets	5	3,849	3,513
Marketable securities	6	3,175	4,109
Cash and cash equivalents	7	6,822	6,757
Current assets		39,472	**38,035**
Prepaid expenses	8	73	**58**
Surplus of pension and similar plan assets over liabilities	9	1,261	**1,086**
Total assets		57,640	**55,819**

»

Figure 3.5 BMW balance sheets for year 2020 (BMW, 2020).

3.4 Financial Reporting from Economic Aspect

The advisory committee of U.S. Securities and Exchange Commission's (SEC) formulated for the suggestion of improvements to the financial reporting have actually defined the complexity of the financial reporting (Chychyla et al., 2019). The difficulty has been described that for preparers of the financial statements it is difficult to apply the GAAP in United States and transmit or convey the economic transaction items and events, and the financial standing of the company (Chychyla et al., 2019). The difficulty can be realized for the accountants in preparing the financial statements of complex economic activities while keeping in view the needs of the users. The continuous conflict of short terms interest between management, directors and shareholders further complicates the situation.

The global financial stability is very much affected by the randomized trend of the economic activities. The external balance sheets of the emerging or developing economic states are the evidence of this trend (Akyüz, 2021). Currently, the balance sheets of the emerging economies have expanded, and the possession of low yielding assets and high yielding liabilities have resulted in the involvement of such types of economic activities that contribute directly to the global financial instability (Akyüz, 2021).

3.5 Practical Examples Related to the Financial Reporting

The financial reporting as explained above does have forceful impact on the decisions of the management, investors, and stakeholders. Including the performance of the business, the financial reports and the statements does impact the decisions of the investors to either invest in a firm or not, if investment decision is positive, then how much should be invested? It all depends upon the representation of the numbers on the financial statements. Different case studies related to financial accounting theories and techniques have been summarized by the Walter in a thesis submitted to university of Mississippi (Kearney III, 2018).

The case study presented here consists of the financial statements of the two companies that perform same operations, and both provide the small heating units to the homes (Kearney III, 2018). These companies are Eads Heaters, Inc. and the Glenwood Heating, Inc. (Kearney III, 2018). Both of these companies operate in the same way, the difference lies in the accounting practices selected and supervised by the management of the companies (Kearney III, 2018). The purpose of the case study is to present the financial statements of both companies and evaluate from the investment point of view that which company would be better for the investment decision from the investor's perspective (Kearney III, 2018).

Table 3.1 presented below shows the Glenwood Trial Balance (Kearney III, 2018).

Table 3.1 Glenwood Trial Balance (Kearney III, 2018)

Glenwood Trial Balance		
	Debits	Credits
Cash	426	
Accounts Receivable	99,400	
Allowance for Bad Debts		994
Inventory	62,800	
Land	70,000	
Building	350,000	
Accumulated Depreciation, Building		10,000
Equipment	80,000	
Accumulated Depreciation, Equipment		9,000
Accounts Payable		26,440
Interest Payable		6,650
Note Payable		380,000
Common Stock		160,000
Dividends	23,200	
Sales		398,500
Cost of Goods Sold	177,000	
Other Operating Expenses	34,200	
Bad Debt Expense	994	
Depreciation Expense, Building	10,000	
Depreciation Expense, Equipment	9,000	
Rent Expense	16,000	
Interest Expense	27,650	
Provision for Income Tax	30,914	
Totals	991,584	991,584

Table 3.2 presented below shows the Eads Trial Balance (Kearney III, 2018).

Table 3.2 Eads Trial Balance (Kearney III, 2018)

	Debits	Credits
Cash	7,835	
Accounts Receivable	99,400	
Allowance for Bad Debts		4,970
Inventory	51,000	
Land	70,000	
Building	350,000	
Accumulated Depreciation, Building		10,000
Equipment	80,000	
Accumulated Depreciation, Equipment		20,000
Leased Equipment	92,000	
Accumulated Depreciation, Leased Equipment		11,500
Accounts Payable		26,440
Interest Payable		6,650
Note Payable		380,000
Lease Payable		83,360
Common Stock		160,000
Dividends	23,200	
Sales		398,500
Cost of Goods Sold	188,800	
Other Operating Expenses	34,200	
Bad Debt Expense	4,970	
Depreciation Expense, Building	10,000	
Depreciation Expense, Equipment	20,000	
Depreciation Expense, Leased Equipment	11,500	
Interest Expense	35,010	
Provision for Income Tax	23,505	
Totals	1,101,420	1,101,420

Tables 3.3 and 3.4 presented below show the income statement of both companies (Kearney III, 2018).

Table 3.3 Income Statement of Glenwood Heating

Glenwood Heating, Inc. Income Statement For Year Ended December 31, 20X1		
Sales		398,500
Cost of Goods Sold		177,000
Gross Profit		221,500
Operating Expenses		
Selling and Administrative Expenses		
Bad Debt Expense	994	
Depreciation Expense - Building	10,000	
Depreciation Expense - Equipment	9,000	
Rent Expense	16,000	
Other Operating Expenses	34,200	70,194
Income from Operations		151,306
Other Expenses		
Interest Expense		27,650
Income Before Taxes		123,656
Provision for Income Taxes		30,914
Net Income		92,742
Earnings Per Common Share		28.98

Table 3.4 Eads Income Statement

Eads Heaters, Inc. Income Statement For Year Ended December 31, 20X1		
Sales		398,500
Cost of Goods Sold		188,800
Gross Profit		209,700
Operating Expenses		
Selling and Administrative Expenses		
Bad Debt Expense	4,970	
Depreciation Expense - Building	10,000	
Depreciation Expense - Equipment	20,000	
Depreciation Expense - Leased Equipment	11,500	
Other Operating Expenses	34,200	80,670
Income from Operations		129,030
Other Expenses		
Interest Expense		35,010
Income Before Taxes		94,020
Provision for Income Taxes		23,505
Net Income		70,515
Earnings Per Common Share		22.04

The ratios are presented below Table 3.5 (Kearney III, 2018).

Table 3.5 Financial Ratio Comparison (Kearney III, 2018)

	Glenwood	Eads
Current Ratio	4.88	4.63
Acid-Test Ratio	3.02	3.24
Gross Profit Margin	0.56	0.53
Return on Assets	0.14	0.10
Return on Equity	0.40	0.34
Earnings Per Share	28.98	22.04
Debt Ratio	0.64	0.71

Tables 3.6 and 3.7 presented below show the balance sheets of both organizations.

Table 3.6 Balance sheet of Glenwood Heating, Inc. (Kearney III, 2018)

Glenwood Heating, Inc.
Balance Sheet
For Year Ended December 31, 20X1

Assets					
Current Assets					
	Cash				426
	Accounts Receivable			99,400	
		Less: Allowance for Bad Debt Expense		994	98,406
	Inventory				62,800
		Total Current Assets			161,632
Property, Plant, and Equipment					
	Land			70,000	
	Building			350,000	
	Equipment			80,000	
		Less: Accumulated Depreciation, Building	10,000		
		Less: Accumulated Depreciation, Equipment	9,000		
		Total Accumulated Depreciation	19,000		
		Total Plant, Property, and Equipment			481,000
Total Assets					642,632
Liabilities and Stockholders' Equity					
Current Liabilities					
	Accounts Payable				26,440
	Interest Payable				6,650
		Total Current Liabilities			33,090
Long-Term Liabilities					
	Notes Payable				380,000
		Total Liabilities			413,090
Stockholders' Equity					
	Common Stock			160,000	
	Retained Earnings			69,542	
		Total Stockholders' Equity			229,542
Total Liabilities and Stockholders' Equity					642,632

Table 3.7 Balance sheet of Eads Heaters, Inc. (Kearney III, 2018)

Eads Heaters, Inc.
Balance Sheet
For Year Ended December 31, 20X1

Assets			
Current Assets			
Cash			7,835
Accounts Receivable		99,400	
Less: Allowance for Bad Debt Expense		4,970	94,430
Inventory			51,000
Total Current Assets			153,265
Property, Plant, and Equipment			
Land		70,000	
Building		350,000	
Equipment		80,000	
Leased Equipment		92,000	
Less: Accumulated Depreciation, Building	10,000		
Less: Accumulated Depreciation, Equipment	20,000		
Less: Accumulated Depreciation, Leased Equipmen	11,500		
Total Accumulated Depreciation	41,500		
Total Plant, Property, and Equipment			550,500
Total Assets			703,765
Liabilities and Stockholders' Equity			
Current Liabilities			
Accounts Payable			26,440
Interest Payable			6,650
Total Current Liabilities			33,090
Long-Term Liabilities			
Notes Payable			380,000
Lease Payable			83,360
Total Liabilities			496,450
Stockholders' Equity			
Common Stock		160,000	
Retained Earnings		47,315	
Total Stockholders' Equity			207,315
Total Liabilities and Stockholders' Equity			703,765

The retained earnings of both companies are shown in the Table 3.8 presented below (Kearney III, 2018).

Table 3.8 Retained Earnings of Glenwood and Eads Inc.

Glenwood Retained Earnings

Glenwood Heating, Inc.
Statement of Retained Earnings
For Year Ended December 31, 20X1

Beginning Retained Earnings January 1, 20X1	0
Plus: Net Income	92,742
	92,742
Less: Dividends	-23,200
Ending Retained Earnings December 31, 20X1	69,542

Eads Retained Earnings

Eads Heaters, Inc.
Statement of Retained Earnings
For Year Ended December 31, 20X1

Beginning Retained Earnings January 1, 20X1	0
Plus: Net Income	70,515
	70,515
Less: Dividends	-23,200
Ending Retained Earnings December 31, 20X1	47,315

The investment decision can be made by analyzing the financial statements of both companies and the financial ratios that can be computed on the basis of the data presented. By analyzing the above presented ratios, it can be inferred that Glenwood Heating is a wise decision for the investment point of view due to the reason that the company is more efficiently handling the revenue based on expenditure (Kearney III, 2018). The net income and the retained earnings figures of the Glenwood Inc. are better than the Eads Heating Inc.

3.6 Conclusion

The financial statements provide the useful information about the company performance to the various entities in the society. There are external and internal users of the financial statements. The financial statements provided to the internal and external users are sometimes framed as per the needs and the interests of the management as well. There are some of the regulatory requirements that compel the companies across the world to release the financial statements. The good financial statements are the ones which provide the data for the calculation of the financial ratios. The financial ratios are the true and accurate picture of the success and the future of the business. The investment opportunities, loans, and the AIS provided by different agencies are based on the performance shown by the companies on the financial statements. The Governments also release the balance sheets to show the financial activity. The financial reporting is one of the key areas that needs attention, and it will augment the process of achievement of the sustainable development goals. There are different types of the financial statements, some of which are the cash flow statements, income statement, and the balance sheet. The Accounting standards also have the requirements related to the financial statements. Financial Reporting is a domain in which the accountants directly contribute to.

The transparency in the business can be ensured by ensuring the transparent financial statements. The details of the transactions, assets, liabilities, and other important parameters should be clearly stated on the financial statements. As mentioned above the financial statements have an impact on the decision of the investors, creditors, and evaluators as well. the management should ensure the transparent, reliable, and meaningful financial reporting in their organizations. Wang after conducting the detailed mathematical analysis on the Taiwan 50 indexed list companies concluded that the sustainability reporting is positively related to the firm's growth (Wang, 2017).

4 Financial Stability

Abstract: Financial stability is basically all the measures required for the institution to avoid instability, to analyzes risks, prices and do an efficient development, a very robust and flawless payment, ability to resolve external risks, imbalance or even take preventive measures, institutions should be stable and durable so much they are able to absorb shocks because of financial imbalance and lastly ability of organization to recover from losses or instability. All these factors define financial stability. Most of financial institutions try to achieve stability by taking steps to avoid financial instability, study and analyze past financial crisis, ensure market discipline. Our study of financial crisis has shown that financial crisis causes a great scale of imbalance in both economic and financial sector all over the world and crisis not only target financial institutions but non-financial institutions also. The main causes of instability are unstable macroeconomic environment, significant distortion in the economy, non-suitable public policy, inefficient financial management and market discipline etc.

Keywords: Financial Stability, Financial Crisis, Financial Continuity, Financial Deviation, Financial Balance.

Financial stability is defined as the ability to expedite and strengthen economic processes, manage risks and nullify shocks. Financial stability is considered as continuous field, varying over time and consistent with the various combinations of the integral elements of finance (Schinasi, 2004).

4.1 Introduction

While covering the topic of financial stability several questions arise such as does financial stability require durability of institutions, stable markets, absence of instability or something basic or something central, can this stability be achieved by doing some individual actions or managed at public sector, are there proper guidelines, frameworks or steps to achieve financial stability? In order to get answers for the last questions definition of financial stability must be comprehended.

From research it has been known that there is not a proper guideline, steps, and models to achieve financial stability. It's been nearly a decade and still there is no practical implemented definition of financial stability. As it is the saying of Governor of the Swedish central bank (Allen and Wood, 2006).

"The concept of stability is slightly vague and difficult to define"

Compared to other fields of economics there is not a proper model to achieve financial stability this is because the research and analysis of financial stability is still in development stage. There are a lot of variables involved making it very difficult to pinpoint single target value. However, it is very clear about the concept of financial stability which is clearly to avoid the downfall of company financially and to reduce the economic collapse to minimum. It means any institution that is very financial stable and able to withstand shocks (Bascand, 2019).

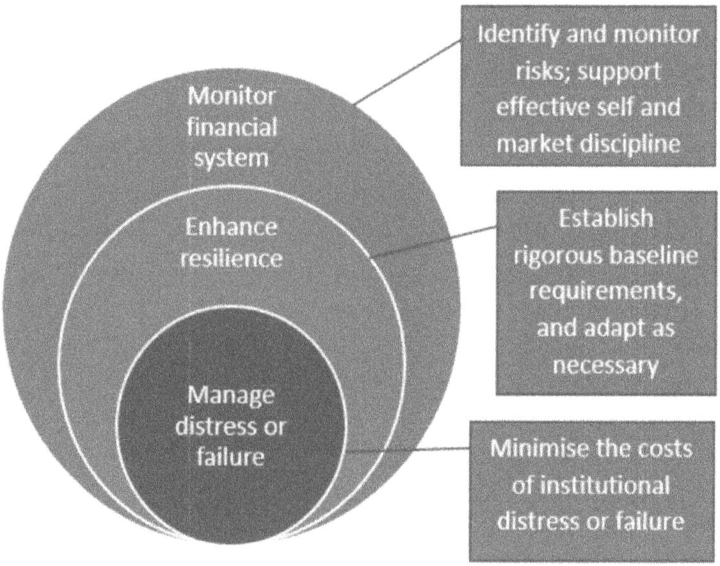

Figure 4.1 Financial stability approach applied by Bank of New Zealand (Bascand, 2019)

If any company wants to obtain financial stability, it should follow the above-mentioned approach. It must have a very sound monitoring system that monitors all the risks, activities and ensure that market discipline is practiced, system must be very resilient, it must be able to withstand shocks and failures.

Before developing concept of financial stability, we need to consider the following concepts which are very generic and play a vital role in economy.

Barter is defined as exchange system in which involved parties do their transaction by offering their services and goods in exchange of services and goods also without using wealth.

Most importantly economy with the feature to spend finances on future real resources is very much preferred over barter economy. Word economic systems deal in actual resources and any sector must have the ability to invest in resources using actual finances.

Processes to achieve financial stability must ensure that all transactions and financial activity must satisfy monetary economy. All transactions must involve money transfer.

Monetary system or economy is method in which participants do the transaction involving money.

Another important economic activity is storage of money. During the transaction of wealth several means are used to transfer the monetary value of wealth. Actual money is only used in cased of emergency and drastic economic fall. This approach has been practiced throughout the human history.

Money and finances also provide service for both private and public sectors. Services provided by finance and wealth are both public and private goods. They benefit private sector such that financial transactions provide benefits to the persons involved in the transaction. In addition, finances also provide benefit to the public. Financial activities and transactions provide public goods that encompasses not only fiat money. Transactions of the fiat money bring out a lot of opportunities such as trade, economic growth and development, production resulting in the social prosperity. In short, all the financial activities ensure that all the members of society get benefit.

Fiat money is the money that is assigned by the government in the form of currency that is not aided by commodity like silver and gold.

A very useful way that finances provide is to introduce trust and human promises. Financial activity involves human trust and promises such that one involved party will pay some amount of fiat money in the future. This system involves a lot of uncertainties about human trust. Modern economic and financial system has transformed this uncertainty into risks such as default risk, market risks, liquidity risks and so on making these risks quantifiable. These are labeled as economic and financial risks and uncertainties.

Conclusion is that finances bring a lot of aspects involving uncertainties of trust which has both benefits and costs. Finances bring a lot of benefits to both social and private life. Private and social benefits of fiat money enhance the pool of liquidity thus facilitating the economic growth and development. Secondly uncertainty of trust has created a large social benefit that is far beyond the reach of fiat money. Through this trust factor, large number of companies are able to develop and extend their relationship thus contributing to positive change in individual and social life, that's why majority of companies spend a lot of investment and energy to build sound trust between people

The disadvantage and major cause are the financial instability is trust factor which is very fragile. lack of trust and doubts have a large impact on financial activity resulting in drastic changes in the market that offsets the balance of the market. Secondly problem associated with the mistrust and doubt can lead to significant issues and problems. The factors such as mistrust and doubt amongst market players and business holders can lead to sudden withdrawal of significant amount of assets. This sudden withdrawal of assets can eventually lead and open way to instability at numerous levels. Lack of trusts can be caused by several reasons, one of major one is any participants not able to fulfill the requirements of transaction. The magnitude of this financial instability may vary depending upon the trust downfall. This financial instability brings exponential change in both private and social life and cause a drastic change in economic development.

4.2 Financial Crisis

Before discussing financial stability in detail, we need to discuss the main reason for implementing financial stability and what caused international organizations such as IRFS, international banks etc. to develop environment that ensures financial stability. As discussed above financial instability has a lot of consequences on financial institutions as well as other institutions, this source of instability on large scale will lead to financial crisis. Financial crisis comprises of large number of situations on broader aspect where liabilities, financial assets lose their value in exponential pattern, these factors will lead to stock market crashes, bursting of financial bubbles, currency and pricing crises. There are three stages of financial stability, first is the initiation of financial instability leading to banking crisis and resulting in Debt inflation. In history there are lot of economic ups and downs, but humanity suffered from global financial crisis five times which resulted in great imbalance in financial and economic activity throughout the globe. Following are the five financial crises on global scale.

4.3 The Credit Crisis of 1772

London was the primary target of this crisis, this crisis spread to rest of Europe in no time. British empire in the 18th century practiced colonization across the Europe and gathered a large amount of wealth from colonial possessions and trade. British banks thought about expanding after such accumulation of wealth. On June 8, 1772 major burst in economic activity started when one of partners of British bankers fled to France to escape his debts. This caused creditors marching at British banks to demand cash withdrawal, which led to great financial crisis across Europe.

4.4 The Great Depression of 1929–39

This was the worst economic crisis in 20th century. It was believed that major cause of The Great Depression was the Wall Street crash of 1929 and bad policy decisions by US government at that time (McCulloch, 20218). This crisis lasted for 10 years causing a great deal of poverty, un employment, income loss on very large scale.

4.5 The OPEC Oil Price Shock of 1973

This crisis began when OPEC (Organization of the Petroleum Exporting Countries) mostly consisting of Arabic countries retaliated against United State by stopping their oil supply to United States. This retaliation was started because US supplied weapons to Israel in Fourth Arab–Israeli War.

4.6 The Asian Crisis of 1997

The crisis originated in 1997 when Thailand decided to alter the currency exchange rate of dollar which it had maintained for so long, this caused a great spike and panic amongst all the institution who spend millions of dollars of investment, this crisis spread all across East Asia until IMF had to step in. This policy was mainly implemented by Bank of Thailand (Jansen, 2001).

4.7 The Financial Crisis 2007–08

The Biggest financial crisis since The Great Depression occurred in 2007–08 starting from US and later on affecting nearly most part of world (Danziger, 2013). It is called The Great Recession and it affected financial markets all around the world. This was the main cause in motivating international organizations to define financial stability, IRFS developed standards of financial stability. This crisis began with collapse of housing bubble in the US (Acharya and Richardson, 2009), the crisis also caused collapse of Lehman Brothers (one of the biggest investment banks in the world). This brought many major financial institutions, banks and business to collapse. It cost billions of dollars of income and eliminated millions of jobs and lasted almost a decade (Danziger, 2013). The main events that caused this crisis are summarized by a lot of researchers which we will briefly discuss. First cause was lowering of interest rate for housing society (Stieglitz, 2010), Federal Reserves lowered the interest rate and therefore encouraged a lot of Americans to fulfill their dream of home owner ship this also led to risky lending (when you lend money to someone and there is a risk that he won't be able to pay it back) which led to housing crisis. Reduced standards for mortgage caused unsafe subprime mortgage crisis. They thought that housing societies and authorities will be able to manage themselves without official intervention. These factors not only led to deregulation of housing market but also investors, banks, investing banks, insurance companies suffered from high deregulation. Bankers working with corruptible rating agencies was another major factor in financial crisis. This financial crisis not only affected US but also countries from all around the world. Many European countries suffered great deal of insolvency; trillions of dollars were lost. Bankers from all around world invested in this housing society and suffered a great deal of loss.

All of these Financial crises discussed above caused a great financial loss at global scale. This made researchers and economist to do analysis and find out the root causes of instability. Therefore, organizations like IRFS set accounting standards to achieve financial stability, organizations did a lot of research on finding the sources of financial instability and what factors may lead to it. In this article we will discuss in detail financial instability, sources of financial instability, financial stability's definition, factors leading to financial stability.

4.8 Financial Instability and Its Sources

In modern capitalist economies, alternating rise and downfall of economy constitute. The boom and bust cycle.

Past experiences have shown that financial crisis or financial downfall cause a great economic and financial imbalance in the society which not only affects the financial institution but also cover every aspect of life. If banking system is collapsed than every party involved in transaction or banking activities will suffer. A Lot of factors contribute to these crises like unstable macroeconomic environment, significant distortion in the economy. Emerging market economies are less diverse and less able to absorbs shocks than mature industrial economies instead they have a great tendency towards boom burst cycles. Poor management in macroeconomic activities is major cause of instability. The root causes of financial instability are found in less efficient macroeconomic activities and failed financial institutions. Problems start with poor management in financial institutions. Mismanagement in internal controls, frauds and insider dealings are source of less reliable financial assets. When owners don't face incentives to act prudently and supervise and guide management, it worsens moral hazards, management tends to apply rules that are not compatible with financial system, all of these situations will cause great shocks in financial institution. There is widely used term weak financial framework, upon study it has been seen that week framework is mainly because of poor management and inefficient governance for example in efficient process for collection of collateral in case of repayment of loan. In adequate information or distorted incentives can slow down performance of discipling the bad performers in financial markets. In absence of market discipline, a lot of responsibility falls on the shoulders of regulators and supervisors who may not have the capacity to do it all.

> *Macroeconomic conditions mainly consist of variables such as GDP growth potential, the unemployment rate, inflation, and fiscal and monetary policy orientations and economic outputs.*

Crisis in the financial sector involved international spill over which affected other institutions as well, so this is a very serious concern for international financial community. There are several cases when countries suffering from financial crisis looked towards international financial community for their aid. This support helped countries to maintain economic balance and to recover from loss.

Banking sector has domestic financial sector problems. Despite the expansion of capital markets in emerging economics banks remain dominant in financial intermediation. In Asia and Europe 80 percent of financial intermediation is done by banks. Banks are most important financial institution in the emerging market economies. This makes financial system too much vulnerable as failure in banking system will cause a major financial downfall. However, banks are not the only source of financial instability, there are other financial institutions as well. the vulnerability of financial institution greatly depends upon its function to transform risks and liquidity. Financial crisis of sector largely depends on these functions. through analysis financial crisis can be traced down to lack of management, incentive structures, market discipline, regulators and financial frameworks.

These vulnerabilities discussed only happens in an unstable macroeconomic environment, failure of economic policies. Macroeconomic and structural instability have a lot of impact on asset price, volatility and incentives. Emergence of unsustainable macroeconomic imbalances, frequently combined with market distortions are a major source of bank crisis.

4.9 Macroeconomic Sources of Vulnerability

Macroeconomic vulnerability and its sources are very vast topic and there is no single approach to understand it (Seth and Ragab, 2012). As there are many reasons for it, but the fundamental reasons are categorized as below.

4.9.1 Instability

Loan portfolios are a large number of loans like pool of loans that banks, investors or even government manage.

Financial sectors are greatly affected by macroeconomic variables in terms of their effect on asset price volatility and allocation of financial resources. Financial institutions can create a barrier for themselves against volatility, same cannot be said for macroeconomic risks or volatility. Therefor in financial downfall banks can't protect themselves against the decaying quality of loan portfolios which affect their capital position.

Encouragement of economic growth like loose policies may benefit banks on shorter term but may cause destabilization of bank on medium terms if they result in price bubble of prices and inflation.

Inadequate risk management by financial institutions, investors and banks may become a cause of macroeconomic instability and financial misallocation. Rapid expansion of domestic credit during suitable economic conditions and increased lending to high-risk sectors leads to asset price bubbles, this is basically due to over-optimism. In Europe before financial crisis, it was observed that banking system credit was growing rapidly relative to GDP.

Developed and emerging economies are more likely to face macroeconomic instability than industrial countries. The main cause for this instability is that these economic policies are less diverse and are exposed to structural disorder, incomplete markets. In this way they are more exposed to economic shocks and less likely to absorb the damage.

Macroeconomic instability doesn't reflect the structure of economy. Instability is mostly caused by macroeconomic mismanagement. Boom bust cycles are result of sudden change in macroeconomic policies, accumulation un sustainable wealth and many other factors.

Macroeconomic instability because of mismanagement will also lead to instability in exchange rates. Exchange rate disturbances is linked with foreign exchange position of banks. There is also indirect linkage of changes in exchange rate to the performance of borrowers. While increase of local transaction in dollars causes reduction in banks' direct foreign exchange exposure, this is often coming in expense of loss for lenders with increased credit-risk. Borrowers service their foreign exchange dominated loans in the event of instability.

Financial systems may become a target of structural changes and policies regimes such as liberalization. This happens when institutional failures prevent financial institution from adapting to new environment.

4.9.2 Inflation

Non-neutral tax system is the one that provide incentives to promote purchase of health insurance.
Float Payment is payment or deposit into the bank that is not yet cleared or processed and is kept in hold state. This type of hold benefits financial institutions.

Non neutral tax system, inflation and incomplete market are the factors that make incentives of buyers and sellers distorted thus making financial system unstable and fragile. Financial institutions particularly banks are very adaptive when inflation happens. They adjust to the environment of inflation in such a way that they protect their profitability. They use index lending techniques in which they shift and adjust prices, loans, payment and interest rate periodically according to their profitable needs. They also take interest in those assets whose price have increased and led to inflation such as foreign exchange, because with increased inflation the value of currency goes down. The financial sector is weakened a great deal due to inflation. Several factors lead to these weaknesses. First is the high share of income by banks. Banks receive high share of payment by using techniques like float payment (Anon, 1994), tax on unpaid (work without pay) deposits and foreign exchange. These prices and payment decrease with decrease in inflation. Secondly, high inflation downplays information analysis for business planning and management. It causes the banks to lose interest in credit analysis and concentrate more on their earnings by foreign exchange. Bank's credit assessment skills are compared in case of inflation and stable environment and deduction is made on the base of this comparison. In history inflation in Russia and Brazil showed bank's true color. Banks further increase interest rate up to a large value which discourages the demand for bank loan. Financial market is weakened by use of long-term maturities in debt instruments. Lastly in the presence of non-neutral tax system, most of institutions deviate towards over borrowing.

Monetary tightening is sharp increase in the interest rate of loans and credit. Monetary loosening is the opposite, sharp decrease in the interest rate.

There is another perspective regarding inflation which is controversial but is attested by many researchers. One of major reason of financial crisis is too much reduction in rate of inflation. This statement doesn't suggest high inflation but to maintain perfect balance. Monetary tightening can lead to exponential rise in interest rate which can result in decline of asset prices. This will create banking problems as borrowers no longer want to service their loans.

4.9.3 Liberalization

Liberalization proves to be very fruitful and has many important benefits, it introduces many new ideas and create an environment of creativity thus providing great benefits to financial system. Financial liberalization (when government stops intervening in financial matters) cover many aspects including capital account liberalism (government stops the movement of capital in and out of the country). Liberalization can lead to financial instability because sometimes it increases the exposure to credit and foreign exchange risks taken in an unstable macroeconomic environment. Liberalized financial systems lack experience to handle risks. If financial and capital liberalization together in parallel with the prudential regulators, they can improve the incentives to handle these risks. There is another aspect to this approach which is observed in many countries. Sometimes working and strengthening of regulators does not keep pace with financial and capital liberalization

4.9.4 Design Failure of Macroeconomic Policies

Quasi-fiscal responsibilities are responsibilities imposed by government to state-owned bank and enterprises and some private sector. Prices are less compared to market rate.

Policy making plays a crucial role in maintaining stability in any kind of system. In financial institution macroeconomic policies are very important in maintaining stability. Macroeconomic stability largely depends on the design of fiscal policy. Most important factor is how fiscal sustainable an institution is and also how its fiscal policies will withstand economic and financial shocks. Fiscal policies through efficient tax system of financial institution play a vital role in strengthening financial institution. Tax system can make banking system perform soundly by altering asset prices and opportunity of borrowers to service their loan. Fiscal policy by imposing quasi-fiscal responsibilities on the banking system weakens the banking system (Mackenzie and Stella, 1996). This happens by directed lending without any compensation or incentives to monitor risks.

Market based instruments are policy instruments that use economic variables like markets, prices to reduce negative environment created by negative external entities.

The choice of monetary policies and central banks facilities and incentives can affect the soundness and the vulnerability of the banking system. Lender of last resort (source that companies turn to when they have used every other option) is very important and absence of such facility will cause great instability in payment system and cause illiquid banks to suffer from insolvency. The development of financial system has allowed to move towards market-based instruments of monetary control.

4.10 Features of Financial Stability

In the previous sections we have discussed financial instability, crisis and what factors may lead to instability. Now we will cover the topic of financial stability in detail. Financial stability covers a wide range of features which are as follow

- The most comprehensive and vital term that defines financial stability is "benefit or welfare". The financial stability should ensure that financial framework is designed and implemented in such way that it benefits individual and public, furthermore it has a considerable welfare cost.
- Financial stability's state of affairs must be very "noticeable" meaning those entities that are responsible for maintaining financial stability and economic development can analyze the status of their work, whether financial stability is succeeding or not
- Public authorities should be able to monitor and have a complete influence and control over financial stability as without these public policies can't be formulated
- Legitimate and comprehensive political entities should have authority on policies of financial stability, meaning financial stability should come under authority of government whether that is at federal level or state level. Some relevant policies may fall under authority of individual states and some policies concerning monetary and fiat money are monitored by federal authorities like in United States.
- Another point of view that is very important is that from downfall and collapse of financial institutions or business entities, they are not the only one that

suffer rather they affect many other institutions as well resulting in the distress of social welfare. Emergency Officials not only provide support to financial institutions but also to nonpolitical companies

- Financial stability should not be so demanding that it classifies any change as evidence of instability because as we know that small to large losses can occur financially. Financial structures need to adapt with the variation in the economy. If any entity tries to stop that kind of change than it may result in great imbalance.

4.11 Key Principles of Defining Financial Stability

Financial stability includes a vast variety of concepts. Some comprehensive and concise principles are designed to define financial stability. Following are the principles that can be used to define financial stability

- Financial stability is a very vast concept encircling variety of aspects of finance system like infrastructure, markets and various entities. Private and public sectors play a vital role in participation in markets and in important components of financial system like official frameworks for supervision and surveillance. This system further involve government to ensure stability of monetary systems, payment plans and implementations, oversee the mobility of monetary system, official agreements, conventions and contracts as well as convention of private financial activities. Turbulence in any one of these aspects can cause instability in the system. The system instability can be caused by private actions or institutions and can also be caused by official institutions and actions or both of these simultaneously.
- Financial stability not only ensures allocation of resources, utilizations and mobility of savings, development and progress but also monitoring the system of payment. All the transactions and payments throughout the economic activity functions without any disturbance whether this payment is done at private sector or at official level. In order to achieve this goal, it should be ensured that central bank money along with its substitutes like bank accounts operate flawlessly. Bank deposits, cheques and other activities are performed soundly.

Liquidity injection is achieved when central bank issue a loan to a member insititution for very short time.

- Another important principle for financial stability is precautionary approach to avoid major instability. Framework and models are designed in such a way that appropriate steps are taken before undergoing a huge imbalance in financial activity. One very good approach is to intervene quickly through liquidity injections. The financial stability requires encompasses preventive and remedial dimensions (De Walque et al., 2010).

- A very vital principle is close monitoring of threats and potential consequences. Minor turbulence in financial market or individual institutions can't be classified as a threat to financial stability as long as they don't affect the economic activity at large. For example, closing of one financial institution, turbulence in financial markets can be caused by competitive institutions or self-correcting mechanism.

4.12 Definition of Financial System Stability

It is the ability of financial system to do efficient allocation of economic resources, ensuring sound economic activities such as growth and development, to analyze risks, prices and do an efficient development, a very robust and flawless payment, ability to resolve external risks, imbalance or even take preventive measures.

Very concise definition of financial stability is as follow:

Stability of financial system is achieved when system is able to empower economic development and able to dissipate and resolve any disturbance caused by un foreseen events.

When we discuss stability, it is very important to consider range of stability. From research and observation, it is of important notice that financial stability's most important requirement is continuum. The continuum of financial stability is comprised of large set of variables which can be quantified and observed. It includes a large set of variables such as quantification, how framework of finance ease economical and financial processes such as investment, prices, development and growth. If any of financial institution complete these set of variables then they fall into range of stability.

Another phrase that falls within defining range of stability is process of optimizing the performance of economy. Finance is also contributing to wealth creation, trade, investment, savings, entails and many other features.

There is another phrase that is very important for continuum, it is "demolish financial imbalances" meaning for continuum of financial stability it is very important to dissipate any imbalance in financial institutions which may be caused by un foreseen event.

Lastly it is very crucial to define range of financial instability and what its impacts are

- A financial system is approaching instability whenever it threatens to decrease or slow down economic growth and development
- A financial system falls within the range of instability if it disturbs the economic cycle and there is no development or any measures to stop it and it continues to dissipate the balance
- Due to this instability whole, financial system may collapse affecting other financial as well as non-financial systems causing a great imbalance in cycle of economic activity

4.13 Practical Impact of Financial Stability

While maintaining the cycle of financial stability, it may face a lot of problems and threats. These threats and problems have different magnitude depending upon the cause and will have different impact on social and financial systems. These problems are categorized as follow

- Hurdles and difficulties that occur at individual institutions or singular financial institution that don't have any broad consequences for financial systems.
- Problems that involve several important financial institutions and markets associated with it and their contagious affect to other institutions and markets as well
- Problems that spread at large magnitude and affect a large number of institutions and also unrelated markets for liquidity such as equity markets
- Problems that spread so large number that they affect vast number of financial institutions along with its non-financial institutions also causing a great imbalance and great distress in economy leading to instability.

Problems occurrence that falls within these categories requires different kind of efforts, mechanism to resolve it which may be from nothing to changing entire financial framework depending upon the magnitude.

4.13.1 Developmental Policies of Financial Stability

In defining financial stability and objectives to achieve it, there are wide range of methods that need to be kept in mind. For development and policies regarding financial stability there are certain rules and regulations that are of worthy notice

- Development of financial stability can't be measured and quantized as a unit. Unlike price stability there is not a single unit that can be used to measure financial stability. This shows that financial stability is multi-dimensional with variety of variables

- Financial stability's development is very difficult to predict and anticipate. In financial stability there are stack of variables that need to be considered. By achieving the state of stability not only variety of imbalance in financial situation is considered but also the factors that may lead to such distress. Prediction of financial imbalance is very difficult because of numerous factors like slipover effect, dissipation of trust and non-linearities in dealings. This cannot be predicted by doing conventional mean, median and mod of the outcomes rather whole distribution need to kept in calculations. Thus, the financial indicators and frameworks used by central banks and international organizations indicates that the relationship between financial stability rules and these indicators is very difficult to accomplish thus making the forecast not very efficient. As with everything development of new frameworks, usage of optimum statistical data and artificial intelligence forecast of such un anticipated event may be possible
- The policies that are designed to give security to financial stability have other goals also besides making stability as its priority such as safeguarding interests of deposit holders which may be private also, implementation of price stability, promoting a very efficient transaction (devise policies for swift payments and govern it). Furthermore, financial stability is always the target of financial shocks and imbalances ranging from natural occurrence to un anticipated disturbances in the market.
- Policies devised to ensure financial stability sometimes require a very good balance between efficiency and endurance. Measures and expenses taken to achieve optimum allocation of financial resources come in expense of sacrificing institutions resilience to withstand economic shocks and vice versa. So, a perfect balance should be created and resources must be assigned in order to achieve that. Uneven distribution of any of these two comes with a tradeoff
- Policies used to make institution financial stable are time varying. Short term financially stable system may come at the expense of long-term stability loss. Deposit guarantee may sabotage the market discipline thus create moral hazards or contrary selection.

4.14 Public Policy and Financial Stability

As we have discussed before those events of financial instability have a lot of effect on relative financial institutions as well as non-financial institutions also. Financial stability is a critical public good; hence is needed to prevent loss in the system (Fell & Schinasi, 2005). A public will also intervene in order to contain all the consequences if financial instability occurs despite all the precautionary measures. The policies that are warranted to protect financial stability have some variables and tradeoffs that need to be kept in mind for example some public policies designed to achieve financial stability create unwanted reduction in incentives and facilities for private parties to achieve their own financial stability by good behavior. A very good example is found in the field of bankruptcy, if a particular jurisdiction has a more creditor friendly law than the person who suffers from bankruptcy will be at great loss thus creating financially stable environment for jurisdiction. However, with the implementation of such laws it is more likely that this will create environment of less risk taking, investments resulting in affecting economic growth. The fear of bankruptcy and its laws will make it very difficult for the new or old business entities to invest. So, this is very big tradeoff between two very important factors that is economic growth and financial stability. Because there is a very big tradeoff between financial stability and other financial objectives it is very difficult for anybody to minister responsibility of financial stability. Price stability has opposite concept. There is normally no significant tradeoff except between price stability and other policies. Because of this, Government of United Kingdom and other countries have made Parliament to supervise the responsibility of price stability and offer the authority to central banks. This delegation is not possible in case of financial stability since there is a very big tradeoff, still in United Nation "Treasury" which is part of government is responsible for delegating financial stability. They participate in certain financial stability functions and delegate them to Bank of England and Financial Services for example emergency official support for financial collapse.

4.15 Preventive Measures

Since implementation of financial stability is very crucial, all preventive measures should be taken to ensure that system doesn't moves toward instability.

4.15.1 Law

Commercial laws are formulated for every jurisdiction. Clear set of guidelines is introduced in case of transactions, investments or any other commercial activity.

Formulation and implementation of the law influence all the parties involved in the commercial and financial activity. These provisions of the law are very important for economic and financial activity. They give more or less motivation to implement prudent behavior in finance. With the efficient prudent financial behavior there may come discouragement of enterprise behavior or some other private behaviors.

4.15.2 Official Agencies and Their Rules and Regulations

Legislation in many countries have their policies to protect and maintain financial stability. They assign and allocate official agencies for that purpose. Central banking systems for example Federal Reserve System in America are assigned this task. With the further development in the financial systems a new system is devised and implemented in many countries where there are official agencies besides Central banks that delegate financial stability. The International Monetary Fund (IMF) does a very multidimensional analysis on financial situations of the institutions. They classify vulnerabilities and gaps in financial structures and provide optimum solution.

Financial institutions not only follow commercial law as their primary objective but they are directed to follow supplementary laws as well which are made specially for them such as these financial institutions must be subject of supervision done by official person. That person has the authority to monitor institutions. Official regulators face a problem, they may sometimes use formulaic approach which proves to be challenging for everyone. They set precise financial and other criteria which they require financial institutions to meet. If institutions meet their demands than they get approval from official. The main problem with this approach is business models and frameworks keep on changing with time and it is very difficult to meet the criteria of regulator, still institutions are able to meet the criteria of officials. The institutions accomplishing this precise goal and fulfilling the criteria fail over time. Therefore, in many countries with advanced financial systems this approach is not taken into consideration rather regulators adapt with time, they inspect the management system and are able to adapt with respect to demand. They get comprehensive overview of the whole management system and even risk management systems also and they devise and suggest "best approach" to nullify these risks. The problem also arises in this comprehensive approach. When regulators try to impose this best approach in the financial institutions there comes a negative result which weakens the industrial system. When regulators introduce this defined approach to risk management system but financial institution may still fail to protect their systems than they would suffer from a heavy loss also by following imposed practices they will lose their ability to overcome problems and resolve any kind of issues, by following these practices their approaches and creativity will start to weaken which will benefit competitors at a very large scale

There is no specific way to resolve issues in both formulaic and comprehensive approach. Nobody can be sure that method of "best approach" is durable or not.

4.15.3 Market Conventions

In order to avoid conflict in any transaction, market experts develop market rules and conventions for price and other factors. Through this they seem to be unfavorable to any parties in the transaction thus making an important role in maintaining financial stability. Such conventions are very adaptable, they can be altered according to the needs and changes in the financial environment. These alterations are done without the involvement of law and legislations. They are not under the jurisdiction of public authorities or official regulator; however, authorities keep a positive communication with them and keep in up to date with them and sometimes suggest efficient solutions to overcome problems.

4.15.4 Official Information Supply

Macroeconomic conditions mean all the economic conditions comprising of economic variables and trends in the country e.g unemployment rate, GDP growth potential, inflation etc.

Public authorities supply information on economic and financial matters, information supply include the publications of information on macroeconomic conditions and all the anticipations and forecast done by central banks and government to support financial decision. Furthermore, these publications include reviews about financial stability. These reviews comprised of detailed analyzes of financial stability and all factors associated with it. Agencies formulating the reviews focus mainly on the risks to financial stability as perceived by them. They do a detailed analysis on the future events that are most likely to cause financial instability. These reviews don't include any actions taken by the agency or institution on which the review is done so the purpose of these reviews is not accountability rather they are source of influence to private and public sector by indicating them the factors and risks that may lead to financial instability. Through this influence, all the related parties are able to analyze and get a deeper understanding of factors that they might have overlooked. However, there is a great disadvantage if these organization's analysis of risks and other factors move to large financial institutions. When financial institutions rely too much on the analysis run by agencies or even central bank, they lose their own initiatives to do risk analysis. Since institutions rely too much on the publications done by agencies, outcome may or may not increase the factors leading to financial instability.

4.15.5 Physical Infrastructure and Financial Framework

Physical infrastructure and financial framework play a crucial role in economic activity thus considered a very important factor in bringing financial stability. The design of physical infrastructure and framework of a financial institution play affect not only themselves but also other institutions involved in the financial activity. Bad design of infrastructure and framework may cause a substantial damage to other financial institutions as well leading to financial instability, for example lack of efficiency or bad management in payment system affect large number of institutions involved, because of this delay or any other problem in the payment not only stops the participant involved in the transaction but may stop financial activities in many other institutions. If one bank stops their transactions or any other operations many other banks may have to suspend many activities. With increase in development the real time gross settlement (RTGS) has replaced old banking system (Summers et al., 2009). Each payment done at interbank level is done at real time centralized at central bank. In order to avoid any failure central bank, allow intraday payments unlimited. Through this approach the payments between two banks are independent and does not affect any other banks or institutions outside the transaction. Central bank also keeps in record and analyze the situation that sufficient payments are made, thus implementation of RTGS is sponsored by central bank

By using all of these preventive measures financial institutions can manage to maintain financial stability, still these are preventive measures, by researching we have seen that financial stability involves a lot of variables. Institutions analyze the factors and do a thorough study on the factors that may lead to instability. If there is a threat of financial stability or conditions arise that may seem to lead institutions toward instability.

4.15.6 Remedial Measures

Insolvency is the state when company or financial institution is unable to pay their debts to their creditors.

Financial instability may emerge for several reasons whether it is a minor fault in preventive measures that may lead to significant results or errors in calculations or informed by agencies or experts that the preventive measures for financial stability is too costly. Companies normally often don't pursue stability because the cost that it's going to take to achieve stability is too much and they use their resources to achieve other kind of objectives and follow other policies. If there are predictions or signs that institution is going to face instability there is always need of financial intervention from external entities.

Insolvency law is created to make a mechanism for all the creditors to get equitable treatment in case company is unable to pay back their debts to all the creditors.

In case of financial instability, financial downfall affects both financial and non-financial institutions. if external intervention doesn't happen than **commercial insolvency** comes into play. Generally speaking, as a result of insolvencies or company who is insolvent have to face various consequences depending upon their financial conditions, they may have to pay penalty like disqualification from management or heavy fine, company undergoes liquidation in which all their financial assets are sold to pay back creditors resulting in the shutdown of their business. The company doesn't lose their name, but their status is switched to liquidation. In some countries government regulates the companies who are unable to pay their debts to creditors.

Commercial insolvency is the state of illiquidity where even though assets of company may exceed its liabilities company is still unable to pay creditors debt.

With this detailed discussion about insolvency and commercial laws there are remedial measures to forestall the financial instability. As discussed before commercial laws are only applicable if there is no financial intervention. This kind of support is referred to as "lender of last resort" (Daniel, 2003). Simple definition of this terminology is that any organization that person or organization request for support in case they have exhausted all kind of resources and are unable to pay debt on their own. These supports are classified into two categories one is liquidity support and other is solvency support.

4.15.7 Liquidity Support

Liquidity support is lending financial support, resources like cash or fiat money to those how are unable to restore themselves by using their own financial resources or they can't afford any help from private sectors. With the development in financial sector, it is possible that "the demise of the gold market" doesn't affect the liquidity, because of the companies with sufficient security for loan is able to get liquidation if needed. Now a days companies are not only dependent on small amount or just one institution for support, if they are unable to collaborate with one institution because of trust or policies issues they can go to some other organizations for support, development has introduced a lot of opportunities and diversity in the market.

Lender of last resort is an institution that companies turn to for financial support in case they have run out of all options, mostly this organization is central bank.

Emergency support or "the lender of last resort" is still applicable despite all the preventive measures or efficient support by institutions. Several problems may arise that may cause hurdles in way of liquidation, for example mode of payment or department of payment is very crucial for smooth deployment of liquidity support, if because of some reasons like server shutdown, IT problems or any other issues the method of payment is compromised than liquidation process is stopped which will create shortage of liquidity support, in that case lender of last resort is the only action taken to provide support. In most of countries it is practiced that individual institution's financial downfall doesn't affect other institutions and doesn't become contagion. It has been made official that only financial institutions provide financial support to non-financial institutions and no other parties are involved in this support.

4.15.8 Solvency Support

Huge problems arise when financial and non-financial institution becomes insolvent, normally there is a very important concept that should be considered, should there be law in which insolvency processes are allowed to fulfill their processes without official intervention. Solvency support's main objectives are very comprehensive, some company's economic activity is very important and any minor delay or stop in these activities may bring consequences on a large scale so solvency support provides immediate support to such distressed institutions. Large financial institutions are given priority if creditors from important financial institutions face setbacks than they are prioritized and given support because discontinuity of operations in such institutions may cause economy to suffer on a large scale. Through this support, effect of one distressed company is very small on other institutions thus it avoids contagion. There is also a very important role of support in minimizing the purchase of distressed company by foreigners. Involvement of foreign companies may cause a lot of effect on economic development of state.

Fiscal policy is the use of government resources, revenue collections, assets and financial resources to improve economic condition of an institution.

There are some drawbacks and tradeoffs when implementing solvency support. The company suffering from state of instability is already in state of distress and at large financial loss when it receives support its debt is increased substantially. It involves a great consumption of public assets thus a lot of risks are involved, if during the solvency support no risk in involved than collapsed company would have done an efficient job of raising financial assets and there would be no need for emergency support but in reality, support team has to face significant risks thus making it as an act of fiscal policy. By utilizing this support there is emergence of big issue, if supporting institution e.g., government demonstrate their objective of helping and supporting a particular collapsed company either by publications or any other means of communication than creditors or lenders predict and perceive this issue and use it for their advantage. They can see that risk is now substantially removed by involvement of government so they lend large amount of money and on very lenient terms, thus making distressed company a target of instability.

4.16 Conclusion

From our detailed study we have come to conclusion that financial stability is a very vast topic and lot of research is required and still undergoing. But there are many points that can be derived from conclusion. There is not a proper definition for financial stability or a quantitative scale to measure financial stability. Financial stability is basically all the measures required for the institution to avoid instability, to analyzes risks, prices and do an efficient development, a very robust and flawless payment, ability to resolve external risks, imbalance or even take preventive measures, institutions should be stable and durable so much they are able to absorb shocks because of financial imbalance and lastly ability of organization to recover from losses or instability. All these factors define financial stability. Most of financial institutions try to achieve stability by taking steps to avoid financial instability, study and analyze past financial crisis, ensure market discipline. Our study of financial crisis has shown that financial crisis causes a great scale of imbalance in both economic and financial sector all over the world and crisis not only target financial institutions but non-financial institutions also. The main causes of instability are unstable macroeconomic environment, significant distortion in the economy, non-suitable public policy, inefficient financial management and market discipline etc. Lastly, we have seen that there are many steps to prevent instability and ensure sound financial system, amongst which the worth mentioning are as follow, commercial and financial laws must be created and implemented which ensures smooth transactions and financial activities inside and outside of an organization. Institutions must have professionals that have a very important job to monitor stability and take all the steps to avoid imbalance. There must be market laws in order to avoid any spike in transactions, all the steps must be discouraged that may become hurdle in maintaining market discipline.

5 Role of Accounting in Financial Stability

Abstract: There are two approaches for maintaining sound accounting standards one is principle-based accounting standard and other is rule based, both have their pros and cons, principle based is mostly used because it ensures creativity and intuitiveness in organization by providing them set of principles and they have to use their own methodology to achieve them. The second most important criteria are reliable and accurate accounting figures since they play a very important role in economic activities. One more criteria worth mentioning is very professional and efficient analysis of risks since this analysis is the building block of durability for financial institutions. Besides these standards there are many standards that are defined by IRFS (a non-profitable organization) to ensure financial stability, these standards are practiced throughout the world, of all the accounting standards IRFS has considered transparency as the most important one, all the transactions, financial and economic information and statements must be transparent for a sound financial system. Transparency has its risks and disadvantages as giving clear information about your plans may disrupt business plans but that can be avoided through efficient accounting techniques. As a result of this transparency investors and businesses invest more because the information is very reliable and accurate.

Keywords: Financial Stability, Financial Stability and Accounting, Accounting Effect on Financial Stability, Accounting Impact on Financial Deviation.

The financial stability is fundamental for the economic growth and development. The accountants play a key role in maintaining the system transparency, identifying the key parameters, and provide useful financial information that serve as financial business indicators. Laux made it clear that the always blamed fair value accounting has got no role in the financial crisis, and the fluctuations in the mortgage market, and other complex reasons were the main cause (Laux, 2012).

Liang and Zhang have performed research on the social value of accounting objectivity on financial stability. The researchers concluded that for the generation of the more objective accounting report, the accounting system should be designed in a way that the less managerial interventions are in place (Liang and Zhang, 2018).

Schwarz et al. demonstrated by using the results of the European Central Bank (ECB), that the annual profit and financial buffers of a central bank could be considerably affected by accounting profit distribution and loss coverage rules (Schwarz et al., 2015). Moreover, in terms of financial stability, the accounting frameworks and the workflows implemented by commercial banks affect their behavior, but also the financial markets. Researchers provided the evidence that accounting frameworks enhanced pro-cyclicality during the recent crisis, and which posed the risk to the financial system stability (Schwarz et al., 2015).

5.1 Introduction

Financial statements are records and data in written form that keep track of all the business and financial activities, financial behavior of company.

Accounting plays a vital role in financial stability. Financial stability is a very large domain that comprises of various variables. Before discussing role of accounting, it is very impertinent to discuss about financial statements and its role in accounting. Economy is very much dependent on financial statements. Financial institutions and organizations make their planning and a lot of decisions based on these statements. It can contribute to efficient flow of business activities in markets, banks and financial institutions thus playing a very important role in growth and development of economy. Through the efficient usage of these statements, it enables the financial system comprising of markets and markets infrastructure to withstand shocks and deformities in the financial system. They play a crucial role in deviating system from instability.

Prudential filters targets those impacts on capital that are undesirable from business point of view.

Accounting standards and their efficient usage are building blocks of optimum quality of financial statements. European Union (EU) formulated a very efficient accounting framework based on International Financial Reporting Standards (IFRS). This framework should be taken into consideration and implemented in financial sectors and banking systems because it has a very positive impact on European financial statements as well as financial sector. Accounting standards have a significant effect on financial and banking sectors. They form the basis of calculation of financial and regulatory variables. Any inefficient use of accounting rules and standards bring a large change in the financial institutions that use these kind of accounting rules. Changes in accounting standards affect market standards and data analysis that supervisors and experts use to analyze the situations of central and other banks. Accounting figures are altered by experts to achieve their objectives e.g., use of prudential filters. These filters are mostly used in calculation of funds, payments, credits. Institution financial stability is largely dependent on the accounting standards followed by that institution. These two variables are under discussion by large number of financial institutions and lot of research is done to create an optimum relation between two. The ECB (European Central Bank) and Basel Committee on Banking Supervision coordinated with each other and came to a decision point about amendments of IAS39 regarding importance of financial stability.

The Banking Supervision Committee (BSC) of the European System of Central Banks (ESCB) thoroughly studied and analyzed that accounting standards are worthy to establish and maintain financial stability. We will discuss the outcome of that analysis in this section.

Some of the researchers have examined the banks' disclosures and loss recognition and then identified core issues for linking between accounting and financial stability (Bischof et al., 2021).

5.2 Criteria for Accounting Standards to Maintain Financial Stability

The fundamental analysis of report highlights criteria for accounting standards to maintain financial stability. In these criteria a new framework is deigned which will serve as guidance in order to check whether these accounting standards are eligible or not and how positive is their standards to maintain stability.

As a starting point bank were chosen as field of study for measuring the criteria in the accounting standards. From financial point of view many financial and non-financial institutions are dependent on banking system. Therefore, in order to achieve financial stability all, the parties provide a very comprehensive financial statement. This criterion defines the objectives the accounting standard must accomplish in order to maintain a sound financial environment. They also target other economic entities, users of financial statements. The investment and interests of economic agents must be kept in mind whether they are interested in long term or short-term activity. Traders are most interested in the short-term output while investors in pensions funds are looking for long term, still both type of investors play a crucial role in development and growth of economy.

In literature various measures related to the financial stability have been explained. And the researchers have also differentiated the measures according to the sector (Gadanecz and Jayaram, 2008). For example, GDP growth is a measure of the financial stability in the Real Economy, similarly, the Household debt is a key measure of the financial stability in the Household sector (Gadanecz and Jayaram, 2008).

5.2.1 Criterion 1- Dependency on Principle Based Accounting Standards

Principle based approach defines the set of principles and require the institutions to follow those principles in their own intuitive way.

There are two types of accounting approach, one is principle-based accounting standard and other is rule based accounting approach. Both have their practical applications and pros and cons. Most common practice is principle-based approach but some countries use rule-based approach also. Accounting standards must be designed in such a way that they generate financial statements that give detail explanation of economic substance of activities. With the fast pace of development in finance and economics it is very difficult to achieve such a goal. Rules based approach may give clear guidance and clear set of actions to follow. It would be very suitable just to follow those rules and complete objectives. There are certain issues that may arise by implementation of such approach. The most important one is that rules become obsolete in an ever growing and developing market. Rules based approach can become tiresome, complex and large set of rules may cause a lot of complication in preparation of financial statements such as people that follow set of rules given may lose their own initiatives to obtain anything, they may lose their innovative and creative approach and lastly having strict rules sometimes force accountants to start their own company.

Rule based approach defines set of rules to follow. These rules are already defined and company has to follow them in that fashion.

A principle-based approach is very adaptive and innovative as it gives set of principles to accountants which they have to follow using their own initiatives to achieve goals. However, principles are generic in nature and they require strict discipline in implementation both from employee and employer point of view. To ensure the implementation internal and external efficiency is required in accounting e.g., effective audits both internally and externally. It is very important factor in financial stability that financial accounts effectively play their role in underlying economics.

5.2.2 Criterion 2: Usage of Reliable and Relevant Figures

Arm's length transfer mostly refers to transfer of property, in this transaction buyer and seller are independent of each other.

Economic decisions and operations largely depend on accurate accounting figures. Therefore, they should have a very precise and meaningful representations for economic authorities. Accounting figures must be so efficient that it ensures smooth settlement of "arm's length transaction". These figures must be consistently good in quality, information extracted from such figures must be so efficient that they reflect good performance to both internal and external economic agents and users of financial statements.

Quoted price are latest and updated price or bid between buyer and seller. It is the closing price of Stock market.

Official quoted price is not the source of valuable information. This is most likely to occur in those markets which are not properly developed or have insignificant liquid. In these markets quoted prices don't follow the fundamental principles. Some markets have not reached such level of development which is sufficient enough for their long-term liquidity.

Mark-to-model is accounting method in which outcome of financial models forms pricing of assets. Financial model historical prices forecast determines the values for these pricing.

As we have seen that market prices are not source of valuable information and are not reliable, there is another approach that is marked-to-model measurements. These measurements should be able to reveal economic and financial values of different elements of transaction and their degree of influence. The issue with model-based approach is that measurements include some decisions and variables whose efficiency is not satisfying all the time.

Mark-to-market is an accounting method that estimates the value of as asset based on its market value.

Accounting figures and their measurements should do an efficient reflection of trading. All the significant entities must be analyzed and taken into account. The block holdings shock will be very difficult to absorb in the market and financial and economic values could be compromised substantially if holdings are sold at the same time. Another accounting approach is Mark-to-Market. Through Mark-to-market tool, assets values and prices may vary with time depending upon several factors mostly conditions of market. This method defines the true value of asset as it is decided with respect to current market price. As in this approach the prices of assets depend upon the market, the main problem occurs if the market-based measurements don't reflect the true value of an asset.

Reliability and efficiency of both these approaches is uncertain and variable. It is very important from financial stability perspective that prices of assets and their adjustments play a vital role in reflecting economical and financial values and they serve as a pipeline for financial frameworks. As the macroeconomic conditions demand, these measurements should not deviate from underlying economics. Failure to do so this may cause significant financial risk leading to imbalance in pricing and great consequences.

5.2.3 Criterion 3: Analysis of Allocation and Magnitude of Risks

The analysis of allocation and magnitude of risks between different economic entities is of great financial importance. The quality of these analysis determines durability and shock resilience of an institution thus affecting the overall efficiency of financial system. An institution deviation towards financial stability or instability depends very much on how the company is able to absorb shocks or show resilience or ability to restore after financial setbacks. Financial statements should provide a clear picture about allocation and magnitude of risks. They should provide a clear reflection on allocation of risks and what would be their effect on financial institutions. They should cover all the angles including those risks which market can't assess themselves. Accounting figures should reflect the impact of risks on economic effectiveness.

5.2.4 Criterion 4: Comparable Financial Statements

Financial stability also requires that accounting framework must be very cooperative. This harmonized framework enhances overall efficiency and capital allocation through impressive comparability of financial statements of different institutions and ease the reasonable allocation of resources thus make a huge contribution in economic development and maintaining financial stability. Relative approach in price is more preferred in marketing than an absolute price. Therefor the need of comparability for prices is essential. absence of this comparability may cause loss of credibility in financial information resulting in reducing market confidence. Comparability is more advanced when this method is applied to similar or highly similar economical and financial operations. Through this approach it is recognized that similar financial institution may be target of different risks and therefore separate records must be kept.

Comparability is very much practicable in banking system especially European banking system where framework of banking system is very large and there are lot of cross border operations. Comparison allows system to reduce risks that may arise from misinformed national or international transactions.

5.2.5 Criterion 5: Presentation of Clear and Understandable Financial Statements

An efficient accounting framework should ensure market discipline by implementing transparency though provision of clear and understandable financial statements. Building block of financial statements is very precise and comprehensible presentation. This practice ensures market discipline. These statements are not only comprehended by accountants but also to analysts and market participants. Presentation of such clear statements is challenging in case of complex financial instruments because their methodology is very complex and their working should be comprehended by financial and accounting analysts.

There are two objectives, understandability and reliability. Perfect balance must be done between two. Financial statements should be very clear and precise but should not lose its reliability and relevance. If statements are too simple, they will lose their relevance and do an inadequate reflection of risks. Therefore, accounting standards must maintain a perfect balance between two.

Financial disclosures are very important tool to assess financial situations, they are used as means of correction in financial statements. Statements are either not reliable or clear, disclosures are not used to correct statements. Disclosures can't replace financial statements. From detailed analysis of cases of accounting malfeasance, it has been seen that disclosures that include questionary statements about relevance of figures in financial statements are compromised, that information can be erased or hidden in such a way that it can cause a great discomfort for even professional analysts.

Another import factor for disclosure is precision and conciseness. If disclosures are too lengthy or time consuming, they become less efficient and clear. Disclosures should be so precise that it should not lose clarity while ensuring that important information that could affect the figures should not be excluded.

5.2.6 Criterion 6: Analysis of Financial Situation of Banks

Financial statements should also provide accurate analysis of financial situation of an institution. In both short and long run, three important processes are fundamentals of assessing financial condition. Solvency, profitability, liquidity is the perfect portrayal of financial situations of any institutions especially banks. It would be not recommended to give market assurance of present and future trading process for financial contracts at a fixed price when this case is not valid all the time. This assurance may result in biased decisions by investors and market users. This is suitable for those environments where market decision is based on processes like return of equity.

5.2.7 Criterion 7: Adaptive Accounting Rules and Sound Risk Management

Financial statements should recommend risk management methods thus helping in growth of economic activity and identification of risks faced by that institution. Financial statements including disclosures that are not aligned with efficient risk management methods and practices could provide a negative and false image of effective financial and economic features of institution. Alignment of accounting and risk management system and their direction is very important. It is very good practices that accounting should be aligned with risk management system, failing to do so management will do the reverse process that is alignment of risk management system with accounting which will produce negative results and less efficient risk management resulting in weakening financial institutions. In the light of publications by BCBS risk management system is the key basis for financial statements thus has a crucial role in financial stability.

5.2.7.1 Risk Management System

Risk management system is comprised of several fundamental elements which are as follow:

- It is duty of senior management and governing board to create risk management profile by defining policies, rules and standards. They should also ensure that these policies are implemented.
- Risk analysis, monitoring and measurements must not be limited to any particular branch, rather it must be practiced throughout the institution.
- Clear, concise and relevant procedures must be introduced to measure risks and performance evaluation must be practiced.
- Very sound management system must be introduced in all fields, ensuring adequate accountability, allocating duties between risk management and business functions

5.2.8 Criterion 8: Predictive Analysis of Risks

Herding is defined as the behavior of investors in which investors take similar trading decisions and cause deviation of stock prices from their value thus representing major cause of economic bubbles.

An efficient risk management system is adequate assessments of risks. This assessment is not only limited to risk information and analysis from the past but also insight in the future. A very intelligent prediction for occurrence of risk in the future is also necessary. for accounting professionals to do complete analysis of risk forward looking approach is much needed. Market approach is also forward looking. Capital markets are more efficient in long term and their values will include all relevant public information including forecast approach. Market participants have different behavior, some are focused for short term commitment which in results become a source of short-term price fluctuations, which partly is the result from market imperfections or other short-term factors such as self-inflated market tendencies, anecdotes presented by individuals. Price may also fluctuate due to events like "herding" or "speculative hunt for yield". Market based elements in the models face challenges in the Marked-to-model approach. These prices movements may not follow economic fundamentals, thus are major cause of economic bubbles.

In certain scenarios, "point-in-time" approach is most optimum approach because it defines and explains the condition at that particular moment. However forward-looking approach may avoid many imbalances in financial situations. This aspect is most practiced in Europe Banking system where lack of practice of this approach may cause financial bubbles.

5.2.8.1 Financial Bubbles

Economic bubble is state of economic activity that may end up in sudden collapse due to various reasons. It is also called asset bubble. It represents a situation in which assets prices are variable and are based on inconsistent calculations about the future. It is mostly sudden and rapid increase in asset price which may result in decrease in value, or a contraction, reaching to a condition normally called bubble burst. There are four categories of bubble stock market bubble, market bubble, credit bubble and commodity bubble. Asset price represents an individual stock, a financial asset, or even an entire sector, market, or asset class.

5.2.9 Criterion 9: Evasion from Negative and Encouragement of Positive Externalities

5.2.9.1 Accounting and Audits

Externality is an economic term which refers to a situation that provides benefits or incur costs to third parties. Third parties don't agree to this situation but they have to face the results.

Accounting standards should be designed in such a way that they serve as backbone for avoidance of negative and promotion of positive externalities. we will discuss this implementation in banking system. Accounting standards create opportunities for economic agents to invest or divest in financial instruments which may have a long-term effect on macroeconomics. accounting neutrality is a very good approach to avoid any distortion in allocation of resources.

Accounting neutrality refers to the information in financial statements to be unbiased.

Accounting standards may encourage positive externalities thus strengthening the system of allocation of resources and the resilience of the financial system to shocks. Such standards must be promoted and acknowledged.

5.3 IFRS Accounting Standards and Financial Stability

The IFRS is a nonprofit international organization designed solely for public interest, it is established to design and formulate very high quality, efficient and optimum accounting standards. These accounting standards are practiced throughout the world. Two standard setting boards set these standards. These standard setting boards are the International Accounting Standards Board (IASB) and the newly created International Sustainability Standards Board (ISSB). The main objective of this board is how companies define their financial statements.

This organization defines IFRS standards that aid in growth and development of financial institutions. These standards provide very reliable and accurate information to investors about the financial situation of the institutions, risk factors and other variables. This organization's basic mission is to serve public interest by ensuring trust, growth and financial stability in the global economy.

IRFS provides transparency by giving reliable information about the financial institution thus ensuring that investors make sound economic decisions. These standards provide accountability to financial systems by reducing information and communication gap between investors and people whom they have entrusted their money. They serve as great help to regulators. By using these information investors make efficient decision because they are able to see opportunities and risks thus ensuring growth of economic activity.

5.3.1 IFRS Accounting Standards and Financial Stability

The global financial crisis (GFC) refers to the extreme crisis in global financial markets and banking systems between mid -2007 and early 2008. This was the worst financial disaster since 1929 beginning with mortgage lending crisis in 2007 and expanding into global banking crisis.

Since the global financial crisis, IRFS foundation made a very good policy to set standards for financial stability. These standards are most useful for institutions which are most likely to face accounting volatility.

The IRFS and regulators consider transparency as key element of financial stability. The transparency can be achieved by recent changes in the accounting standards. Primary role of accounting standards is not fostering of financial stability but it's the efficient functioning of prudential regulators whose task is to safeguard the financial health of system.

The transparency has a short-term risk and disadvantage as giving the clear information about financial situation of an institution may lead to instability as flaws and problems hidden within company's sheet are brought to light. However, problems can be resolved through efficient accounting and only way to ensure this process is to identify and paint clear picture of problems. Therefore, to conclude, transparency defined by accounting standards play a vital role in long term financial stability.

Accounting transparency contributes in financial stability in following ways. It gives investors very reliable and updated information to enable them to make a wise decision. It discourages the officials and management to take unnecessary risks by painting them a clear picture of situation. It encourages informed economic decision-making.

Bank runs occurs when banking system appears to be going towards instability and client withdraws their money.

The definition of prudence practiced by traditional accounting methods give rise to smoothing, reducing accounting volatility and transparency. The board revised definition of prudence. The new definition doesn't allow any understatement and over statements of financial assets, liabilities and expenses rather it gives a very transparent report of financial situation of institution. Banks and insurers face challenges while maintaining sound accounting standards. There is an economic mismatch between financial assets and liabilities which may lead to accounting volatility which may lose the trust of clients in business, banks may become unstable and face "runs".

5.3.1.1 Financial Stability and IFRS

IFRS 9 is standard that specifies classification and identification of financial assets and liabilities and contracts for purchase and sale of non-financial institutions. The main clause discussed in IFRS 9 is Expected Credit Loss (ECL). ECL is the weighted estimate of credit losses based on principles of probability. It is calculated based on estimated economic loss of an asset. Before this approach IAS 39 was used as impairment requirements. IAS 39 was a backward-looking approach in which already incurred losses are taken into consideration, whereas IRFS 9 is a forward-looking approach. ECL is calculated using formula. The main factors involved in calculating ECL are Exposure at Default (EAD), Probability of Default (PD), Loss Given Default (LGD), ECL formula.

Amortization is an accounting technique to reduce the book value of loan or an asset. Default is the failure to make payment on time. It refers to a situation where individual or company is unable to pay on time.

- Exposure At Default (EAD): For any asset taken into consideration EAD is exposure of projected credit risk at a particular time. For example, EAD for a company relating to its investment will be its amortized cost balance at that date
- Probability of Default (PD): This represents any asset projected probability of default.
- Loss Given Default (LGD): This refers to the projected economic loss to a company when company faces default situation. Collateral existence and valuation form the basis of computation of this factor.
- ECL formula: ECL formula for any asset is ECL= EAD x PD x LGD, formula can be refined and revised based on specific requirements of each company.

ECL approach is very beneficial as it is forward looking and provide timely information about risks and other factors so that appropriate actions may be taken to prevent failure. Support of ECL provides transparency thus reducing volatility.

Procyclicality refers to the positive and negative fluctuation in the financial variables around a trend. It also refers to business cycle fluctuations in gross domestic product.

This implementation faced some contrasting reviews. Some agencies think that ECL is very complex as it is forward looking approach and a lot of predictions are done to achieve this objective, Provisions are made too early without realizing the actual situation and they are volatile. This model leads to procyclicality.

Available for sale securities are category of securities that companies invest in with the intent of selling it before it reaches mature stage.

Most of regulators like Bank for International Settlements (BIS) have different point of view. According to them ECL indicate loss recognition which reduces procyclicality. ECL provisions will enable banks to practice better risk management techniques. Provisions that are transparent, highlight risks which result in improving credit risk management and pricing. IRFS 9 made amendments in equity investments by removing IFRS 9 removes Available for Sale (AFS) category for equity investments. In IAS 39, AFS category defined the assets in fair value on balance sheet. The main critics of fair value is that it doesn't highlight long-term nature of investment. IRFS board made a conclusion that AFS delayed the recognition of losses which increased procyclicality and caused a great effect on performance.

5.3.1.2 Financial Stability and IFRS 17

IFRS 17 is based on accounting volatility and insurance contract. IRFS 17 will contribute to financial stability through following principles.

- Efficient and more reliable accounting techniques for assets and liabilities resulting in increased assessment of insurance risks and enhancement in comparability.
- Constant principles for analysis and recognition of revenue and comparability of profit with other industries. This results in greater comprehension of insurers 's financial performance.
- Enhanced transparency and reduction of cost of capital which results in promoting market discipline and improved functionality of capital allocation.

5.3.1.3 Financial Stability and Prudential Regulators

Prudential regulators consider transparency as fundamental element for ensuring market discipline for financial institutions. The two standards set by IFRS, ECL model under IFRS 9 and accounting volatility and insurance contracts under IFRS 17 played a vital role in understanding the risks that financial institutions face hence enhancing market discipline. There is another aspect to this disclosure, these transparencies affect the confidence of financial institutions hence damaging financial stability. Regulators see changes introduced by IRFS as positive implementation. They view information gathered by assets and liabilities under IRFS 9 and IRFS 17 as an adequate fundamental for financial stability and market discipline. The regulators will develop rules based on their analysis of new regulations among which most important is that they will develop new methods to address the effects of accounting volatility rather than conceal the volatility. Foundation work with regulators to ensure financial stability. Foundation has a very important role to ensure that all information is provided on timely basis and it is very reliable and comprehensible. They work with prudential regulators as they develop rules on relation between accounting and regulatory measures of capital.

It must be mentioned that the primary goal of the accounting standards in not to foster the financial stability directly, it is the responsibility of the prudential regulators, however, the accounting standards if followed inculcate and foster transparency, that is then necessary for and contributes to the financial stability (Hoogervorst and Prada, 2015)

5.4 Financial Stability and International Organizations

Valuation is analysis of determining current value of an asset or a company. An analyst defines the value by analysing business management, market value of its assets.

The International Accounting Standards Board (IASB) and the US Financial Accounting Standards Board (FASB) classified number of flaws in accounting standards and their applications that emerged during financial crisis and affected credibility of financial reporting. These issues included: trading valuations of instruments in illiquid markets, complex classification of financial instruments, negligence in recognition of credit loss by financial institutions, inefficient accounting procedures for insurance contracts.

Procyclicality is fluctuations of financial variables around trend. These fluctuations can be positively and negatively correlated with business cycle fluctuations in gross domestic product.

Accounting standard setters have taken these weaknesses into special consideration. Special attention has been given to recognition of credit loss, which is main cause of procyclicality, accounting treatment for insurance contracts and performance of insurance companies (Financial Stability Board, 2021).

External auditing is auditing done by independent accountant in accordance with certain rules and regulations of financial statements of a company. These audits are done by company to receive certifications.

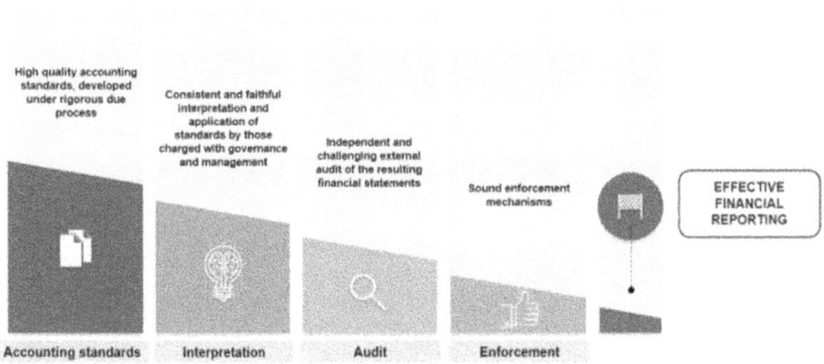

Figure 5.1 Accounting standards, financial reporting, and effective enforcement (Financial Stability Board, 2021).

The FSB (Financial stability board) acknowledges the importance to financial stability. As the member of FSB, IASB regularly updates FSB about their accounting developments. Consistent and reliable external audits form the basis for efficient financial reporting. In 2003 several international organizations including FSB established Monitoring Team to monitor the development of auditing standards that are connected to reliable financial information, resilience of financial institutions and financial stability.

FSB convenes meetings with several international organizations such as global audit networks and the International Forum of Independent Audit Regulators (IFIAR) to promote constructive communication and ensure efficient auditing. We will discuss small details about FSB and its working in the next section.

5.4.1 Financial Stability Board (FSB)

Financial stability board is an international organization that analyzes, monitor and make recommendations about maintaining financial stability internationally. Several countries are part of this board. The boards design practical measures for ensuring the financial stability at international level. The financial stability board establishes connections, co-operations, and coordination frame works with localized national financial institutes, and international standards defining organizations to develop a massive, properly designed, and well connected legal, monitory, supervisory and other financial measures in different areas of financial policies. To ensure the financial stability at global level, the co-operation of the national financial institutes is required. The intention of the board is to develop a culture that promotes and motivates the uniform and same phased implementation of the policies in different regions that supports the common cause. There were various reasons that the FSB has been created, and certain goals were defined to achieve in future through the working of this boards. The board was created for the following reason:

To evaluate and analyze the existing gaps, weaknesses, and issues that have an impact on the global financial framework and system.

5.5 Examples Relevant to Financial Stability

Fong et al. have studied the impact of the of long-term organizational investors on the financial stability (Pak Wing Fong et al., 2022). The impact of the investors' contribution on the stability and instability of the Hong Kong and International stock markets have been evaluated by the researchers (Pak Wing Fong et al., 2022). A dataset based on the funds issued by the insurance companies and pension funds globally was used. The analysis of the data revealed that these types of the investors change the funding flow dynamics in the time of financial stress (Pak Wing Fong et al., 2022). And in the time of the financial stress the fund flow diverted to the developed countries economies increasingly associates with the other countries. The investment pattern of the investors during the favorable and stressful times and the associated impact on the stability and instability of the markets was also highlighted. The long-term investors which stabilize the decline in the global markets at the time of normalized market conditions actually destabilize the stock markets in the developed countries at the time of stressed market situations (Pak Wing Fong et al., 2022). Figure 5.2 presented below shows the Composition of insurance and pension funds with Hong Kong's equity markets.

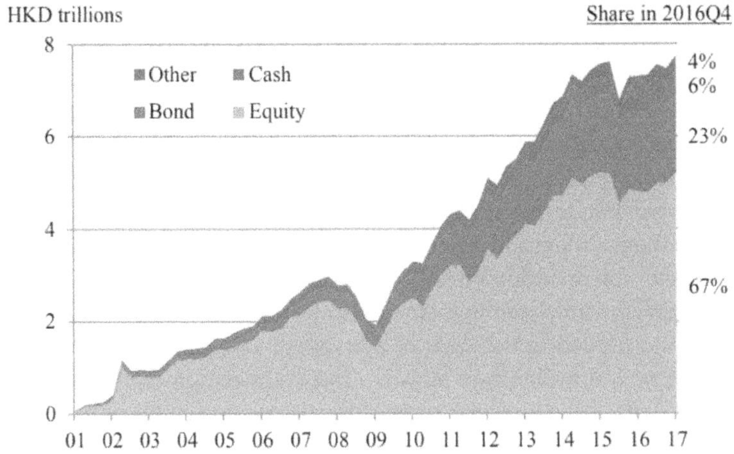

Figure 5.2 Composition of insurance and pension funds with Hong Kong equity market exposure. (Image source: Pak Wing Fong et al., 2022).

Figure 5.3 presented below shows the aggregate growth of insurance corporations and pension funds for 29 economies in size in terms of percentage (Pak Wing Fong et al., 2022).

Figure 5.3 Aggregate growth of insurance corporations and pension funds for 29 economies in size in terms of percentage (Pak Wing Fong et al., 2022).

Accounting plays an important role in the financial inclusion. The Micro, small and medium-sized enterprises (MSMEs) are the main and important contributors to the national economies. The MSMEs often face issues related to the access to the economic and financial services. The access to the financial services is not available in vast majority of the companies. The financial services and facilities are critical for the growth and the development of the MSMEs. One of the major obstacles that MSMEs face in terms of the services is the setting up a proper business account and meaningful financial statements. Both of these items are necessary for the achievement of aids, grants, loans, and other incentives from the governmental and non-governmental agencies. The policy makes and designers are needed in the areas of accounting and insurance regulations to assist the financial inclusion of MSMEs. This is the reason that the accounting for MSMEs have been a regular topic of the debate during the annual sessions of UNCTAD's Intergovernmental Working Group of Experts on International Standards of Accounting and Reporting (ISAR) which is the United Nations focal point on enterprise accounting reporting matters. For addressing the needs of MSMEs and fulfilling the requests of its member states, UNCTAD-ISAR have devised the Accounting and Financial Reporting Guidelines for Small and Medium-sized Enterprises Level 3 Guidance (SMEGA level 3) (International Standards of Accounting and Reporting, n.d.).

Malik et al. have studied the role of the financial inclusion and the Governance quality on the financial stability of the Asian nations (Malik et al., 2021). The financial sector is an important contributor of the economic system. Financial sector can accelerate the mobilization of the capital for highly efficient and yielding projects by financial intermediation between the loan providers and the loan receivers as well (Malik et al., 2021). The Asian financial crises and the global financial crisis have provided the lessons and also highlighted the unsuitable aspect of the global financial integration that have got spillover impacts on the financial stability (Malik et al., 2021).

> *Financial inclusion means that every adult in the population has an easy and affordable access to the financial services. And these financial services should be designed as per their needs* (Malik et al., 2021).

The financial stability is attained when the financial system works efficiently without any interruption and impact, and the risks are calculated and controlled in the systematic way to minimize the impact of the systematic crises (Malik et al., 2021). The economies around the globe struggle to incorporate and enhance the financial inclusion in the system as a plan to develop the economic and financial sector and to aid the businesses by providing the financial services.

The emerging Asian markets are considered as the most rapidly growing markets in the world. And the issue is that only 33 percent firms have got an access to the line of credit and loans (Malik et al., 2021). Using the stakeholder theory, the researchers have studied the connection between the financial stability, financial inclusion and the governance quality (Malik et al., 2021). The researchers have performed Principal Component Analysis to determine the Governance quality relationship with the Financial Stability and Financial Inclusion in Asia and the mediating role that financial inclusion can play in between (Malik et al., 2021). The period and the number of the countries were selected on the basis of the data availability from 2009 to 2017 (Malik et al., 2021). Forty countries were selected for the study (Malik et al., 2021). The data for the bank z score, credit to deposit ratio, liquid assets to deposit ratios, and the ratio of the short-term funding was obtained from the Global Financial Development Database (GFDD) provided by the World Bank (Malik et al., 2021). And the data related to the governance parameters and indicators was collected form the sources and data base provided by the World Bank and International Monetary Fund (Malik et al., 2021).

The study concludes that in the Asian region, Governance and Financial inclusion have a significant positive relationship with the Financial Stability, but the Governance quality has a negative impact on the financial inclusion (Malik et al., 2021). The negative impact of the bureaucratic processes, red tapes, and the policies and regulations that cause the difficulties for the financial inclusion process actually hinder the economic development in that particular state. The population should be able to avail the financial services for their benefit, and the financial services should be clearly and transparently described to the public.

5.6 Conclusion

There are a large number of methods to obtain and maintain financial stability amongst which accounting is one of most importance. Some of the researchers have provided evidence that the accounting models are helpful in anticipating the credit crisis and economic recession (Bezemer, 2010). The main core of accounting is financial statements which means proper record of transactions or financial activity must be stored and maintained and can be retrieved at any time without any failure and accurate information. These statements play a vital role in accounting which in result is very essential for financial stability. There are accounting standards which must be maintained in order to achieve financial stability and for these accounting standards there are list of criteria defined. There are two approaches for maintaining sound accounting standards one is principle-based accounting standard and other is rule based, both have their pros and cons, principle based is mostly used because it ensures creativity and intuitiveness in organization by providing them set of principles and they have to use their own methodology to achieve them. The second most important criteria are reliable and accurate accounting figures since they play a very important role in economic activities. One more criteria worth mentioning is very professional and efficient analysis of risks since this analysis is the building block of durability for financial institutions. Besides these standards there are many standards that are defined by IRFS (a non-profitable organization) to ensure financial stability, these standards are practiced throughout the world, of all the accounting standards IRFS has considered transparency as the most important one, all the transactions, financial and economic information and statements must be transparent for a sound financial system. Transparency has its risks and disadvantages as giving clear information about your plans may disrupt business plans but that can be avoided through efficient accounting techniques. As a result of this transparency investors and businesses invest more because the information is very reliable and accurate. Besides IRFS many international organizations such as The International Accounting Standards Board (IASB) and the US Financial Accounting Standards Board (FASB) classified a number of flaws in accounting standards such as trading valuations of instruments in illiquid markets, inefficient classification of financial instruments, negligence in recognition of credit loss by financial institutions, inefficient accounting statements. Accounting standard setters gave special attention to the recognition of credit loss as it is the main cause of procyclicality.

6 Bankruptcy and Insolvency

Abstract: Companies or individuals may see some downfall in their finances whose magnitude vary depending upon the situation, when such situation arises affected parties may go into large amount of debt, in such cases instead of stopping operation or business at once there is a legal process to get some relief from debts. That process is called bankruptcy. There are many types of bankruptcy which are mostly classified as Chapters. The most practiced ones are Chapter 7 and Chapter 13. Chapter 7 is mostly used by individuals and can sometimes be used by businesses also. This chapter is mostly about liquidation of your assets, all the assets are liquidized in order to settle the debts. Chapter 13 is mostly used by businesses as by using this plan you don't have to sell all your assets; in this chapter all your financial situation and debts are thoroughly analyzed by professionals and they formulate a plan for your payments and how you should manage your finances in the future. It has many advantages and some disadvantages as well, by getting most of your debts or all of your debts removed you can start a new business and start from the beginning with new ideas and methodology and learn from your mistakes

Keywords: Bankruptcy and Insolvency, Bankruptcy and Accounting, Insolvency and Accounting, Bankruptcy and Financial Statements, Insolvency and Financial Statements.

Bankruptcy and Insolvency in the businesses are the practical concerns in which the accountants actively play their roles. Accountants as the financial advisors propose methodologies and strategies to improve and recover from the financial distressed conditions. From the economic developmental point of view the role of accounting in the bankruptcy is significant. The accounting information is useful in the prediction of bankruptcy situations. In this chapter, bankruptcy and insolvency is explored.

6.1 Bankruptcy

Bankruptcy is a legal process in which a person, organization or business gets a relief in case they are unable to pay their debts to creditors. They get relief from a portion of their debt or may be all of it depending upon various situations. In very simple terms, Bankruptcy can be associated to the situations in which the company is not able to pay its debts, and the bankruptcy law is concerned with such situations (Hart, 2000)

The Accounting based measures can be used to find the probability of bankruptcy. The Z-Score and O-score summarize the publicly available information about the probability of bankruptcy (Hillegeist et al., 2004). The information available for the analysis plays a key role in the prediction. Leon and Robert highlighted the importance of the loading on information for the prediction of the corporate bankruptcy, as it has always been a discussion in the research-based platforms that weather the accounting or market-based information should be used for the prediction of bankruptcy (Li and Faff, 2019).

One of the useful areas in which the research has been performed is the prediction of bankruptcy resolution. After the filing of the bankruptcy, the distressed firms in the United States are placed under the court supervision, and the firms that have filed for the bankruptcy have got similar financial distress characteristics which make it difficult to predict the final resolution (Barniv et al., 2002). For this purpose, Barniv et al. have worked on the classification and prediction of the final bankruptcy resolution (Barniv et al., 2002). Researchers have used the data from the non-financial large companies from European Union for the period 2006 to 2015, and evaluated the predictive capacity of factor analysis based over discriminant analysis by using five models for assessing bankruptcy risk. These models are Altman, Conan and Holder, Tafler, Springate and Zmijewski (Bărbuță-Mişu and Madaleno, 2020)

As in the upcoming text, the bankruptcy will be further discussed. Accountants play a significant role in bankruptcy situations as financial advisors. These financial advisors are involved in the bankruptcy proceedings, and the advice of the financial advisors is required to consider the alternatives that can transform a business from the distressed state into the profitable again (Newton, 2010).

Some of the researchers have worked on the consumer bankruptcies, and the researchers have highlighted that personal bankruptcy has witnessed a rise of 1.4 per thousand working age population to 8.5 from 1970 to 2002 (Livshits et al., 2010). The researchers concluded that the innovations in the credit market results in the decrement in the credit cost of lending and a decrease in the cost of bankruptcy can account for the rise in the bankruptcy (Livshits et al., 2010).

6.2 Insolvency

Insolvency is more of a state of financial stress in which person, organization or even business is unable to pay back the debts. When faced with insolvency companies or individuals contact the creditors directly and define and restructure ways to clear the debt. The IRS made a very simple and good criterion for insolvency. When a person or company's total liabilities exceeds total assets than they become insolvent. Person or company being insolvent arranges meeting with the creditors and design a very reliable plan to pay back the debts.

When a company is declared insolvent, it stops its payment plans, this is the notification to the creditor that you are going to surrender your estate. This record will be published in the government gazette and you no longer will have any dues. Companies become insolvent in two ways

Liquid assets are property or any other asset that can be converted easily into cash without substantial loss in its value.
Illiquid or non-liquid assets also known as fixed assets are those that are held long term such as land, home.

- Cash flow Insolvency: When business doesn't have sufficient or accessible cash to pay back your debt but it still has illiquid assets.
- Balance Sheet Insolvency: if amount of debt is greater than the company's total assets (liquid and illiquid).

6.2.1 Examples of Insolvency

There are many situations that can lead to insolvency for example

- Cash flow crisis: lack of management in spending of assets or customers make delayed payment
- Loss of business contract: your so trusted and healthy client suddenly change suppliers
- Loss of customers: your customer or client may find some other products interesting which may be because of several reasons particularly with the maintenance of quality and upgradation with the changing demands.

6.2.2 Act of Insolvency

There are eight acts that count as an act of insolvency. These actions are signal for the creditors that debtor will be unable to pay back the debt, so legal proceedings must be started. These acts are way of knowing for a creditor that debtor is insolvent.

Following are the eight actions that count as an act of insolvency

6.2.2.1 Offer of Settlement

It is the written document that you submit either to a court or lawyer which shows about the amount of money that you owe to the creditor. After showing that document you suggest offer for the creditor in order to settle the debt

6.2.2.2 Inability to Pay the Debts in Written Form

The very common way of declaring yourself insolvent is that you write an official document in which you declare that you are unable to pay back the debts. This is your admittance of insolvency. This step should be taken very carefully because there may be severe consequences so it's best to consult the legal personnel in this matter.

6.2.2.3 Evading from Debt Payment

If you leave your home country with the sole intention of avoiding the debt than you declare yourself insolvent, there are laws which vary in each of the country. In this case it will be very difficult for the creditor to prove that you left the country in order to evade from the debt, this condition of evading is called abscond

6.2.2.4 Unable to Satisfy a Judgment

If a creditor is assigned with the judgment against you and you are unable to justify or satisfy that judgment than you declare yourself insolvent.

6.2.2.5 Benefiting One Creditor over Others

It is an act of insolvency where you pay your debts to one creditor while ignoring the debt of other creditors.

6.2.2.6 Not Proceeding with Sequestration after Notice is Published

Once you have declared that you are unable to pay back the debts but you don't proceed with the sequestration of assets than this is an act of insolvency

6.2.2.7 Sale of Your Business

If you have applied for the sale of your business but you are unable to clear your debts than you will be considered insolvent and creditor may liquidate your business.

6.2.2.8 Hiding Assets

If you hide or sell your assets in order to evade from attachment than you are declaring yourself insolvent.

6.2.2.8.1 Factors Leading to Insolvency

There are a large number of factors that may contribute to insolvency like bad management or in adequate and efficient staff. Inappropriate construction of company's budget by accounting manager is also one of important factor that may lead to insolvency. If the outgoing money is greater than the incoming money than expenses of the company add up which may lead to insolvency.

Another factor that contributes to the increase in insolvency is the rise in the vendor cost. If in a company or business, prices of assets, services and products may increase due to several factors, when these prices are presented before the customer, they are not satisfied with the prices instead of doing negotiations they move their dealings and purchase to someplace else or some other companies.

Some customer uses lawsuit for their damages associated with the companies. This may lead to insolvency as the business may end up paying a large amount of money in case of damages, this amount is so enormous that it will stop company's operation. When company's operations stop whole of the business goes down and the company becomes insolvent.

Some companies become insolvent because they are unable to satisfy the customer's need. Customer's need keeps on changing and their demands too. So, it is very important for the company to keep their products and services up to date. Their services should meet all the customer's requirement. Companies failing to do so lose their customer and become insolvent. Customers turn to other companies that meet their requirement.

The accounting information on the costs of the bankruptcy situations are the most important ones. The accounting information is also very useful for the insolvency specialists (Bauer and Jan, 2020).

6.3 Bankruptcy Vs Insolvency

The main difference between bankruptcy and insolvency is as follows

- Bankruptcy is the process that is carried out by court order while insolvency is the state of financial problem that can happen to company or individuals.
- Insolvency has many types, one of them is bankruptcy
- Bankruptcy in most of cases target individuals and traders but insolvency is applied to both companies as well as individuals.
- A person or individual can be insolvent without being bankrupt, but they must apply for bankruptcy if situation goes for a long time.

Bankruptcy is a relief and help through court order to give debtors a fresh start. This process is done by liquidation of assets. Bankruptcy not only help individuals or one institution but can be a great source of protection for financially unstable business.

The process of bankruptcy begins by petition filed in court. Bankruptcy laws and matters are handled in the federal court. The petition can be filed by debtor or his/her spouse which is most common method but this petition can also be filed by creditor which is not that much of common. The whole organization can also file a petition by following court proceedings. Everything is done by court and there are large set of documents and rules and regulations in this process so it is best recommended to consult an expert attorney.

Bankruptcy process after filing the report starts out by liquidation of assets, which is done by following certain steps

- Debtor (individual or an organization) consult lawyer or accountant
- Do a very thorough analysis for the assets and inventory and do a proper preparation for these items to sale.
- Secure goods by consulting respective security agencies.
- Establish an official liquidation value (it's the price of an asset when it is given insufficient time to be sold in open market) for an asset.
- Choose proper time, place and quantity for your assets.

Liquidation on larger scale may involve shutting down the company and selling all its assets to get relief from debt. It allows great freedom for debtors and also provides opportunity for creditors to get back their debt. Theoretically this bankruptcy scheme helps in the growth and development of economy by providing debtors a second chance to restart their business and give repayment to creditors. All bankruptcy cases are settled in federal court where they are observed by bankruptcy judge.

Debts are not usually paid in full when someone is bankrupt. They are paid by two processes which are sale or liquidation of assets or compulsory payment which is set and agreed upon by debtors and creditors and court by taking all variables into consideration. There are many kinds of debts that may or may not be discharged through bankruptcy.

6.4 Types of Bankruptcy

There are several types of bankruptcy that are identified in the form of chapters. They vary from liquidation of assets to payment plans and many other options. PricewaterhouseCoopers has provided a comprehensive Bankruptcy and liquidation guidelines, under which 6 types of bankruptcy filings under the bankruptcy codes, and the description has also been provided for understanding purposes (PricewaterhouseCoopers PwC, 2021)

Table 6.1 Bankruptcy Codes and Filings (PricewaterhouseCoopers PwC, 2021)

Type	Filer	Description
Chapter 7	Business/Individuals	Provides for the orderly liquidation of the assets of the debtor for the satisfaction of some or all of its liabilities to its creditors
Chapter 9	Municipalities	Provides protection to a municipality from its creditors while it renegotiates a plan to adjust its debts
Chapter 11	Business/Individuals	Allows for reorganization of the business and a "fresh-start," most likely with reduced liabilities, or in certain cases an orderly liquidation
Chapter 12	Individuals	Provides for the adjustment of debts of a family farmer with regular income and limited debt
Chapter 13	Individuals	Provides for the adjustment of debts of an individual with regular income or a qualified small business
Chapter 15	Ancillary and Other Cross-Border Cases	Allows for cross-border insolvency cases to be governed on a uniform and coordinated basis

6.4.1 Chapter 7

Chapter 7 is all about liquidation. It is also known as straight bankruptcy. It is the most common bankruptcy that is practiced by companies and individuals. The main important variable in this type of bankruptcy is *trustee* which is appointed by court. When this trustee is assigned several contracts and agreements are signed from court and debtor side. The main clause of these agreements is that debtors take complete control over your assets. He uses anything that has value to pay debts to creditors. This type of bankruptcy removes unsecured debts like credit card and medical bills but not all the debts are cleared through this kind like student loans and taxes. Assets liquidation depends upon state of living of debtors meaning debtor will sell the items cash-based on condition of his livelihood. Chapter 7 can only postpone foreclosure; it can't eliminate it. The ones having assets like antique collections, stocks and bonds must liquidate their property to repay some or all of their debts. Person is only eligible for Chapter 7 bankruptcy if the court decides that person doesn't make enough money to pay back the debt. Proper tests are conducted on the court order where person's monthly income is compared with state average. If income is too much below the average and person doesn't have any decent amount of money to pay back the debt than he may file Chapter 7. If anyone files for this Chapter than he/she has to attend several meetings with creditors to discuss all the financial situations and time estimations. One very great disadvantage is that this filing stays on your record for 10 years meaning it will be a bad impression for business and you won't be able to file for it again until 8 years have passed.

Unsecured debts are that kind of debts that are not backed by some kind of item and there is no collateral if debtor is unable to pay back the debt. Person will more likely face lawsuit. Foreclosure is a legal process in which creditor has authority to sell asset of debtor as a collateral in case debtor is not able to continue his payment.

6.4.2 Chapter 13

Individuals or businesses who wish to remain in business find Chapter 13 as most suitable as it doesn't sell your assets. This chapter is very much about organizing and management of budget plan and resources. This allows a company and individual to reorganize their budget create plans and cut costs. Individual or company is only eligible for this chapter if they make sufficient amount of money and they meet the requirements set by court.

In secured debt there is a collateral, any amount of money that a person borrows is backed by some item. Creditor has the ownership over that item.

The court approves the payment plan which can be set by person or by professional also. This payment plan allow debtor to pay back some of unsecured debt and all of the secured debt. The monthly payment amount is approved by the court by looking at the financial situation and monthly salary or earning and how much debt person has. There is a strict rule that is applied to this chapter, it is that court manages finances and put person on tight budget and all transactions and spending will be monitored. Unlike Chapter 7, you don't have to sell your assets or face the process of foreclosure, instead time is given to update your mortgage. This chapter allows individuals to carry out their business objectives without any interruption while managing debt repayment plan. There is a threshold that is defined by the court for both secured and unsecured debts. If a persons secured and unsecured debts fall below that threshold than he/she is eligible for filing this chapter.

6.4.3 Chapter 11

Unlike Chapter 13, this chapter is more about organizing whole business or organization rather than individual finances. Debtors or business in debt come up with the plan, there is a proper meeting between court, debtors and creditors in which creditors and court thoroughly analyzes the financial situation of involved party or parties. KPMG in the Handbook has provided the accounting and financial reporting consideration at different stages of Chapter 11 bankruptcy (KPMG, 2022).

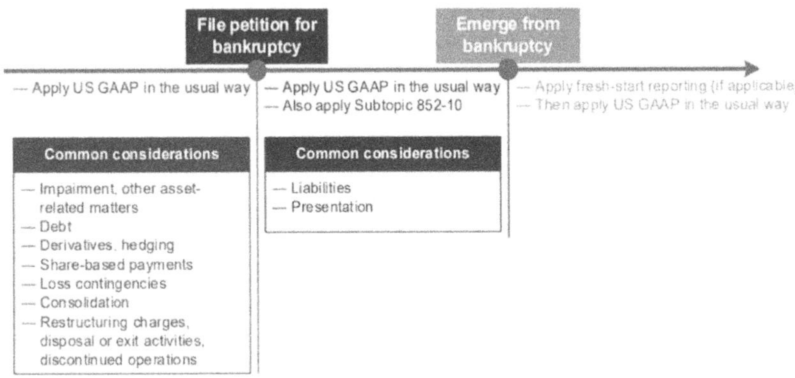

Figure 6.1 Chapter 11 Bankruptcy considerations (KPMG, 2022).

6.4.4 Chapter 12

This chapter is very much similar to Chapter 13 but it's more likely in the interest of farmers and fishermen.

The other two types are Chapter 15 and 9 which mostly target international bankruptcy issues and repayment plans for town, cities and districts respectively.

Very important questions arise when filing bankruptcy for example who can file for bankruptcy, what kind of bankruptcy is suitable.

6.5 Eligibility for Bankruptcy

Before filing for bankruptcy, one should look into set of variables, analyze the situation and file for bankruptcy very efficiently. Chapters 7 and 13 are most commonly used bankruptcies, so we will do a short comparison for both of these.

6.6 Chapter 7 (Liquidation Bankruptcy) Vs Chapter 13 (Reorganization Bankruptcy)

- **Who can file for bankruptcy:** Chapter 7 is more suitable for individuals and businesses while Chapter 13 is only suitable for individuals (including self-employed)?
- **Who is eligible:** Debtors are only eligible for Chapter 7 if their income is below a particular threshold and financial situation, while Chapter 13 doesn't have any income requirement but there is particular limit to debt?
- **What happens to unsecured debt:** Chapter 7 gets rid of most of unsecured debts except student loans, government taxes, child support. Chapter 13 gets rid of unsecured debts by repayment plan over time.
- **What happens to secured debt:** Debt is cleared by sale of non-exempt assets in Chapter 7. Chapter 13's dealing with secured debt is same like non-secured debt which is through a repayment plan.
- **Foreclosure Condition:** Chapter 7 can delay foreclosure but it will be brought into effect. Chapter 13 can stop foreclosure.
- **How long does it take:** Since Chapter 7 is more about liquidation of assets so it doesn't take that much time, it takes around 4–6 months, while Chapter 13 takes 3–5 year to complete repayment plan?
- **How long does it stay on your credit report:** Chapter 7 filing stays on the credit record for 10 years while Chapter 13 stays on the record for 7 years?

6.7 Advantages and Disadvantages of Bankruptcy

Filing bankruptcy has many benefits like clearing your debts, save home and assets, create a new fresh start, keep business going depending upon the type of bankruptcy that is filed. The main disadvantage for any kind of bankruptcy is that it stays on credit record for years depending upon the type. This record is a very bad impression for business and individual reputation since it will be very difficult to get loan, mortgage, credit or buy property.

6.8 Effect of Bankruptcy on Investors

As discussed above bankruptcy is classified into two categories, one is at individual level whether person is doing a job or self-employed and he goes bankrupt. The other type of bankruptcy is business or corporate bankruptcy. This kind of bankruptcy affects both the company and individuals who have invested in the company or have shares.

If company is approaching to bankruptcy, no one will invest in that company, when company analyzes its situation and declare that it is going bankrupt than liquidation of assets or repayment process starts, company continues its trading of stocks and bonds at very low prices. This will result in creating unfavorable situation for shareholder as they also suffer badly since there is substantial decline in the value of shares. Once company goes bankrupt there is very strong possibility that investors will not get back their full investment and there are also many cases when investor will lose their full investment.

Investor financial status will depend largely on company comeback, some companies don't maintain their status after going bankrupt while some can, in most of cases investors never fully get back what they have invested. The amount is always lessened.

When company files for bankruptcy there is a notice that is sent by court to all the creditors, and court makes bankrupt company's outstanding debt as an important priority.

6.9 History of Bankruptcy

6.9.1 In Ancient World

Debt slavery is a pledge of person's service in exchange of repayment of debts. He and his family will serve the creditors as their master for limited time unless he finds a mean to repay back his debt.

In ancient world (like Ancient Greece) bankruptcy and such advance rules did not exist. There was not leniency in debt payment. In ancient Greece if any person is unable to pay back the debt, he and his family will go into debt slavery. In this state creditor gets his debts back by utilizing physical labor. In many advanced states of ancient Greece there were rights of debt slaves, their debt slavery was limited for five years and they were given life protection. However, there came many situations in which creditors extend the deadline of five years and force the debtors to work for more time and sometimes even for a lifetime.

6.9.2 Roman Law of Bankruptcy

The law of bankruptcy was not as lenient as it is today even in Roman empire. Like most of our field's legislation, finances and economies traveled very large journey of growth and development. Laws which we find today as suitable and favorable are the result of very long research and study.

In Roman empire because of its ever-going wars, lot of soldiers faced debt problems and even subjected themselves to slavery or even become a prisoner. This situation happened so often and the reason was quite simple, Roman citizen-soldiers bore heavy weight of debts as they were serving the empire in the battlefield, no one was there to look after their crops and other kind of farming, when they came back to their homes after war they were already in state of debt.

"Nexum" was the roman contract for debtor bondage. In this contract debtor himself is the collateral if he is unable to pay back his debt on given time. He himself is the collateral. If the debtor is unable to pay back his debt on given time than creditor by law can seize him and force him for slavery. Nexum was put to an end and replaced by a new law Lex Poetelia Papiria. In this kind of contract debtors completely pledged themselves to the service of creditors, these debtors were set free during the course of war, they serve in the ranks and when the war is over, they return to the service of creditors. The twelve tables declared and upgraded laws related to debt payment.

- Thirty days will be allowed for payment in case of admitted debt
- After the completion of thirty days, if debtor is unable to pay back the debt, he/she will be arrested and presented before the magistrate.
- Debtor will be given a chance that if he still can pay the debt, if he is unable to do that and no one comes for guarantee of payment in his place, then the creditor has the right to capture him and bind him in thongs whose weight is less than fifteen pounds.
- The debtor will have the option to live according to his own means or the creditor will take responsibility for him to offer him sufficient portion of food for each day.
- After this settlement, debtor is given sixty days to pay back the debt and he will be presented before the praetor in three successive days and amount of debt will be made public. After the third market day the debtor will be sentenced to death or sold beyond the Tiber.
- After the third day creditor may have the option to cut several parts of body of debtor.

6.9.2.1 Lex Poetelia Papiria

The situation of nexum and Table iii of the Twelve tables continued for quite a time until Lex Poetelia Papiria was introduced to ease the situation of debtors. There were many provisions to that law but the most significant were three that were preserved. They were as follow;

- Thongs or any kind of fetters around arm or neck will only be used on prisoners or those who have committed a crime
- Even if one is debtor and he has borrowed money he will never be a nexum to his creditor
- Killing was prohibited, right to kill debtor or be sold by creditors was banned.

In all of these provisions debtors were given relief but they were still held in confinement unless they clear their debts.

6.9.2.2 Late Republic and Early Empire Laws

These laws continued for a long period of time. From period of nexum to closing of Republic, debtor and creditor laws kept on alleviating and damaging lot of debtors. There were minor variations in the laws but their main objective proved to be difficult for debtor class. Some of these laws promoted growth of economy and increased currency value, others wiped out nearly 75 percent of debt.

6.9.2.2.1 Using Property of Debtor for Repayment of Debts

In all the laws of Roman Empire there was no procedure in which creditor could reach out to debtors' property or even hold some item as collateral. Most of laws revolved around imprisonment and harsh treatment and even death for debtors. Even there was procedure designed to reach out for debtor's property there was still an option to hold the person in imprisonment in case of unsettlement or outstanding debts. There were two kinds of approaches to this property reaching method

- Portion of Debtor's property.
- Whole of Debtor's property.

6.9.2.2.1.1 Portion of Debtor's Property

This law was practiced under the rule of emperor Antoninus Pius. Magistrate had the authority to sell sufficient portions of debtor's property in order to pat back debts.

6.9.2.2.1.2 Whole of Debtor's Property

In Roman republic or even before there was common practice of escaping by the debtors. The only way for the creditors to get back their debt was in the form of imprisonment or using the debtor to perform labor activities but everything was related to physical existence of person. Debtors found a way of escaping creditors, that is mainly through hiding or moving to another place, in that way creditors would get nothing. So Roman Republic introduced new kind of rule that was greatly in the favor of creditors if they were dealing with escaped debtors. In that rule Magistrate under the authority of emperor introduced and enforced a new rule in which creditors would get all of the debtor's property if he escaped. This method was called the Rutilian Procedure. The purpose of this procedure was to maintain and preserve debtors' property who has escaped and distribute this property among all the creditors. The Rutilian process was simply possession of debtors' property (missio in possessionem) and sale of that property (venditio bonorum).

6.9.2.2.1.2.1 Missio in Possessionem

The Missio in Possessionem was implemented firstly for the debtors who were a fraud, the ones that hide instead of paying back their debts, this rule was implemented to confiscate the property of such debtors who fail to appear before the magistrate or any representative come in their place. When method of sale for the property of debtor was introduced, several clauses were also implemented. This possession of property for purpose of selling the debtor's property was extended to many cases

- If debtor died without any hair or legal successor or any person that was to be instituted heir. However, this possession of the property can be stopped if anyone would give security in defense of the deceased or any heir or pupil that defends the action against debtor's property. Pupil could also claim the inheritance and possession of the property if Praetor allows it. He allowed it by taking many things into consideration. If the sale of property is beneficial and the value of property exceeds the debts than the surplus amount can be possessed by the heir or pupil by permission of Praetor.
- If the defendant failed to appear before the magistrate on the appointed day as promised and paid in security by the defendant.
- The defendant was considered to be absent even if he/she is captured by bandits or absent because of business matter or he was a pupil. However, he would be pardoned and not considered absent if he was captured by enemies, in that case his property was temporarily put in the possession of supernatant until his freedom or return.
- If debtors were part of corporation or corporation themselves and if they were sued and no defendant or representative for that corporation appeared.
- If any person was sued and he failed to appear or representative failed to appear in his place.

- If person was in exile as a punishment or because of some other reason and no one appeared in his place.
- If debtor admitted the claim and failed to pay within the agreed upon time set
- Where there was a voluntarily assignment of the property by the debtor

This possession of the property was in nature of arrest. In order to justify this claim of property debt must be absolute and actually due. Only if these conditions were met than creditor was given the possession of the property. There is very important point that must be kept in mind that this possession of the property was not completely owned by the creditor instead it was a joint possession.

The creditor had to manage the possession properly, he was bound to manage the property and all the functionality of it like let the business or sale activity going. He could recover his expenses. The creditor was in possession of the property which he could use as mean of business activity or means of income.

This temporary possession of the property continued until debtor found reasonable amount for security or he himself or somebody in his place settled all those claims.

6.9.2.2.1.2.2 Venditio Bonorum

At the end of thirty days of possession of property, if nothing had been done from debtor's sides to clear the debts or if debtor is dead after fifteen days than process of sale of property starts. This property was not given into possession of creditors rather there was a price set by Praetor and magistrate and creditors and it was sold in the market. After these allocated days the creditors elect and appoint a "magister" to handle this case. After the election of this magister all the rights of debtor over his property were vanished and it was not his property anymore. The elected magister had the following jobs

- Act as a liquidator
- Make an inventory of the property.
- Make lists of all owing debts
- Mark this property for sale and make arrangements with the respective buyer known as "emptor"

This arrangement would take ten days if debtor is alive, five in case if he is dead. After the arrangements, with the consent and approval of Praetor the process of transferring the property to emptor starts which would take another ten to fifteen days. During all these processes debtor still had the chance to save his property by clearing his debts or anyone cleared the debts in his name. Sale of this property can be stopped by privileged bidders also which are prioritized in an order starting with largest creditors, other creditors and lastly relatives of bankrupt. They were given priority and they could avoid the sale by offering the suitable price. The one who offered the highest dividend to creditors was considered the highest bidder.

This magister was simply a person elected by the creditor and in no sense was the person appointed by the Praetor or had the authority of public officer. There may come a case where there were more than one creditor and if any of the creditor did not take part in electing this magister than he would be in same position and rank as the person who was involved in electing the magister.

6.9.2.3 Justinian's Legislature

Justinian made few changes in the laws of bankruptcy. It was mostly similar to Late Republic Laws with only few changes.

- Under the legislation of Justinian judgment debtors were still imprisoned. However, they were imprisoned in a public prison rather than in creditor's dwellings.
- There were no bankruptcy proceedings in case of seizure and sale of the property, however this was ordinary execution of court order by the public officer
- If debtor had enough resources or he could manage later on he could ask for more time. If he believed that he could meet all his requirement if more time is given to him than there was leniency introduced by Justinian. This would stop the process of possession of property. This had to be done by writing a personal letter and special application to the emperor. After filing this petition, creditors had to decide by the vote under the supervision of magistrate what to do, they could proceed at once to the surrender and sale of the property or they could do otherwise, if they could do proceedings steadily than the debtors were given no more than five years to clear the claims in full.

6.9.3 Bankruptcy in Middle Ages

6.9.3.1 Origin and Evolution of Bankruptcy

In the Middle Ages the first phase that appeared on the statue of bankruptcy was "One made Bankrupt" instead of "One becoming Bankrupt". This concept is very important as it shows a lot of information about the situation of bankruptcy and origin of this concept in 16th century.

The debtors who were defaulters and fled from the creditors were called fugitives. It was very common for debtor to flee from his creditor in those centuries so much that it became a custom. There were two reasons for that, one was harshness of the medieval laws for debtors in case of their insolvency despite of their honesty, second was the ease with which debtors can fled from the creditors which was basically due to lack of communications and political barrier. Now a days people sometimes go into bankruptcy voluntarily, same was the case in middle century people do voluntarily flight, this flight from the country or fleeing from the market was considered very essential and a part of definition of bankruptcy. By fleeing debtor was making himself bankrupt voluntarily that's why that phrase of making bankrupt was very common.

Thus, after seeing this English legislature became very serious about these bankruptcy laws. They knew about the debtor's behavior and how they *became bankrupt*. In whole of the parliament a special attention is paid toward the phrase "Debtors or Merchants that run away with other people goods". There was bill passed concerning this phrase. There was one more practice to evade creditors or any legal proceedings, that is "keeping the house". There was an old English Maxim that a person's house is his castle, he would use his house as a protection, consumes all goods of creditors and he will be protected from legal proceedings. Thus, in the first statue of bankruptcy two of practices by debtors were greatly targeted. One of them was Continental flight of escape "to parts unknown", second was "keeping the house".

The second statue of Bankruptcy was passed in the reign of Elizabeth in which these laws were improved but these implementations did not stop debtors, they added more methods in order to evade from the creditors like taking asylum in the sanctuary, voluntarily subject oneself to arrest, by doing all these things debtors were able to get away from the creditors and avoid the confiscation of one's property. The act of voluntarily arrest was done very smartly and using the advantage of laws regarding the criminals. The last act was not unintentional rather it was done wilfully by debtors by letting his friends arrest him on a false and bogus claim. There was very important and highest priority law that debtors used for themselves when they let themselves arrested it was "capias ad satisfaction" (a process done by commanding officer to place person under civil arrest in order to answer to a charge). By law this was highest execution as the person was placed in arrest and deprived of his liberty. Therefore, he can't be sued nor he has to answer for his creditors. He used his freedom for a long time in exchange of sacrificing his property. The main important question was that why would anyone go for a long imprisonment in order to save his property, the answer was quite simple he could easily obtain his freedom after being arrested. In the year 1626 group of creditors filed a complained against a debtor particularly a certain individual who was in imprisonment for 14 years yet he had the liberty to travel wherever he pleased, he only had to keep one person to act as his keeper which was normally selected by him, and he was not questioned for payments of his debts.

It was in the late 17th century that bankruptcy legislation thought about making laws for these kind of debtors as it was a great source of both social instability and financial problems. Therefore, at that time the word bankruptcy was originated and act of bankruptcy was incorporated in Anglo-American law. It was in that century that legislature extended the idea of extending the idea of liquidity, this method was introduced in the first statue but it was only for default debtors who did not flee nor they were imprisoned. Instead of making separate laws for those debtors who were imprisoned he thought about extending the concept of bankruptcy and making this concept more generic. The problem with the first statue was that creditors had to go through a very long, tedious and expensive procedure in order to prove their claims and outstanding debts. There was never a case when whole of the property of debtor was executed. The law provided the facility to liquidate debtors' assets real and personal. This method was even more troublesome when number of creditors increased. The new amendments included the imprisonment of any person who was bankrupt for six months or more depending upon his arrest. This imprisonment was completely different from the one that debtors did voluntarily. For those who were able to flee or remain imprisoned for fictional claim they were dealt severely. Those merchants who somehow got the chance to flee to other parts of Europe did not have any rights to their property any longer, their property was liquidated and all the debts were settled, in case of voluntarily imprisonment debtors were not pardoned from their debts, even in that kind of imprisonment person had to find a way to clear his debts.

6.10 Conclusion

English bankruptcy law did not evolve as much before 17th century. Most of creditors felt repressed and they were not faced with the favorable situations. All of laws and situations let to anti market situations until two additions to the law were brought into action. First, debtors were offered a friendly environment for debt discharge. Secondly there was an introduction of environment that supported negotiations among the parties. In the large companies, bankruptcy can be caused due to poor management, inappropriate sale forecasting, inexperienced management, and rapid technological advancements, and changes based on preference (Bărbuță-Mișu and Madaleno, 2020). The general quality of the accounting systems, quality of the warning systems (early) and properly written recognition plans positively impact the court supervised reorganizations of SMEs (Kuttner et al., 2022).

In the above section we discussed in detail the bankruptcy, insolvency, factors leading to insolvency and difference between these two. We also discussed in detail the history and laws of bankruptcy in Roman Times, Greece, and Colonial Period. Companies or individuals may see some downfall in their finances whose magnitude vary depending upon the situation, when such situation arises affected parties may go into large amount of debt, in such cases instead of stopping operation or business at once there is a legal process to get some relief from debts. That process is called bankruptcy. There are many types of bankruptcy which are mostly classified as Chapters. The most practiced ones are Chapters 7 and 13. Chapter 7 is mostly used by individuals and can sometimes be used by businesses also. This chapter is mostly about liquidation of your assets, all the assets are liquidized in order to settle the debts. Chapter 13 is mostly used by businesses as by using this plan you don't have to sell all your assets; in this chapter all your financial situation and debts are thoroughly analyzed by professionals and they formulate a plan for your payments and how you should manage your finances in the future. It has many advantages and some disadvantages as well, by getting most of your debts or all of your debts removed you can start a new business and start from the beginning with new ideas and methodology and learn from your mistakes. The biggest disadvantage is that when you become bankrupt even for once, it will go into your financial records which stay there for a long time. So, this becomes very difficult for getting a fresh start as looking at your record investor will less likely invest or you will less likely get a mortgage or loan but with period of time this bankruptcy is removed from your record. While bankrupt people can get a very big relief in their debts a very important question comes to mind that what will happen to investors, how they will get back their payments and what will be the effect of bankruptcy on investors the answer is very simple that when a company goes bankrupt than all the investors and shareholders that invested in this business will also be effected as they will not get back all of their investments or if they invested in the company that becomes bankrupt once but is not able to do business again, in these cases investors may suffer from loss so like always there is always a risk in investment.

Insolvency is more of state in which company or individual is unable to pay back their debts, so they contact the creditors and discuss some kind of payment plan. The very simple criteria defined by IRS is that when a company's or individuals total liabilities exceeds total assets than they become insolvent, and they will contact with their creditors and arrange for a meeting to design a payment plan. There are many factors that may cause company to go insolvent starting with bad management of finances or inefficient spending of company, if outgoing money is more than incoming money than company will go insolvent, some other factors are increase in the vendor price, if due to some factors price of the product increase customer starts to lose interest and looks for other businesses in order to get desirable price for the product. The last factor is the expensive lawsuit, some companies use lawsuit to deal with the damages, sometimes when damages occur these lawsuits becomes so expensive that company will be unable to manage its assets and will go insolvent.

The last discussion on this topic is difference between bankruptcy and insolvency. Bankruptcy is a legal process that is carried out by court order while insolvency is the state that can happen to individual or company. Insolvency has many types among which one is bankruptcy.

7 Accounting for the Sustainable Development

Abstract: By ensuring the transparency, auditing, accurate and meaningful reporting, and consultation, the efficient and proper utilization of economic and non-economic resources can be ensured. The economic development in the under-developed regions across the world is not possible without the integration of social, economic, and environmentally sustainable goals, and all of these activities are interlinked with each other. A special emphasis has been laid in the United Nation 2030 agenda to generate, increase, and appreciate the financial services in the rural and under-develop areas. The access to the financial services will result in generating the awareness related to financial management. In this way the general public in the under-developed regions will be able to manage their economic resources in an efficient way. And the corporate representatives will not be able to use them solely for their own purposes. The starting of the financial services in these regions will also provide loans to the farmers and agriculturists. The agro-economic approach if implemented in the rural areas will result in the efficient utilization of the natural resources, including crops, fertile land, etc. IFAC has identified eight goals of the sustainable development which are related to the accounting professions. By focusing on these goals and associated targets, accounting professionals can aid the process of achievement of sustainable development.

Keywords: Accounting for Sustainable Development, Business and Sustainable Developments, Financial Statements and Sustainable Development, Accounting Role on Sustainable Development.

The idea and concept of the sustainable development is not a new one. Keeping in view the depletion, wastage of the resources, and other ways of constructing and designing things that can pose a threat to the current and future inhabitants of the planet, the approach for the sustainable development has been worked out. Since the human activities, economic and non-economic have a greater impact on the society as well as the future generations.

Sustainable development is easy to understand using the environmental aspect of sustainability. The developmental activities performed by the human society if not feasible for the environment will result in the climate change, and this climate change will impact the lives of the current human societies as well as the future generations. As a consequence of the climate change, the environmental conditions for the future generations would be tough. As a consequence, in order to withstand the harsh environmental conditions, the human beings have to take measures and employ the technology. And this will directly or indirectly change the workflow of the economic activities. The Economic transactions in the field of technology related to environment and human comfort such as heating and cooling systems for homes and workspaces, will eventually increase.

7.1. Definition and Description of sustainable development

The sustainable development can be defined in multiple ways. As per the definition of the sustainable development from Oxford Languages, **"conductance of economic activities without the depletion of natural resources"**. The definition provided covers a broad spectrum and relates to the economic activities that involve the usage of natural resources, in particularly the resources that are depleting. The definition can be explained in a way such that the all of the industrial development occurring in the human society is related to the product development and services. The industrial development of the products has got an economic incentive, and this product when reaches the market, it results in the generation of economic transaction. The product that is developed in the industry should not involve the natural raw material that is depleting, or the method of acquiring the raw material should not result in the depletion. Moreover, the industrial process and operations should be based on the principle of environmental friendliness.

Another definition that is broader and simplifies the concept of sustainable development was the one that is available on the website of International Institute for Sustainable Development (IISD). "**Sustainable Development is the method of development that is based on the fulfilment of the current needs, without compromising the capability and ability of the future generations to fulfil their needs** "(International Institute for Sustainable Development). The economic, environmental, and the production activities should not affect the potential of the future generations to perform these activities. The ability and potential are a broader term that is being used here. It also covers the existence and availability of the resources, feasible and suitable economic environment, as well as the climate that supports the production and developmental activities.

International organizations in particular UNESCO, world bank, and UN itself is emphasizing on the practical implementation of the goals of the sustainable development. The sustainable development directly and indirectly affects the method and workflow of all the human activities. According to UNESCO, the concept and description of the sustainable development was first provided in the report of the Bruntland Commission published in 1987 (Brundtland,1987). The report presented by the commission was very comprehensive and different aspects of need and characteristics of the sustainable development haven been discussed. The main elements that can contribute towards the sustainable development are the technology and society as indicated by the report, and more precisely the social organization.

UNESCO highlighted four main dimensions of the sustainable development, these are, the society (social organization), environment, culture or norms, and economics (UNESCO). All of these dimensions are linked to one another. With reference to the scope and the purpose of the book, the main focus would be on the economic aspect of the sustainable development. There is always a confusion among the term sustainability and sustainable development at different forums of discussion. The term sustainability can be referred to a long-term goal or aim, which will be achieved by following the goals of the sustainable development itself (UNESCO). And the sustainable development refers to the processes and activities that will ultimately result in the creation of the sustainable society that can ensure the high-quality life for the future generations. It must be mentioned that the term sustainable development is a broader concept that does not only applies or requires the input from the producers or developers, rather the consumers and the customers are also expected to adopt the life style that support the overall process of sustainable development.

Klarin has provided a good explanation related to the concept of sustainable development in the publication (Klarin, 2018). Klarin has linked the sustainable development with the socio-economic development (Klarin, 2018). The socio-economic development should be limited within the boundaries and requirements of the ecological goals. And this development of the society should be based on the adjustment of society needs that ensure the distribution of the economic and non-economic resources in the society are making the quality of the life better for all the society not just the elites. And this would automatically ensure the careful management and utilization of the resources in such a way that these resources when consumed by the future generations should improve the quality of the life (Klarin, 2018). The adjustments of needs and the management of the resources are viable for the sustainable development. Klarin has compared the sustainable development with the triple bottom line, the sustainable development itself is founded on the three pillars or supporting sub-structures of sustainability (Klarin, 2018). As per the explanation provided above, these three pillars can be treated as long term goals themselves. The three main sub-elements of the sustainable development are environmental, economic, and social sustainability (Klarin, 2018). Without the achievement of even the one, the process of the sustainable development cannot be ensured.

The environmental sustainability is associated with the attainment of the quality of the environment so that the economic activities can be performed in an easy and efficient way to ensure the quality of life for the people. The environment should be feasible for working, growth, and development. The environment term can be extended to ecological as well as the working environment of the workplaces, markets, industries and institutes. The ecological quality includes the air quality, water quality, atmosphere, and general environment so that the human society can work with full pace to achieve the productivity and efficiency as well. The virtual working environment can be referred to as the environment that provides growth and development for the whole human society. Environment in which people belonging to all the age groups can find opportunities and contribute to the development and prosperity of the society. Social sustainability is relatable to the change in the behavior and the approach of the acceptance of others. The social sustainability requires the promotion and appreciation of the equal rights for all human beings and the consideration of the human rights. The social sustainability can be achieved by the respect and preservation of the cultural identities of the human beings, acceptance of the diversity in race, culture, religion, and ethnicity. The economic sustainability is associated with the maintenance of natural, social, human, and intellectual capital that is essential for income, production, and living quality life (Klarin, 2018).

7.2. UN 2030 Agenda for Sustainable Development

As mentioned above, the global monetary and peace institutions are determined to implement the concept of sustainable development, and require the active involvement of the state members. In the seventeenth session of the United Nations General Assembly, a resolution named as "Transforming our world: the 2030 Agenda for Sustainable Development" was adopted on 25th September 2015 (United Nations, 2015). The detailed agenda of the sustainable development 2030 was published and is also available at the website of the United Nations sustainable development goals. The term universal agenda was used for this, and it requires the participation of governments, partners, and stake holders at the implementation level. In the agenda, 17 sustainable developmental goals and 169 targets were declared (United Nations, 2015). The goals are needed to be integrated with the three main dimensions of the sustainable development, which are economic, social, and environmental (United Nations, 2015). Since the agenda was finalized in 2015, and it provided the operations and implementation strategy for the next fifteen years, till 2030 (United Nations, 2015). The means of the implementation were also described. The seventeen goals defined by the United Nations in the context of the sustainable development are associated with economic, social, and environmental aspect. The sustainable developmental goals are associated with the end of poverty, hunger, availability of the clean water and energy, and reducing the gaps based on the consideration of inequalities. Sustainable infrastructure development is a principle that can help in the achievement of the many goals of the sustainable development. The first goal for the sustainable development is the eradication of poverty from the globe by 2030, and the definition of the poverty was also defined, that is person living below 1.25 $ for a day. The targets defined under the eradication of the poverty goal especially addresses the poor and vulnerable population of human society. Moreover, the targets also include that by 2030 it should be ensure that all the men and women should have access to the basic services, and ownership to the property including lands, and access to the technology as well as the financial services and facilities. As we have seen in the villages and sub-towns of Asia, the farmers, and other people belonging to rural societies usually do not have access to the basic financial system such as banks and other micro-financial services. The target 1b is related to the creation of policy frameworks at the national and international level to promote investment that supports the eradication poverty (United Nations, 2015).

One of the infrastructure related sustainable development goals is based on the assurance of universal access to affordable, reliable, and sustainable energy at the universal level (United Nations, 2015). Moreover, the contribution of the green energy and renewable energy in the global energy generation should be increased (United Nations, 2015). The energy efficiency at the global rate should also be doubled by 2030 (United Nations, 2015). It means the efficiency of the energy generation and transmission should also be increased. This target is closely associated to the definition of the sustainable development itself. As the non-renewable sources of energy generation are also depleting, and this can endanger the availability of the resources for the future generations. The strategic goals include the increase in the investment in the green energy and cleaner sources of energy generation and increase the international co-operation in this matter by 2030 (United Nations, 2015). The target 7.b addresses the developing, least developed, island based, and landlocked countries, and the technology and infrastructure should be modified and upgraded to ensure the availability and generation of clean and green energy in these regions as per the support programs of the countries (United Nations, 2015).

As mentioned previously, the consumption patterns of the products and resources are also very relatable to the achievement of the goals of the sustainable development. The twelfth target is associated to the sustainable consumption and production pattern globally (United Nations, 2015). By 2030, efficient management of the natural resources needs to be ensured.

7.3. Sustainable Economic Development

The more relevancy in the context of the sustainable development and this book is related to the economic aspect of the sustainable development. It must be mentioned that at the end of the last century there was a change/revision in the conceptual thinking of the development and the interpretation of the agreed conventional concept of the economic development (Barbier, 1987). The new approach of the concept developed has the main motive of fulfillment the needs of the poor people, appreciates the concept of the cultural sensitivity, and the promotes the participation in the developmental process at the ground level (Barbier, 1987). Moreover, the main concept that it advocates is that the development and changes in the developing and under developed regions across the world is not possible without the implementation of environmentally sustainable policies and strategies (Barbier, 1987). In this way it was made clear that the environmental and developmental goals have common purpose that is the welfare of the current and future human society, and there exists no conflicts among the goals of two (Barbier, 1987).

The concept of the sustainable development is very difficult to describe in the analytical terms (Barbier, 1987). There existed a need for the sharp definition of the unique ecological, economic, and the social characteristics of the sustainability that are sufficient enough to provide the meaningful tools and methods for the analysis and the policy making (Barbier, 1987). Prior to the conceptual understanding the details of the sustainable economic development, it is necessary to understand the characteristics of the economic development itself. Barbier has mentioned the agreed upon features of the economic development and also the definition of the economic development (Barbier, 1987). The economic development as per the non-Marxist thought can be defined as the processes and activities that contribute to the increment of the per capita income of a country or state, over a longer period of time, subjected to the condition that the poverty does not increase and the unequal distribution of the income is not increased (Barbier, 1987). The definition of the economic development that has been presented has already contained the characteristics and features that are meant to be achieved by the sustainable economic development, which are the, poverty eradication, and the equal distribution of income and wealth.

Barbier has provided an explanation while citing the literature, that the interpretation of the economic aspect of the sustainable development should be based on the definition of the sustainable development as presented by the World Commission on Environment and Development and also presented in the agenda of sustainable development 2030 (Barbier, 2007). The definition has been presented in the text above. The definition is very suitable and understandable by the economists as well, as in simpler terms the economic prosperity and achievement of well-being today should not be based on any method or technique that can result in the reduction or decrement in the prosperity tomorrow (Barbier, 2007). The future generations should be able to utilize at least the same level of economic opportunities and enjoy at least same level of economic prosperity and welfare that the current generation has (Barbier, 2007). In economic terms, the per capita welfare should not decrease over the time. The same kind of explanation of the per capita income we have studied above in the definition of economic development as well. Barbier has described the concept of sustainable development using the diagram (Pearce and Barbier, 2000). The Figure 7.1 presented below contains the diagram for the sustainable development (Pearce and Barbier, 2000).

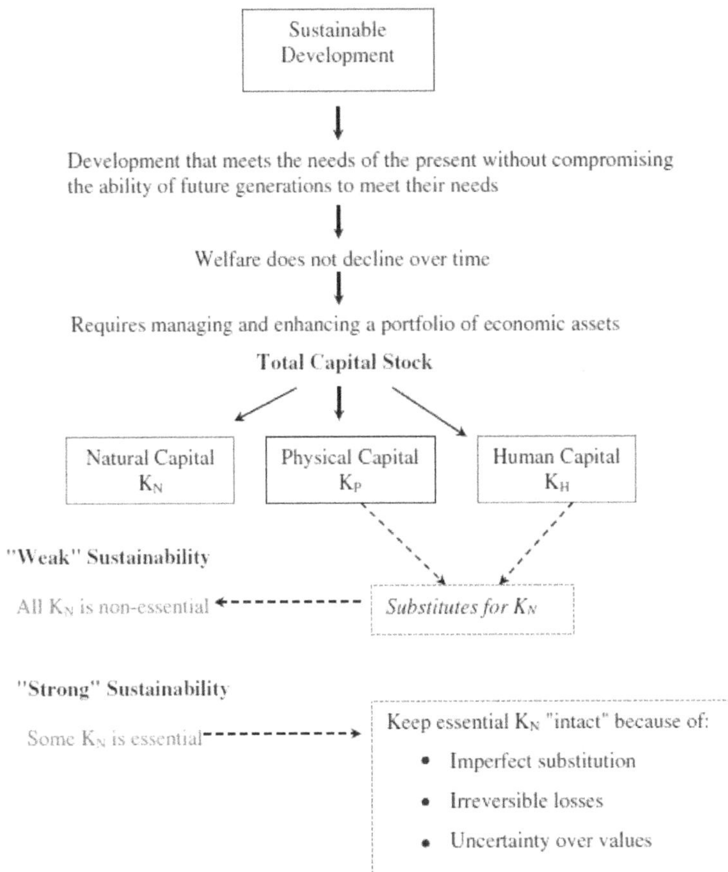

Figure 7.1 Sustainable economic development model. (Image source: Pearce and Barbier, 2000).

In the figure presented above, the utilization of the resources, and the economic sustainability concept has been explained in terms of practical economic measures and resources. Barbier has explained that the total economic opportunities and welfare, and the prosperity for the future and current generations is dependent upon the total stock of the capital (Pearce and Barbier, 2000). The human society has to make decisions related to the utilization of the total capital stock today for fulfilling the needs of present, generate economic and production activities, and manage welfare, and how much of that stock should be saved for the future generations (Pearce and Barbier, 2000). As the concept of the consumption, and utilization has also incorporated in the sustainable economic development model. The total capital stock is formed by the summation of Natural, physical, and human capital. The intellectual and human capital are both utilized in the modern economic system. The relationship between the utilization and consumption of the resources is not just as simplified as explained above. The constituent elements of the total stock capital matter a lot, and it is currently debatable within the context of the sustainable development that in which compositions or ratios that individual capitals are contributing to form the total capital stock. Wither the development and welfare is being done on the expense of major utilization of the natural capital, then this will result in the depletion of the natural resources. The fact described can be explained well using the example of the poor countries and the communities. The development occurred at the expense of the natural capital completely will cause the environmental problems. Barbier has explained that one of the greatest contributions of the sustainable development is the realization of the concept of combined causation of phenomenon and the elements are the poverty, environmental devastation, and under-development (Barbier, 1987). The poor people residing in the geographical areas that are associated with the extreme climatic conditions are involved in the struggle for survival, and this survival war forces these communities to do activities that have got an environmental damage. The survival moves these people attempt to made have long-term disadvantages associated. The continuous grazing of the animals on the cultivated crops, and usage of the agricultural lands for other purposes and cutting of the forest trees for using the wood for fire purposes are the examples of extreme measures that the poor people are forced to take. Moreover, in certain regions there exists an extreme condition of weather for 3–6 months in a year, the poor villagers have to collect and stock the wood, food, and other necessary items for that period of year. Moreover, the roads in the certain regions are highly under-developed, villagers have managed their own transport for traveling to the main highway. The bad road conditions and extreme weather conditions make it difficult for the outsiders to travel to these villages. The scenario presented here shows the strong relationship between under-development, poverty, and unsustainable consumption of the natural resources. The way the poor people are consuming the natural resources, which they are forced to use will result in the extreme conditions of weather in the future. And these natural resources such as forests, agricultural lands, and fertility associated with the land may not be available for the future generations. Using the concept of sustainable economic development, the goal is to eradicate poverty, ensure the development in the far-situated areas, and the promote the proper utilization of the natural resources.

7.4. Role of Accounting in Sustainable Development

The businesses and the entrepreneurial established units are the fundamental units of the economic systems. The methods of doing businesses and business operations are critical in defining the frameworks of the economic systems. The skills and the role the accountants have acquired all across the world have resulted in the creation of responsibility and potential to bring change in the society through effective planning, management, and implementation of the strategies in the organizations that meet the goals of sustainable economic development. The private businesses and the organizations are one of the major contributors of the economic system. Multiple businesses have more than one office in different countries and each of the office has hired the professionals from the local regions. These businesses are growing due to the contribution of the local society members. So multi-national businesses are formed and developed due to the contributions of multi-national professionals who are working for the growth of the businesses. In other words, the multi-national businesses have got a great impact on the society. And if the goals of these businesses are aligned with the sustainable development goals, then automatically their economic and social contribution to the world would have a significant impact. There is a huge share of the private sector in the GDP.

There is a huge role that management accountants can play in the modification of the businesses. In this section the role that the accounting profession can play in the achievement of the sustainable development and in particular the sustainable economic development will be explored.

In simple words the accountants act as an economic actor to meet the requirements and expectations of the public and act in the following roles: Associate, employee, governmental official, customer relations manager, banker, and investment (Sorina-Geanina et al., 2018). The way the accountants are involved in the businesses today, they certainly have significant impact on the businesses as well as the economic system. Accountants can play a critical role and act as a lever in the process of sustainable development of a business (Sorina-Geanina et al., 2018). They can design the business strategies, they know the methods, and they have the experience, and also have the mathematical values of the parameters (Sorina-Geanina et al., 2018). Using all the previously mentioned attributes, the accountants know the methods and strategies to convert a normal businesses strategy into a sustainable business approach. Successful businesses have the management accountants at the key management positions in the company. The example presented in the previous chapter (Role of Accountant in Businesses) consists of the successful auto-mobile company of the premium auto group. The company has management accountant as one of the senior members of the management, and the responsibilities included management of the technical as well as the non-technical resources. The role that management accountant has been playing in the company has got an impact on almost all the operations of the company.

7.4.1. Sustainable Reporting

One of the key duties that accountants perform while doing their jobs is the financial reporting. The financial reporting as discussed in the previous chapters have a key role in forecasting as well as the decision-making process of the businesses. The importance of the corporate, transparent, and useful financial reporting in achieving the financial stability as well as the sustainability and particularly in the achievement of the sustainable development goals was acknowledged and recognized at the thirty-second session of the UNCTAD Intergovernmental Working Group of Experts on International Standards of Accounting and Reporting (Makarenko and Plastun, 2017). The accountants are actively involved in the process of the financial reporting. They accurately measure, analyze, and report the progress of the company in terms of achievement of the sustainable development goals (Makarenko and Plastun, 2017). The accountants guide the companies and act as the translators of the triple bottom line analysis using the concept and terms of the corporate sustainability (Makarenko and Plastun, 2017). The corporate sustainability is an approach that is used for the creation of the long-term stakeholder value of the business by the implementation of a business approach based on the moral, ethical, environmental, social, economic, and cultural factors.

One of the key areas of reporting in which the accountants play their role is the reporting of the environmental information. The traditional financial method of the environmental reporting is insignificant in providing a complete and the clear picture of the environmental impact of the business or any entity (Sorina-Geanina et al., 2018). In order to address this issue, environmental and social information reporting method guidelines have been developed and provided to the businesses to ensure that sustainable achievements can be reported and presented properly (Sorina-Geanina et al., 2018). The guidelines also help the managers to obtain the reports based on the internationally approved concept, and the data reported can be comparable and understandable by the users of the accounting reports (Sorina-Geanina et al., 2018). The common reporting methods will enable the shareholders that are contributors of the sustainable development goals to compare the progress and exchange the information with each other, and relative progress of achievement of the sustainable development can be compared. The sustainable reporting is based on the guidelines and methods guided by the Global Reporting Initiative (GRI), as well as the other international bodies have proposed the solution to the problem of the common social and environmental information reporting methods (Sorina-Geanina et al., 2018). International Federation of the Accountants (IFAC) has acknowledged as well as identified that the sustainability achievement and enhancement are directly linked to the role that the accountants play, ethical and moral values and their implementations, codes of conduct, information reporting methods, commitments and interests of the shareholders, and the transparency in the accounting procedures (Sorina-Geanina et al., 2018).

IFAC has issued the sustainability framework 2.0 in 2011, that provides the guidelines related to the role that accountants can play in their respective organizations to enhance the ensure the sustainable development (IFAC, 2011). The methods and guidelines proposed in the sustainability framework 2.0 can be implemented at all the entity levels, irrespective of the complexity of the organization and business procedure. The framework has proposed the implementation of the strategies and integration of the sustainability characteristics from three approaches, these approaches are, business strategy, operational, and reporting (IFAC, 2011).

The environment of stakeholders is promoting and driving the sustainability, Economic, Social, and Governance (ESG), and integrated reporting methods (IFAC, 2011). The reporting based on sustainability indicators is important for the share and stakeholders, and it results in highlighting the appropriate and useful information related to the impact of sustainability, issues and problems of ESG, risks, and opportunities that can be availed to enhance the sustainability (IFAC, 2011). As the concept of the sustainability has evolved, there is always an increasing pressure on the organizations to report the sustainability and highlight the ESG issues, and the pressure comes from the regulators, stake and shareholders, stock exchanges, investors, customers, and the NGOs as well (International Federation of Accountants (IFAC), 2011). At several legal jurisdictions and the states, the security regulating authorities have acknowledged the importance and need for the firms to report the ESG issues that would be able to provide the investors useful information and especially fundamental in highlighting the following aspects (IFAC, 2011):

- Financial liabilities associated with the environment and social responsibilities
- Financial and operation impact of the environmental protection and especially the requirements
- Policies related to the protection of the environment and especially the risks

The information related to the sustainability and impact of the sustainable development is very necessary for the investors. A major portion of the economic sustainable development goals require the investment from the investors and stakeholders in the areas that require the development. From the financial point of view, the investors should be satisfied about the impact of the investment on the society, environment, as well as on the finances so that the investment can be ensured. The IFAC has provided the **Jurisdictional Requirements** section in sustainable framework 2.0 in which the regulatory requirements in different countries have been mentioned to report the sustainability and ESG related issues (IFAC, 2011). In Sweden and China, it is mandatory for the State-owned Enterprises to report the sustainability (IFAC, 2011). The purpose of these regulations is to encourage the organizations to provide the reports based on the non-financial parameters, and these reports should be based on the factors that are critical in achieving the sustainability. Since the companies are reporting the sustainability factors, the next step that is logical to follow is to achieve high scores and values related to the sustainability parameters. 12 countries have developed and signed the principles of reporting the non-financial and sustainability parameters (IFAC, 2011).

IFAC in sustainable development framework publications has also provided the guidelines that the accountants can follow to provide the useful reports based on the progress of the sustainable development achievement by their firms and organizations (IFAC, 2011). These guidelines have been mentioned below (IFAC, 2011). And each of these methods have been explained in detail in sustainability framework document (IFAC, 2011)

- Developing a reporting strategy that provides the complete description of the organization's performance, and the reports should be useful for a different range of stakeholders. The organizational report should not fulfill the needs of only investors, or stock exchange bodies, it should be equally understandable, and useful for the government officials as well.

- Representing the sustainability impacts in the financial statements, especially the environmental impact on the assets, liabilities, income, and profits etc.
- The transparency in the reports should be ensured, and the reporting gaps should be minimized. The actual picture of the organizational performance is necessary for the stakeholders and investors to understand. The details related to the internal and external reporting needs have been mentioned in the chapter of the financial reporting
- Understanding and re-applying the approaches to the sustainability reporting and materiality
- Developing an approach so that the external audience is satisfied from the organizational reporting, and the reporting provides the internal benefits as well such as the improvement of the performance, and improvement of the reporting methods as well.

7.4.2. Role and Responsibilities of Accounting Profession in Sustainable Development

After the approval and adoption of the sustainable development agenda in 2015 and 2016 respectively, IFAC has identified eight goals which the accounting profession and the professionals can focus and contribute significantly to the implementation of the new sustainable development agenda of united nations 2030 (Nechita, 2019). As a consequence of the agenda, at the end of 2016, two meetings were held by IFAC to discuss the capabilities of the accounting profession and the way accounting professionals working in different organizations can contribute to the achievement of the sustainable development goals (Nechita, 2019). Nechita has mentioned those eight main goals of sustainable development and the adjacent goals that IFAC has determined so that the change can be made in the organizations and the society through the accountants working in different roles across the world (Nechita, 2019). In this section these goals and the adjacent objectives have been mentioned. The same goals have been published and explained by the Chartered Professional Accountants of Canada (CPA Canada) (CPA Canada, 2016).

7.4.2.1. Quality Education

The fourth sustainable development goal is the Quality Education (Nechita, 2019). As mentioned previously, there are targets associated with each of the goals.

And the targets that IFAC has determined and are relevant to the accounting profession are 4.3 and 4.6 (Nechita, 2019). 4.3 states that it should be ensured that all the men and women should have equal access to the affordable, and quality technical, vocational, and the tertiary education including the university education (Nechita, 2019). Similarly, the 4.6 adjacent goal ensures that all the young population, and as well as the substantial population of adults including men and women achieve an appropriate level of literacy. Both of these targets are more rigorously needed to apply in the developing countries. In developing countries and particularly the culture sensitive regions especially South East Asia, and some parts of the Arab countries the concept of equal education for both genders are not appreciated. Traditionally, the parents think that the women are ultimately married to someone, and the need for the education and investment of the resources is not fruitful. Moreover, mentally and psychologically the professions are reserved for the genders. The male population of youth in these countries are more likely to adopt the STEM fields as compared to female young population. If the Gender diversity and enrolment in the accounting profession is observed in India, there exists a clear gender biasness trend. In Institute of the Chartered Accountants of India, the male to female percentage is found to be 66 %: 34 %. This means that 66 percent of the students registered or enrolled for the accounting education are male and 34 percent of the students are female. The percentage difference is almost double. Similarly, the recruitment and the HR strategies adopted in various accounting organizations are still gender dominated which results in the discouragement of the female population to adopt and pursue the accounting career (Atena and Tiron-Tudor, 2019).

Moreover, in the developing countries due to the safety and security concerns, the female population is hesitant to struggle and think or move out of the box to acquire the advanced skill and education. The accounting profession has made serious actions to ensure the quality accounting education. The profession is working towards meeting the global demands for the qualified and professional accountants, and the professional accounting bodies are ensuring that the future accountants are equipped with the leadership, entrepreneurial, and business skills (CPA Canada, 2016). Moreover, the accounting profession is providing support to the accountants in continuing the education throughout the career so that the relevancy and the specialized skills can be obtained (CPA Canada, 2016).

There also exists a strong need for the incorporation of the sustainability in the accounting curriculum of the degrees offered in universities across the world. Bergner et al have performed a survey in 2016 to search the courses devoted entirely to sustainability at the accounting departments in colleges and universities in USA (Pippin et al., 2016). Surprisingly only 17 out of more than 900 universities offered a course that is completely based on the sustainability.

Various measures have been taken to ensure the commitment of the accounting profession to the quality education. Skills Future is an initiative that was taken by the Association of Chartered Certified Accountants (ACCA) and the Institute of Singapore Chartered Accountants that is based on providing more opportunities for the persons who are intending to become an accountant and meeting the growing needs of the professions (CPA Canada, 2016). High quality professional trainings are offered to students from the various technical and polytechnical institutes and also the professionals who are already adopting the career (CPA Canada, 2016).

YES Bank, the Bombay Stock Exchange (BSE), and the Institute of Chartered Accountants of India (ICAI) have combined together and decided to improve the financial education, literacy, and understanding by offering financial literacy camps (CPA Canada, 2016). There are many other practical initiatives that have been taken by the accounting professionals and bodies in different regions of the globe to ensure the quality educational access to all of the population (CPA Canada, 2016). There exists a strong need in the society for the skilled accounting professionals who understand the public as well as the corporate narrative. The skilled accountants play a fundamental role in the management and monitoring of the economic resources in businesses.

7.4.2.2. Gender Equality

The sustainable development goal number 5 corresponds to the gender equality. The associated target and the adjacent goal are 5.5. the target 5.5 relates to the accounting profession, and it requires the assurance that complete and effective women participation for the leadership at each level of the decision-making process in the political, economic and public matters of the life (CPA Canada, 2016). Some of the description related to gender equality has been presented in the above section. The gender equality is associated with allowance of both genders to contribute to the development of the society. The discipline or profession will be able to utilize the full talent and the deliver to the society with full potential if the participants and the leaders are selected from the wider range of pool talent (CPA Canada, 2016). Inclusion of women is associated with incorporating the diversity into the business operations. The women are fully capable of pitching unique and useful ideas in the businesses, and in the past, we have seen many examples where the women leaders have provided new energy and explored unique dimensions in the businesses. It is important that women are allowed to fully participate in the process of development, and in this way the better opportunities of education and employment for the future generations of the females would be possible.

As mentioned above, in many states the participation of the women in the field of accounting and finance is low (CPA Canada, 2016). Moreover, the rate and chances of the women to reach the leadership and obtain the key management position in accounting and finance sectors are low (CPA Canada, 2016). However, there are many countries in which the society and the corporate culture has embraced the diversity and gender equality very well. In Singapore the women contributing to the accounting profession make up to 75 percent of the total accountants, and 69 percent of the accountants in the Philippines are females, and more than half of the new Certified Public Accountants are females (CPA Canada, 2016).

Accepting and embracing the concept of diversity is fundamental in achieving the sustainability by ensuring the sustainable development. The sustainable development approach requires creativity, innovation, and making the actions possible which were not done in the past. It is worth mentioning here that some of the regions of Asia and Africa are included in the one of the poorest and least developed regions in the world. However, the contribution of Asia and Africa in the implementation process of the sustainable development is remarkable. Policy and decision makers in Asia and Africa have started promoting the methods and practices of sustainable development in business by introducing new mechanisms such as Corporate Social Response (CSR), and the members of this committee are particularly focusing on the targets and deliverables of sustainable development goals (Cicchiello et al., 2021). Gender diversity is increasing and the women participation in the emerging and growing markets of Asia is also increasing (Cicchiello et al., 2021), women are now holding 9.3 percent of the corporate board seats and 4.2 percent of corporate board chair positions, and there is an increase of 1.5 percent to 1.6 percent respectively from the 2016, which is indeed a positive change (Deloitte, 2019). The presence of the female population in the leading roles in the tech industry in Asia particularly the IT industry is also increasing.

When the accounting discipline is considered in the developed countries, the conditions of presence of the female population in the accounting profession and holding the leadership position is far better than the developing countries, however, overall, the percentage of the females serving as the leaders in the finance industry in the developed countries is still low (CPA Canada, 2016). The accounting professionals and regulatory bodies have also taken the practical steps to address the gender gap in the accounting profession. The Women's Accounting Leadership series is a newly designed series that consists of events of continuing education for the women in accounting and finance (CPA Canada, 2016). The series is co-sponsored by the Institute of Management Accountants and Pace University, and the events give women working in finance and accounting industry having different experience duration and type to discuss the career and technical aspects of their profession (CPA Canada, 2016). American Institute of Certified Public Accountants (AICPA) Women's Initiatives Executive Committee is determined to retain and promote the growth and advancement of women in the accounting industry (CPA Canada, 2016). One of the appreciable activities of AICPA is the arrangement of Women's Leadership Summit (CPA Canada, 2016). This helps the women in developing the advanced skills related to the development and progress of the business, mentoring, network and connectivity, and client service. The characteristics and attributes that are fundamental for the leadership in the accounting can be learned using this forum. The institute of the Chartered Accountants of India has created a portal for the Women to provide power to its women members, and the portal will be helpful in the management and implementation of the plans and policies that are focused for the development and facilitation of its members (CPA Canada, 2016).

The need for the participation of the women in the accounting and finance profession in the developing countries is more intense. Women in these regions can contribute to the economic system and also attain self-sufficiency in terms of economic resources, and in this way, they can support their families to have a better quality of life.

7.4.2.3. Decency in Work Patterns and Economic Growth

The eight-sustainability development goal is the Decent work and the Economic Growth (CPA Canada, 2016). In detail the goals states and requires the promotion of sustained and retained, inclusive, and sustainable economic growth patterns, full employment opportunities that ensures the productivity, and depicts the decency in the work for all (CPA Canada, 2016). The adjacent accounting goals and the sustainability targets are 8.1 and 8.3. the target 8.1 states the requirements of sustaining the per capita economic growth as per the national scenarios and the circumstances, and particularly, at least 7 percent of the growth per year in the least developed countries (CPA Canada, 2016). The target 8.3 states the promotion of the development-based strategies and policies to support the productive activities, job creation that is decent in nature and beneficial for the development and the society, entrepreneurship, creativity, and innovation, and the encouragement of the formulation and growth of the micro, small and medium sized entrepreneurship and enterprises, while ensuring the full access of all to the financial services (CPA Canada, 2016). The economic growth, equal and efficient distribution of economic resources, and the proper utilization has a direct impact on the elevation of poverty. And the eradication of poverty is the main and the fundamental goal of the UN agenda for the sustainable development.

In order to meet the first target, the accountants around the world are working in the business intensive environments to help the management in formulating policies that are essential for sustainable business growth. The sustainable development practices fully incorporated in the businesses will automatically ensure the growth in the economic system. As discussed above, the major portion of the economic system and GDP is composed of the private businesses and the economic activities that are occurring in the market constitute the framework of the economic systems. To ensure the per capita growth, and sustaining the growth parameters, Accountants are needed to utilize their skills, expertise, and the experience to help to encourage the resilience and responsibility in the organizations. As the accountants are the professionals who are directly associated with the decision-making process in the businesses and companies, they need to ensure that the decisions making process considers the long, medium and short term financial, social, environmental, and the influential consequences (CPA Canada, 2016).

The accounting profession is directly associated with the prosperity and improved quality of life and living standards (CPA Canada, 2016). Centre of Economic and Business Research conducted research for the IFAC, and the research highlighted the role of Accountants in the economic development (IFAC, 2020), the research has corelated the size and the development of the accounting profession as well the growth of the discipline with the economic development (CPA Canada, 2016). It is worth mentioning here that the accountants working in the governmental and non-governmental roles are ensuring the transparency. The economic corruption is avoided by the accountants by the fair representation of the financial information on financial statements. Overall, the accounting profession has got a direct contribution to the economic growth and imparting decency in the workflows at different types of the industries. The accountants can directly contribute to behavior modification in the work environments that will lead directly to the productivity and efficiency.

7.4.2.4. *Other Sustainable Development Goals Associated with the Accounting*

As mentioned earlier, there are 8 goals that the IFAC has determined which are relatable to the accounting profession. Three of these goals have been mentioned and explained above, the SGD 9 will be discussed in this section.

7.4.2.4.1. *SGD 9 Industry, Innovation, and Infrastructure*

- Adjacent Goal and target 9.4 are associated with the Accounting and the goal is related to the upgradation and modification of infrastructure and restructuring and modification of the industries to ensure the sustainability, with the enhanced resource usage efficiency, and the adoption of the clean, and the environmentally friendly technologies, methods, and processes (CPA Canada, 2016).

7.5. Practical Examples Related to the Sustainable Development

Lamberton has performed a case study on the city farm to study the role of accounting model in the sustainable development (Lamberton, 2000). The activities performed by the organizations that lead to the environmental crisis include production and generation of the industrial waste, pollution, and the utilization of the natural resources. The city farm is a small business that has got an objective of the achievement of the sustainable development by the adjustments of its economic, social, and environmental goals (Lamberton, 2000). The city farm has three independent business operations which are organic seeding nursery, organic fruits, vegetables, and garden of herbs, and the community supported agriculture (CSA) (Lamberton, 2000). Figure 7.2 presented below shows the operational design of the City Farm (Lamberton, 2000).

The operations of the community supported agriculture and the farm's nursery were independently managed. The Nursery sales its seeds to the Organic Garden of the city farm and other customers as well. The CSA purchases the products from the local growers and the CSA ensures the sustainability by buying products form the local organic growers. In this way, the active involvement of the community and the alignment of society's common goals are ensured. The Garden is operated and managed using permaculture strategy in which the agricultural system is maintained, and the system is biologically diverse and resilient (Lamberton, 2000).

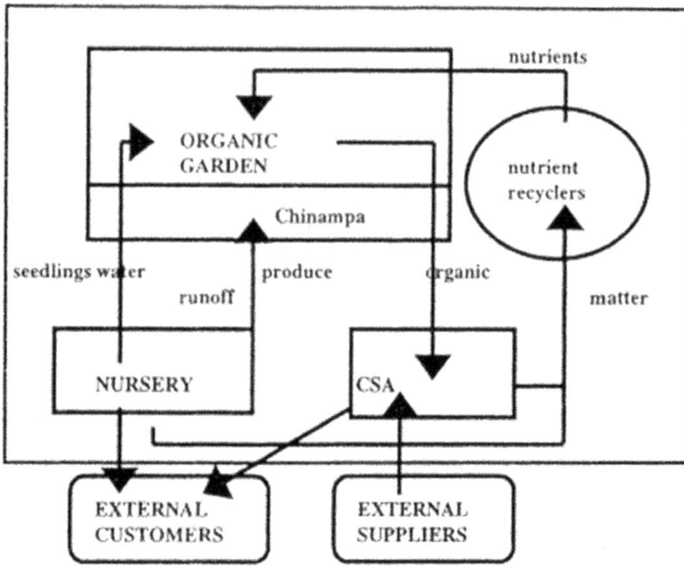

Figure 7.2 Operational design of the city farm (Lamberton, 2000).

The operational and the strategic design if the city farm appreciates the concept of the industrial ecology, in which the industrial system and design is based on the natural system. As mentioned in the figure posted above, all of the three main operations of the farm are situated on the same site which ensure the closeness between the producer and the consumer, and the waste products of the one of the industrial agricultural operations to be recycled and utilized by the other operations (Lamberton, 2000). As shown in the figure posted above, the nursery provides the seeding products to the Garden, and the Garden provides the product or produce to CSA, this overall recues the transport requirements and the economic costs of procuring the inputs of the operations (Lamberton, 2000). The waste from the Nursery and CSA is recycled back in the form of the nutrients to the Garden (Lamberton, 2000). The wastewater from the nursery is then recycled into the Garden's chinampa (Lamberton, 2000). The operational design of the site and business conserves the natural resources and reduces the operating costs.

The environmental performance indicators have been mentioned in the Table 7.1 posted below to highlight the eco-efficiency of the business (Lamberton, 2000).

Table 7.1 Environmental Performance Indicators of the City Farm (Lamberton, 2000)

Performance category	Performance indicator	Actual value	Efficiency targets	Sustainability target
Recycling	percentage materials returned for reuse		Reduce cost and usage of materials inputs	100% recycling of all outputs
	CSA			
	boxes	21%		
	plastic containers	5%		
	Nursery			
	trays	95%		
	inserts	95%		
	punnets	nil		
	percentage of reusable material available at end of product's lives	100%		
Waste management	emissions (kg per week)		Reduce cost of waste disposal Reduce volume of waste	Eliminate waste
	CO_2	701		
	HC	0.99		
	CO	15.8		
	NOx	1.97		
	HCFCs	0.019		
	solid waste produced (cubic litres per year)	4		
	cost of waste disposal	nil		
Water management	town water usage	712 litres per week	Reduce cost and usage of water	Sustainable use of own supply
	nursery contribution margin per litre of water consumed	$0.105		
Electricity management	total electricity usage per week		Reduce cost and usage of electricity	Switch to non-polluting renewable energy sources
	kW h	263		
	cost	$42		
	percentage of energy usage reliant on fossil fuels	100%		
	CSA contribution margin per kW h of electricity used	$1.30		
Transport management	petrol consumption per		Reduce cost and usage of transport services	Switch to non-polluting and renewable energy sources
	week	188.7 litres		
	$1 of revenue	0.14 litres		
	distance from suppliers to City Farm (km per week)	859		
	distance from City Farm to customers (km per week)	1 028		
	revenue earned per km travelled	$0.61		
Compliance	fines imposed	nil	Avoid fines	Beyond compliance
	percentage compliance	100%		
Performance category	Performance indicator	Actual value	Efficiency targets	Sustainability target
Land management	land cleared at City Farm site	0.5 ha	Increase production per hectare	Maintain biodiversity
	cleared area required to produce one standard box per week for one year	0.02–0.04 ha		
	transformation of land	100%		
	native vegetation	minimal		
	area eroded	nil		
	land irrigated	100%		
	number of species planted	> 50		

The detailed evaluation of the sustainability relates parameters have been mentioned in the publication (Lamberton, 2000). The comparison was made by Lamberton of actual performance and the sustainability targets (Lamberton, 2000). The Table 7.2 presented below shows the comparisons (Lamberton, 2000).

Table 7.2 Actual Performance Vs Sustainability Targets (Lamberton, 2000)

Category	Comparison	Comment
Recycling	Actual return and reuse rates were below the sustainability target of 100%	A new design of nursery punnet could make 100% reuse or recycling of all outputs feasible.
Waste management	Emission levels below sustainability target of zero waste	Zero emission, energy, transport and refrigeration options are required.
Water management	Reliance on town water supply results in failure to achieve target of sustainable use of own supply	City Farm's Nursery operation is dependent on the town water supply. Usage of town water by Nursery beyond City Farm's catchment capabilities. Reliance on external supply necessary given scale of Nursery operation.
Electricity management	Performance below sustainability target due to 100% reliance on electricity generated from non-renewable sources	Option to switch to electricity generated from renewable source is available from regional supplier. It is not known whether this source of electricity is ecologically sustainable. Possibility of generating own electricity has not been investigated.
Transport management	100% reliance on conventional transport methods results in performance being below the sustainability target	City Farm needs to reduce reliance on ecologically unsustainable modes of transport. Options available include • exploring alternative fuel sources • using local suppliers and customers • purchasing a low impact vehicle for transporting inputs and outputs.
Land management	Land cleared for food production resulting in loss of biodiversity and hence failure to meet the sustainability target	A small proportion of the products sold by City Farm are produced using permaculture techniques which utilise biologically diverse farming systems for food production. Organic farming methods are used to produce the remainder.

By analyzing the above case study, it can be seen that implementation of the sustainable development practices at every scale is possible. The city farm is a very good example of efforts in the right direction. The model presented above shows the association of the community to a common cause. These types of activities create the general awareness in the other parts of the society about the sustainable practices and businesses.

Another practical example that needs to be mentioned here is the steps that the global food company Mars is taking to promote the sustainability. The scientists and the researchers at the Mars are doing research on the nutrition, genetics, genome, an agriculture to reveal the positive impact of the food and promote the best sustainable agricultural practices in the society.

Mars is one of the founding members of the African Orphan Crops Consortium which is an initiative to improve the nutritional content, output, and the resilience of 101 crops in Africa (CGMA, 2018). The crops were primarily grown by the women in the rural areas of the Africa, and these crops have not been included in the Research and development previously (CGMA, 2018). The improvement in the agriculture will ultimately eradicate the stunting, which is caused by malnutrition, the cost of which Africa bears is 125 billion USD per year (CGMA, 2018). The Consortium is actively involved in gathering, combining, and altering the genomes of the crops, the data is shared in the public domain which will help the plant researchers and breeders to develop highly nutritious, yielding, and resilient crops (CGMA, 2018). The sustainable development efforts of the Mars can be understood by the 2020 score card. The scorecard has been presented below to show the efforts made by the company.

Figure 7.3 Mars 2020 scorecard. (Image source: mars.com).

7.6. Conclusion

The sustainable development requires the efficient utilization of natural and economic resources in such a way that the opportunity and the natural resources remain available for the future generations as well. The Unite Nation sustainability agenda 2030 is an excellent guide that provides the frame works of practical steps that need to be taken in each of the domain. The targets set by the United Nation corresponding to the goals further explain the achievement parameters. The relationship of the environment with the economics cannot be ignored or neglected. By the careful utilization of the resources, and circulation of the economic resources in the society, the poverty can be eliminated. Elimination of the poverty is the topmost priority of the United Nation 2030 agenda. The accountants working across the world can play a positive and exemplary role thorough their profession. The Accounting profession is directly associated with the economic development. By ensuring the transparency, auditing, accurate and meaningful reporting, and consultation, the efficient and proper utilization of economic and non-economic resources can be ensured. The economic development in the under-developed regions across the world is not possible without the integration of social, economic, and environmentally sustainable goals, and all of these activities are interlinked with each other. A special emphasis has been laid in the United Nation 2030 agenda to generate, increase, and appreciate the financial services in the rural and under-develop areas. The access to the financial services will result in generating the awareness related to financial management. In this way the general public in the under-developed regions will be able to manage their economic resources in an efficient way. And the corporate representatives will not be able to use them solely for their own purposes. The starting of the financial services in these regions will also provide loans to the farmers and agriculturists. The agro-economic approach if implemented in the rural areas will result in the efficient utilization of the natural resources, including crops, fertile land, etc. IFAC has identified eight goals of the sustainable development which are related to the accounting professions. By focusing on these goals and associated targets, accounting professionals can aid the process of achievement of sustainable development. And one of the key areas of the sustainable development is the sustainable economic development which is directly linked to the accounting profession.

8 Modern Technology and Accounting

Abstract: The methodology of accounting has been advancing throughout the ages. In the past accounting was very difficult and required a lot of work and manpower. There were a large number of records of all the transactions, personnel, entities and operations and all of them were handwritten and stored in storage rooms. Such a large number of records required a lot of resources for the company and there were greater chances of humane error in storing and retrieving records. Also, there was a greater risk of theft or stealing of records. The advancement of technologies made a great improvement in all fields especially in accounting, now a days large number of data is stored inside servers and can be retrieved very quickly and efficiently, for security purpose large number of firms have developed protocols so that data is secured. Computing devices have also reduced traveling and infrastructures costs, in the past in order to transfer record from one place to another people have to use transportations and they have to deal this in person, now a day internet has made lives a lot easier, data can travel through internet all over the world. Now a days with a centralized system all the businesses are very advanced and can be modularized very efficiently.

Keywords: Modern Technology and Accounting, Computerized Accounting, Digital Era and Accounting, Financial Statements and Digital Era, Financial Statements and Digital Technologies.

In the modern globalized world, the tools and the methods associated with the production, control, and almost everything is digitalized. This type of the economic system is also referred to as the digital economy. The more automated methods are being used and the processes and the workflows are monitored using digital tools. The digitalized world uses modern tools such as cloud computing, cloud-based operations, data analytics, machine learning, and artificial intelligence. The globalization and digitalization both complement each other in the current era, and as a result more fast, efficient, and connected processes are achieved. These methods mostly rely on the computer-based technology and other digital tools and methods. Likewise in other disciplines, Accounting and Economic practices are also being modified as a result of digitalization. The traditional way of accomplishing the accounting functions have been changed and are being replaced with the modern tools and methods, that are more efficient, accurate, and reliable. The aspect of the modularity can be very easily achieved using this method. In this chapter the modern methods and tools associated with the modern accounting practices are being explored.

The software methods, benefits of using such tools, cloud computing, and other techniques and technologies will be discussed.

8.1. Introduction

Language of business mostly refers to financial accounting. This language is used by officials and managers to exchange accounting and economic information with external parties and shareholders.

In the field of accounting, it is commonly known that accounting is the language of business. Like any other language this language has done remarkable journey of development. If we look back in the history, we can see that in the beginning accounting and business management was not that much advanced and proved to be a very difficult job for accountant. In the beginning abacus was used to keep track of the numbers and calculations in business which is not considered a technology in now a day but it proved to be very useful for old times. After that the first notable development in the field of accounting and mathematics was adding machine, this machine was invented by Blaise Pascal. It was used for simple addition and subtraction. After the adding machine calculators were invented which made accountant lives lot easier. Like all fields accounting and business field developed a lot. With the increase in development and enlargement of businesses large number of records were kept. These records were of vital importance and needed precise management and efficient management. Through use of calculator and papers these records were maintained, but this proved to be very difficult for accountant. He was expected to be very exceptional person in every aspect as he had to perform a lot of calculations and keep track of transactions and records.

Towards the end of 20th century like all other fields accounting field advanced a lot with the inventions of modern industrial machines especially computers. Computers proved to one of most important and remarkable invention in history of mankind. Use of modern technologies made accounting jobs a lot easier and eliminated the tasks of sitting behind the desks and maintain plenty of records (Kruglinski, 2009).

8.2. Accounting and Information Technology

Accounting is technique or process that is used by many companies and businesses. It is used to maintain records, keep track of transactions, sales and liabilities. All of these factors are managed in such a way that they must fulfill certain standards mostly known as accounting standards. In old ages all of these records were kept on papers and they were assessed manually. Company's past and current performances were monitored manually by people and a lot of time was taken for evaluation (Ghasemi et al., 2011). Now a days all the performances and analysis are very fast and done by using machines.

8.2.1. Information Technology

Database is the storage of data, it is the organized and hierarchal collection of data. Data is saved in a very secure way which makes it very easy for the software to retrieve this data. Database is only used by programmers and is not visible to end user.

Firstly, we will take a brief introduction of Information technology. Information technology is misinterpreted, it is not only limited to computers, hardware, software and programming. Anything that processes data, analyze the information and present the data in the form of visual format lies in the field of Information Technology. IT professionals have a very versatile job and wide range of responsibilities, such as database management, designing of complex network system, data analysis and administration of entire system. Information technology is spreading rapidly. This development is not only limited to computers but also mobiles, laptops, tablets and automobiles.

8.2.2. Impact of Information Technology on Accounting

Central bank is the financial institution which has the privilege to manage distribution of money and credit throughout the nation or group of nations.
Accounting software is term which refers to generic software which is used by financial institution to monitor and automate institutions financial transactions.

Accounting practices and business methods are changed by use of devices like computers, servers and personal devices like mobile. Transactions are done within a second because of centralized banking system, whereas previously it would take hours or sometime days because of lack of development, because of such fast devices accounting is very much advanced and reliable. There is a very little chance of error as all the operations are performed at machine level. Accounting software play a vital role in business management and playing various functionalities, lot of accounting procedures and calculations are done using accounting software. From managing shops to business software provide a vast variety of features. These features are generic which can be applied to any type of business. This software come with variety of packages which may vary on usage and scale of company. Companies use package of software depending upon their operation. This software is very advanced and linked to one another, company can monitor all of its business operations and various transactions and records without compromising the security features.

8.3. Advantages of Computerized Accounting System

The biggest advantage of IT and computerized system is keeping track of records and transactions as this was a very tedious process and required a lot of time and man power, a lot of accountants would spend most of time preparing large spread sheets and maintaining records. All the handwritten data is transformed into software which can be presented to the respective person within short period of time, data can be presented in any suitable form

8.3.1. Improved Functionality

Computers not only improved the data management but also improved the functionality of business operations and accounting procedures. The most important improvement in functionality is done by increasing quality of accounting information. All the information is very accurate, reliable and free of humane error. Data is analyzed and presented by a professional which gives a very transparent picture of the business operations and status of a company. Financial reports and statements have been improved by the use of computing devices. Loss calculations, predictions, profit margins and many other variables are improved by the field of IT.

8.3.2. Improved Accuracy

In the field of accounting there is no room for errors, as a little error may lead to downfall of a company or business. Computer systems have feedback and check systems to verify transactions before making financial statements. All the financial information is highly accurate and presented after going through advance processing and computation. There is very little chance of error, furthermore financial statements are improved by access management meaning all classified information will only be available to certain accountants who meet certain criteria and have a particular role.

8.3.3. Faster Processing

Higher Speed and processing play a vital role in the development of accounting and financial infrastructure. Data is stored and accessed within a very short period of time. Unlike the old days where it would take a lot of time to create records and statements and even more time to fetch those records computing has made it a lot easier. Data is accessed within seconds or a little more depending upon the size of data. Head offices can access and view any of their branch's data within seconds all because of centralized and efficient computing system. In old times it would take a lot of time to fetch a single record because of big storage of files and sheets and it would be very difficult for accountant to identify the respective document but now a days accountant can easily access the transaction or any other data with just mouse click

8.3.4. Improved Reporting

FreshBooks, QuickBooks Online, Sage Business Cloud Accounting are the most commonly used software for financial reporting.

Reporting is improved by the use of computers and IT. Investors and stakeholders view these reports and make decision whether a company is suitable for investment and business. Reports are generated through advance computing software and tools. These reports are verified at many stages by the use of devices programmed by accountant so that they meet accounting standards.

8.4. Modern Tools in Accounting

With the advancement in the accounting techniques and introduction of new procedures introduced by IT industry it is now very important for Accountant to master computer skills. Many employers have made it a mandatory that entry level employee must have a sound knowledge of IT and accounting software. Accounting is improved by introduction of various methods by IT industry.

8.4.1. E-Business, Intranet and Internet

Intranet is a network connection of computers inside an organization.
Extranet is a network connection of computers used by organization and clients, customers and stakeholders.
Internet is network which creates connection all around the world.
E-business also known as electronic business allows the accountant to use both intranet and internet to perform different activities

Internet is very important nowadays, those accounting professionals who understand its importance will use internet to carry out their accounting activities. Employers by the help of IT professional use intranet to communicate within an organization or company, all the mails and information between employees are exchanged using intranet thus maintaining the integrity and security for the company. In order to carry out business activities with the client companies use extranet. All the communications, transactions and many other activities between clients and company professionals are carried out by using secure internet. By the use of this extranet, travel cost has been reduced exponentially (Laudon & Laudon, 2006).

8.4.2. Data Life Cycle

There is a very common approach in the field of IT which is input, process and output which means any user input the data, that data is processed and will be displayed after some changes as an output. This approach is applied to accounting as well. Both client and company must have a proficient knowledge of computers. Accountants together with system designers and programmers design programs for both the client and company. By using these solutions client can view his information and status and at the same time company can also monitor client activities related to company. For example, company can know about the time and place of transaction that client did.

8.4.3. Cloud Computing

Records storage has always been an issue even from the beginning, as it would consume a lot of space. In trivial times, a large pile of records was kept for transactions and other activities which had many problems like time taken to retrieve those records, records would consume a large amount of space as the business grew and lastly the security, there was a lot of possibility of the records being stolen or compromised by third party or even by company's own employee.

This thing was prevented with the invention of computers. Large amount of data is stored inside computers. There is always a limit to what a single computer can store, when business increases the number of operations is also increased hence all the records and transactions are also increased exponentially resulting in the need of more storage devices, therefore companies have to pay a lot of resources for storing devices.

Database and data management are very important and vast fields in the IT industry. There are many factors that are involved for the operations of data like database design, data storage, storage capacity, data retrieval algorithms. With increase in data, these operations become very costly thus companies always look for cost cutting solutions but there is always a limit to which database operations can be optimized, in the end companies have to bear the cost.

The cloud platform used by Amazon is called AWS (Amazon Web Service), by Microsoft is called Microsoft Azure and by Google is called GCP (Google Cloud Platform).

In order to resolve these issues big companies like Amazon, Microsoft, Google devised new solution. They introduced cloud computing. Many small to medium sized companies and even some larger companies shift their accounting to cloud (Christauskas and Miseviciene, 2012). In this computing every operation is done at the cloud level. Cloud refers to a massive storage place with vast variety of servers that can store millions of data from all over the world. In cloud computing users or developers are offered to create their own databases according to their requirement, programmers implement the logic in such a way that record of any accounting activity or transaction done by a company will be stored at the cloud database and cloud services will be used to perform all the operations related to data, since these are leading companies in the field of IT, so all the operations done at the cloud are state of art. The usage of cloud is very simple, any user or company will have to buy the storage depending upon the size of business or data, after that for cloud computing and database operations company has to pay according to subscription. Subscription plan depends upon the usage and amount of data. In the field of cloud computing by using these services the most important question that comes into the mind of users is that whether these services and their data is secure or not. In order to answer these questions, there is very good policies introduced by those companies in which they highlight about the safety of data. Their operations are performed in such that a way that integrity and security of data is never compromised. Yoon did research on the new technologies used in accounting by taking evidence from Korea (Yoon, 2020).

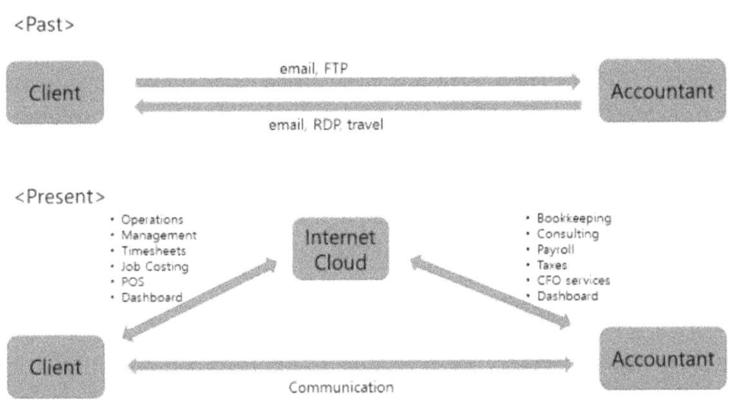

Figure 8.1 Past vs. present models of communication (Yoon, 2020).

In this Figure 8.1 author explained two methodologies used in accounting by using IT methods. Old way of communicating was very expensive and time taking, as constructing and using emails takes time. By introduction of cloud problems of both data storage and communication were solved.

Besides management of data and data computing solutions, these companies also provide the option to deploy company's web applications to their cloud. Thus, company will not have to worry about security of website, malware attacks or any other injection because those servers are highly secure. Many companies use these services to carry out their operations, in fact some of companies' whole operations are carried out by using cloud solutions. There is only one drawback using cloud computing, if by chance server goes down or there is any technical problem at cloud level than company's operation will stop but this is most unlikely because their services are most reliable.

8.4.4. Software Solutions

IT industry provided software solutions to many other industries including banking system, accounting, literature, nearly everything. All fields of life are automated using software and application solutions. From running a small grocery store to international company, IT industry provided very efficient software solutions to carry out operations.

There are many kinds of software solutions among which some are generic and their architecture is used in many businesses like CRM, ERP solutions and tax software. The tax software of today is very efficient and reliable and there is a little chance of error. Tax software calculate taxes and suggest ways for companies to avoid tax penalties and prevent issues with the investors. Previously companies had to hire a professional who would take a lot of resources to calculate taxes, even now a day these professionals are available, in order to reduce the usage of resources IT had provided software solutions for tax calculation. Tax software helps company or user to complete and file the tax using internet. Software will further guide to reduce billings and deductions and many other recommendations. The most famous software is H&R Block Online, TurboTax, TaxSlayer, TaxAct, Credit Karma Tax etc.

8.4.4.1. Enterprise Resource Planning (ERP)

This is very efficient solution designed for Accountants and organization in the 21st century. This is a strategic application that is designed for future endeavors. This application is very hierarchal, in this application all the departments of an organization are integrated on to one system, that system is the core of organization as it monitors and automates the activities between different departments for example attendance systems, all new policies announcement, contacting any employee, declaring new rules. All of this functionality is performed on a single platform (Scapens and Jazayeri, 2003). That platform is called Enterprise Resource Planning. ERP not only manages the activities between departments but also activities related to clients and transactions, sales and finance. It is stated by CIO of Red Hat Company that 96 percent of accounting and financial applications are run by using core ERP.

By integration of data ERP streamlines accounting needs of the company. It provides a clear picture of all aspects of business; thus, it plays a vital role in decision making. By analysis and insight into financial data accountants become more confident and look for cost efficient solution which results in increased financial productivity of an organization.

8.4.4.1.1. Role of ERP in Accounting

In any department or institution ERP is essential in carrying out the operations. In the field of accounting, it is most needed since data is very important and integration and management of data is very crucial, for these purposes we use ERP. Following are the roles of ERP in accounting:

- ERP systems do an efficient estimation of capital and resource management
- Company's budget can be designed and implemented using ERP
- Cost managements for various activities and departments such as labor, installation, transportation and communication
- Payment management, not only limited to employees but also to the vendors and clients
- ERP system can be structured in such a way that it can be used as financial management system. By integration of data financial activities such as client payment schedule and credit management are improved. Since data is saved at a secure place, it is very easy to keep track of bills, revenues, cost and taxes.
- ERP systems can also be used to track and calculate profits made by organization, invoicing, cost analysis and budgeting.
- ERP systems ensure that data is of best quality and very well maintained. The data is accessible to accounting department because of that they can maintain good financial standards. Financial information is also very secured. It is only accessible to those people who have the authority to do so because of hierarchal structure. Those organizations which use separate software and modules for accounting and separate for other activities will have to maintain each of the

module separately, that will require a lot of time and resources whereas EPR is the integrated system where everything is centralized.

- ERP systems provide financial management modules that will keep track of all the financial activities, transactions and revenue, it further ensures that all of the activities are performed according to international standards. In order to communicate and do business internationally ERP systems have the option to switch language and chose firmware that is designed for a particular country.
- ERP systems allows the company to collect data from various department and make detail reports and financial statements. In that way organization can know very quickly that which department is the main source of revenue and which department needs improvement.
- The most important and advanced feature in the ERP system is integrity and security of data. ERP system always provide most secure solutions, data can be only accessible to authorized person, there is state of art encryption involved in transferring of data. Secondly data calculation, storage and representations are free of error. The system doesn't make mistake, there is very little chance that because of humane error data may be wrongly captured like losing focus or entering wrong data. Such kind of minor mishap can lead to bad consequences which may affect the whole organization, in order to solve this problem ERP systems, provide various solutions. The data is always verified before storage, different type of filters is applied while entering the data, for example if any user want to enter birthdate or employee number in the text field, he will only be allowed to enter numbers that match the format of both variables, if by chance he tries to enter characters in "employee number" place than system will either show him a warning or will prevent him to enter characters.

8.4.4.2. Customer Relationship Management (CRM)

ERP system is very advanced, it is integration of data from all the departments of company and automation of operations. ERP is mostly inside the organization, some of its modules are related to customers and transactions but most of it is for Organizational Hierarchy, for any business to run successfully, it must have a very healthy relation with the clients, without a good relationship with the client business may be effected or even collapse, that's why it is very important to keep track of all the customers and maintain healthy relations with them, for this purpose CRM software system is the best solution that is designed and manufactured by a collaboration between IT Professionals and Business Analysts. If any of company or business wants to run their business efficiently, they need to use CRM that's why 70 percent of businesses uses CRM to interact with the customers. This software is the best solution to interact with the customers, keep track of their relation and activities with the company. Customer data is stored and professionals do a lot of analysis on this large amount of data. New strategies and efficient solutions are designed based on the analysis of data. CRM is the best interface software between a company and customers (CGMA, 2013).

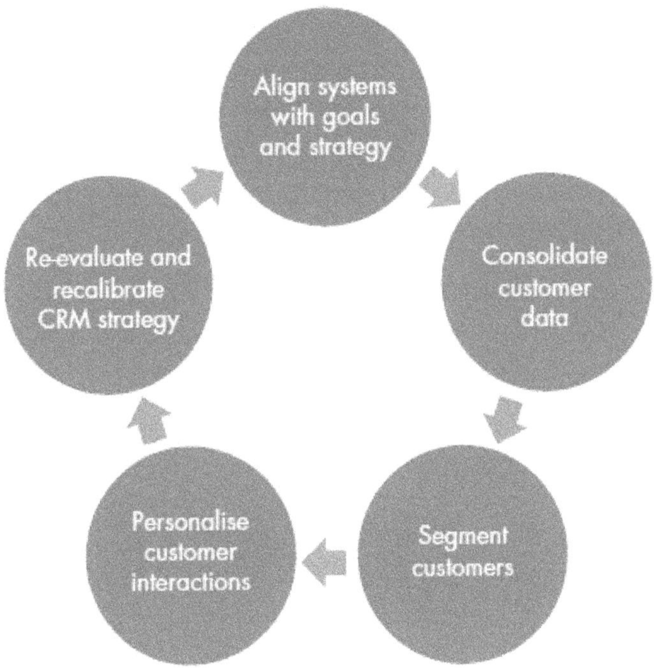

Figure 8.2 Implementation cycle of CRM (CGMA, 2013).

In this Figure 8.2 author explained the cycle of interactions with the customer. The model of CRM can vary from company to company but the main objective is same for all of them.

CRM works in very categorical and modular way, it divides and prioritize clients if they meet certain conditions, for example the client who comes first time to a company are named and categorized, this naming can be redefined by the company according to their needs, after that clients who contact further after first visit are put into another category with their personal data stored in the servers, the next step is very important the client who makes the first purchase is also categorized, another category is made for the client who visit after first purchase and also for those clients who make another purchase. A complete dataset is created with a list of clients and their respective importance, the clients are categorized and prioritized based on the above-mentioned standards. By categorizing the client's company can know very well about the clients that need much work or the clients that need much marketing, CRM gives company a direction, how they should proceed with the clients.

There are three types of CRM software

- **Operational CRM**: management of all the sales, marketing and clients
- **Analytical CRM**: Analysis of large amount of data for better decision making
- **Collaborative CRM:** Enable efficient communication between teams

CRM can be accessed on website or on your local server or on a cloud depending upon your requirement

8.4.4.2.1 CRM for Accounting

CRM is extremely beneficial for accountants since they deal a lot in managing financial and fiscal data. They spend most of their time in calculation, reporting and documentation, in addition to that they also need to maintain good relation with the clients or find new clients, this becomes very difficult for them since they have a lot on their plate, in order to save time and use efficient solution they use CRM.

CRM provides following benefits to accountants

- It creates very good and long-lasting relation with the customer. Among many other benefits this software helps accountant to manage their meetings with the client, keep track of client schedule and generate notifications. Since this software basic purpose is to collect a lot of data about clients so by using that data accounting experts build good relation with the customers.
- It creates a central hub for information. All the information related to customers are stored in a database. Database is categorized efficiently. This software will keep track of the client's journey and record the information in the database. Furthermore, this information is accessible by clients also so that they can view their status and relation with the company.
- It also categorizes and prioritizes company's activities. CRM software presents the data in many forms among which the core representation is in the form of Dashboard which is there when accountant opens up the software. It shows experts their progress with the clients and which client is most profitable for the company, by knowing this accountant can prioritize his/her actions to build healthy relation.

- It also provides tool to make marketing easier by automating data. Sales and marketing professionals can customize their newsletter campaigns to convert leads into opportunities.

8.4.5 Artificial Intelligence (AI) and Machine Learning (ML)

AI is the methodology that enables machine to think like human and solve complex problems by itself without writing long set of codes.
ML is the subset of AI, machine learns about the behaviour by using past dataset.

Artificial Intelligence (AI) and Machine Learning (ML) are the most advance and emerging fields nowadays. In detail functionalities of AI and ML are little bit different from one another but their outcome is nearly the same, their methodologies are different which is too much technical.

AI is used in many of applications, from domestic usage to large applications like avionics and automobile industry also use AI. AI main motive is to replace human thinking and efforts with machines. AI's basic concept is learning and make decision making and everything is done by the machine, humans just have to write the algorithm and provide datasets for the models than machine will learn these models and use this learning to learn about some other data. The most common example is vehicle classification using cameras first IT professionals or programmers provide a large data set of vehicles comprising of different class of vehicles and enable the machine to learn about these vehicles. Humans let the machine run algorithm for a long time (depending upon the size of data and processing power of machine) and after long processing and learning machine will learn about different categories of vehicle, now when cameras are fed live stream it will be able to classify the vehicle based on learning it did from datasets.

Like this traffic, many business analysts use AI to make decision making about the business. AI uses data from the past and present and make predictions about the future. Companies use AI to look at the sales done to a set of customers or clients, time of sale done by the company and then make the decision. For example, top brands of the world use AI for their business, their models are trained by using following variables, number of customers with respect to age, number of customers and their region, number of customers and their interest in a product, sale of a product, number of customer and time of the year and many other variables. All of these variables are taken into consideration and models are trained to provide suggestion. Machines are provided with huge amount of dataset which it uses to learn about customer behavior.

Baldwin et al have argued that the usage of the Artificial Intelligence by the Accountancy dates back to around 40 years (Baldwin et al., 2006). The researchers have applied the artificial intelligence techniques and algorithms for the performing specific tasks and the success was not achieved up to full extent (Baldwin et al., 2006). The initial application of the artificial intelligence with reference to the accounting was related to the financial reporting, analysis, assurance, and auditing (Baldwin et al., 2006). The proper research into the development of the expert systems for the accounting using Artificial Intelligence for the Accounting purposes began in 1980s (Baldwin et al., 2006). The artificial intelligence-based systems were proposed, analyzed, and developed for the auditing, taxation facility, management Accounting, Analysis of the systems, and the financial accounting (Baldwin et al., 2006). The initial attempt to implement the Artificial Intelligence in the field of accounting was a bold move realizing the needs of the future and development of the profession itself.

8.4.5.1 AI for Auditing and Assurance

One of the most suitable applications and the purpose for which the Artificial Intelligence is being used in the field of accounting is the lack of the perfection in decisions and associated uncertainty. In the field of accounting, the tasks and the duties require the intensive decision-making process. The nature of the decisions is structured, semi-structured, and unstructured decisions (Baldwin et al., 2006). The auditing and assurance require the taking of decisions that are very less-structured and the associated analysis contains the element of the uncertainty, which is associated with the lack of information and risk as well (Baldwin et al., 2006). In accounting the significant training, skill, experience, and expertise are required, and very few accountants across the world achieve. The research is done by the accountants who are highly successful in their profession. Two of the main areas of accounting has been mentioned by the researchers are (Baldwin et al., 2006).: The field of auditing and assurance, and the second domain is financial reporting and the analysis (Baldwin et al., 2006). These fields of the accounting are associated with the risk and uncertainty, and the decisions is always not ideal. The intensive environment of the Auditing and Assurance requires the usage of the computer-based decisions. The associated risks, uncertainty. Litigation, and associated financial risk in case of the large companies creates the tension for the both auditee and the auditor (Baldwin et al., 2006). Decisions in the field of the accountancy have got a significant impact on the business as well as the finances. The auditing decisions like the other decisions in accounting have got far reaching consequences, therefore the expert auditing systems and the computer-based decisions would be helpful in increasing the accuracy and effectiveness.

One of the complications related to the Auditing and assurance in which the Artificial Intelligence can help is the Audit tasks. A wide range of the characteristics and specifications are associated with the Audit tasks. Researchers have identified over 400 individual tasks (Baldwin et al., 2006). The chances of the mistakes and clouding of the decision is possible while performing all these tasks for the single audit. The researchers have mentioned the major audit tasks and the associated Artificial Intelligence technique that can aid in the tasks have also been mentioned (Baldwin et al., 2006). These tasks have been mentioned below for the demonstration (Baldwin et al., 2006).

- One of the main auditing tasks is the analytical procedure and review (Baldwin et al., 2006). Auditors perform the analytical review for obtaining the auditing evidence (Baldwin et al., 2006). Koskivaara in 2004 has published an article in which the usage of the Artificial neutral networks in the analytical review procedures have been highlighted (Koskivaara, 2004). The researcher has also highlighted the problems associated with the auditing process, and one of the problems related to the auditing process is the cooking of books (Koskivaara, 2004). Researcher has also highlighted that the process of tool development for the auditors is the consequence of the workload as well as the demand of the auditors themselves (Koskivaara, 2004).
- Some the auditing tasks are related to the classification or belong to the classification problems (Baldwin et al., 2006). The questions related to the classification of debt and legitimacy of the transaction may arise, and for the complicated audit involving a large number of transactions and debt details, it is very difficult to classify each of the transaction or debts into the categories (Baldwin et al., 2006). The researchers have studied the behavior of the auditor in the fraudulent setting and suggested the usage of the genetic algorithm in such scenarios (Baldwin et al., 2006). Various fraudulent activities and false claims can also be detected using such techniques and methods. One of the classification-based tasks are also related to the materiality assessment (Baldwin et al., 2006). Researchers have proposed the expert system and fuzzy based expert system for the assessment of the materiality, especially for the planning stage judgments (Baldwin et al., 2006).
- The internal control evaluation has become an important part of the auditing systems and the frameworks. Watkins et al have proposed an AI based system for the extended decision-making processes (Watkins et al., 1992). Researchers demonstrated the integration of Artificial Intelligence in the context of the

Internal Control Evaluation with major focus on the prevention of the fraud (Watkins et al., 1992). The researchers have demonstrated the integration of the parts of the AI such as Genetic Algorithms, Neural networks, and the Natural Language processing with each other, and also with the DSS (Decision Support Systems). The research is more relevant to the accounting in a sense that the more intensive application for the accounting would be based on the technology that provide the smart and intelligent decisions. The expert and smart systems developed for the internal control evaluation are efficient and effective, and also provide the valuable information to the mangers.

- Various auditing and the general accounting tasks are based on the assessment and evaluation of the risks. The risk assessment is generally based on the matching similar patterns in the data and also the identification of deviations, variations, and diversions (Baldwin et al., 2006). The most suitable tool that seems to be delivering the promising result in the risk assessment is the neural networks. Moreover, the researchers have also used the fuzzy neural networks in this matter (Baldwin et al., 2006). It is the responsibility of the independent auditors to plan and perform the audits for ensuring that the financial statements of their clients are free from the misrepresentation of the facts based on the frauds. The incidents of the frauds have become more common and the measures for the detection of the fraud are just lagging behind (Lin et al., 2003). Sometimes it becomes difficult for the auditors to detect the fraud on the financial statements, as the fraud is mostly associated with the false representation of the accounting records, and the failure of the detection of the fraud especially on the financial statements can expose the auditor to strict legal actions (Lin et al., 2003). As a consequence, the researchers have proposed fuzzy neural networks for the detection of fraud based financial reporting (Lin et al., 2003). A fuzzy model based on the fuzzy clustering was developed by the researchers (Lin et al., 2003).

In general, the auditing and assurance has been one of the main focuses of the researchers who have developed AI based applications for the accounting profession. Since the auditing is one of most important job that accountants perform. The Artificial Intelligence is expected to aid the auditing by increasing the efficiency and the speed (Jauhiainen, 2021). Machine learning and deep learning methods can be applied and trained in the existing data of the auditing to determine that the actions of the reporting that have been performed in the firms and businesses were in accordance to the predefined standards and the requirements (Jauhiainen, 2021). The complexity of the algorithms can be increased and extended so that the text, audios, images, understanding is possible in both structured and unstructured data (Jauhiainen, 2021).

8.4.5.2. *Artificial Intelligence Application in Other Sub-Domains of Accounting*

A large amount of the work in the field of artificial intelligence with reference to the accounting profession has been done related to the bankruptcy prediction. The main supporting and the founding role in the prediction models related to the bankruptcy was played by the Artificial Intelligence and machine learning (Naidu and Govinda, 2018). Naidu and Govinda have argued that the Artificial Neural Network and random forest method are more efficient than the traditional algorithms for a standard algorithm in prediction of the bankruptcy (Naidu and Govinda, 2018).

Viaene et al has done a comprehensive comparison of the techniques that are used for the detection of the expert automobile fraud claim (Viaene et al., 2002). Similarly, the insurance industry is also growing day by day. The private insurance industry is one of the fastest growing industries (Dhieb et al., 2020). The insurance exists for one of most valuable assets such as jewelry, vehicles, homes etc. (Dhieb et al., 2020). The traditional models involve the human beings and their input, and the process becomes very time consuming and the results are inaccurate (Dhieb et al., 2020). An Artificial Intelligence based secure method has been proposed for the automated insurance systems, the researchers have proposed the usage and implementation for extreme gradient boosting (XGBoost) machine learning algorithm for the automated insurance systems and also made a comparison with the other systems (Dhieb et al., 2020). The percentage accuracy of the techniques was also studied (Dhieb et al., 2020). The following machine learning based module pipeline has been proposed by the researchers

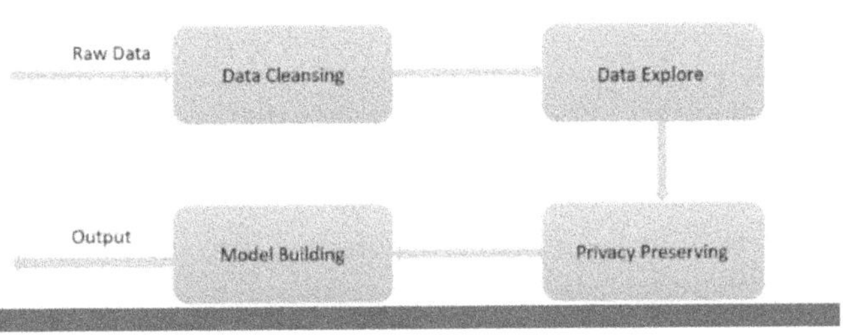

Figure 8.3 Machine learning based module pipeline. The image has been taken from the publication of Dhieb et al. (2020). (Image source: A Secure AI-Driven Architecture for Automated Insurance Systems: Fraud Detection and Risk Measurement).

One of the complex and the potentially useful implementation and integration of Artificial Intelligence is the Cognitive Computing. Marshal and Lambert have presented the cognitive computing model based on the artificial intelligence models to support the process of task automation in the accounting industry (Marshall and Lambert, 2018). The task automation has been attracting the attention of the businesses and have got a huge potential in increasing the efficiency of the processes. Advancements in the fields of data analytics and machine learning has opened those pathways for the accounting and auditing automation (Marshall and Lambert, 2018). The drivers of the task automation in the field of accounting are reduced costs, enhanced speeds, better agility, and increased profit margins (Marshall and Lambert, 2018). The cognitive computing has been designed to augment the process of thinking so that the thinking like the human beings is possible by the understanding of the complexities, interdependencies present in the unstructured data set, and involves the reasoning for generation and testing of the hypothesis (Marshall and Lambert, 2018). By the implementation of the task automation using cognitive computing, the complexities of the accounting profession can be handled with ease, and the decisions would be accurate. One of the emerging powerful tools based on cognitive computing and AI is Watson, and the global accounting firm KPMG is also using Watson (Marshall and Lambert, 2018). In this section various research and development efforts in the field of accounting using Artificial Intelligence have been described.

Machine learning is being used in the accounting and assurance profession, and the machine learning is being gradually applied and extended to review the source documents, analysis of the business transactions, and the risk assessment (Cho et al., 2020). In the academic research field, machine learning has been used in the fraud detection, prediction of bankruptcy, and misstatements (Cho et al., 2020). Bao et al. proposed a machine learning approach for the detection of the fraud in publicly traded US firms using Machine Learning approach (Bao et al., 2020).

As mentioned in the previous chapters, the accounting rations are very useful in taking the meaningful decisions. Some of these ratios have been explained in the previous chapters. The accounting ratios can be used to predict the bankruptcy using the approach of machine learning. Li and Wang have compared the statistical method and machine learning method to predict bankruptcy with utilizing China listed companies (Li and Wang, 2018). The employers of the private assurance and auditing firms are ensuring the well-being of their employees. Antunez et al have used the machine learning approach for the quantification to determine the extent to which JQI variables explain the work-engagement scores, and to determine which JQI variable affects the most the work engagement scores. JQI represents the JOB Quality indexes scores (del Pozo-Antúnez et al., 2021). The overall goal of the research was to enhance the work engagement in accounting profession (del Pozo-Antúnez et al., 2021). Syed has performed a comprehensive review on the Role of Artificial Intelligence in the Development of the Accounting system. The study has analyzed the relative impact of AI on Auditing and Taxation (Moudud-Ul-Huq, 2014).

Various efforts are being done by the accounting regulatory bodies to implement the education target of the sustainable development goals. American Accounting Association had a virtual Annual Meeting on the critical thinking in accounting curricula in the era of AI (Parthasarathy, 2020). Zemankova has performed a comprehensive literature review highlighting the application of Artificial Intelligence in audit and accounting (Zemankova, 2019). The application of Artificial Intelligence in various fields of accounting such as financial and managerial accounting, auditing, and taxation have been mentioned by Ng and Alarcon (Ng and Alarcon, 2020). Zhang et al. have highlighted the role and impact of AI and blockchain technology on the accounting profession (Zhang et al., 2020). Researchers have found out that the usage of AI based accounting software have enhanced the productivity and improved the efficiency (Lee and Tajudeen, 2020).

Ghosh has highlighted the implementation of AI and the Triadic Entry Accounting (Ghosh, 2021). Bertomeu has highlighted how machine learning improves the accounting practices (Bertomeu, 2020). Bertomeu et al. have highlighted how the machine learning to detect the misstatements (Bertomeu et al., 2020). The researchers have also highlighted the role of cloud, big data, blockchain, and artificial intelligence related technologies in modifying and shaping the work of accountants (Moll and Yigitbasioglu, 2019). Cerullo applied the approach of neural networks for the prediction of financial reporting fraud (Cerullo and Cerullo, 1999). Petkov has determined and evaluate the current ability of the accounting functionality to adjust and accommodate the introduction of Artificial Intelligence in an organization (Petkov, 2019). This will help the companies in the introduction of Artificial Intelligence in their organizations. Balakrishnan et al. have studied the impact of AI on the accounting and finance industry, demonstrated the positive changes, and the effect of AI on function and workflows (Balakrishnan et al., 2020). Wu has highlighted the benefits of using AI in accounting (Wu, 2021)

Researchers have also highlighted the challenges associated with the accounting profession currently and discussed the possibilities of future development within the reference of Artificial Intelligence (Stancheva-Todorova, 2018).

All the above-mentioned research and development efforts in the field of accounting with reference to artificial intelligence and machine learning shows the huge potential, and the modern technology can easily increase the efficiency of the processes and innovation can be achieved. With reference to the previous work done in the field of accounting using AI, a considerable development has been done especially in the field of auditing and assurance, and the fraud detection. With the usage of more practical and realistic data for training, more desirable results can be achieved. The usage of cognitive computing methods based on AI will further refine the "thinking" process and would be able to take more complicated decisions. The AI and machine learning can help in improving the decision-making power of the accounting professions, and the overall contribution of the profession in the development of the society will be enhanced. The Artificial intelligence should be the part of the education and training activities of the accountants.

8.5. Practical Examples Related to the Use of Modern Tools in Accounting

Donald Hsu has compiled different case studies related to the usage of financial accounting software (Hsu, 2007). There exists a lack of attention related to the publication of case studies associated with the financial accounting software. The case studies are relevant to the students of accounting, and provide information about software and need for learning this software (Hsu, 2007).

PeachTree is an old accounting software, the Sage group has acquired the company and now the software has been named as Sage 50cloud Accounting. In 2007 it reported more than 2.4 million customers in United States (Hsu, 2007). The software PeachTree in 2007 was not compatible with Microsoft Vista. In 2020, it has been rated as the best accounting software for small and medium businesses (SMBs) by The Blueprint.

Microsoft has launched the accounting software named as Accounting Express and Accounting Professional in 2005 to compete with the PeachTree (Hsu, 2007). In 2006 when Microsoft Express was launched, there were 1.5 million downloads (Hsu, 2007). The software was added as a part in the accounting course. Klovienė performed a case study in 2015 to analyze the impact of information technology on the Accounting System's conformity with the business environment (Klovienė and Gimzauskiene, 2015). A banking sector company was selected for the case study. Researchers have mentioned the accounting system in the form of three variables which are processes, measures, and decision levels in different business environments (Klovienė and Gimzauskiene, 2015). Information technology serves as a tool for developments and improving processes in the organizations. Researchers have highlighted that the conformity in the accounting process can ensure the general conformity of the accounting process with the business as shown in the Figure 8.4 below (Klovienė and Gimzauskiene, 2015).

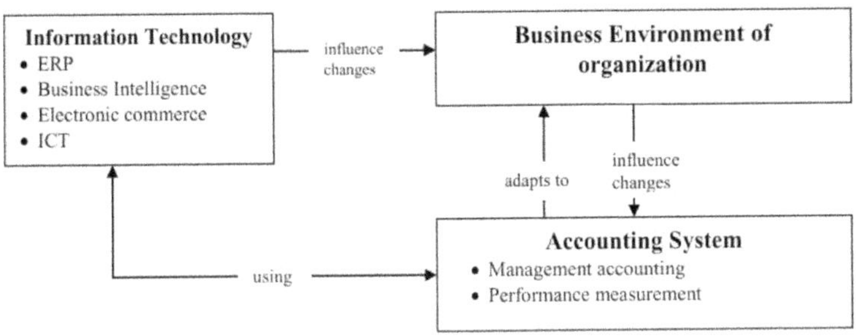

Figure 8.4 Impact of information technology on conformity of accounting system with business environment (Klovienė and Gimzauskiene, 2015).

The Case study was performed in Lithuanian organization to determine the relationship between the accounting system of organization and business environment. Interview was conducted from the management persons of different levels. The researchers have concluded as a finding of the case study that the information technology aids in establishing conformity between the accounting system and business environment (Klovienė and Gimzauskiene, 2015). The case study also reveals that the information technology systems are used for the services and management, planning, control, evaluation, analysis, and other purposes (Klovienė and Gimzauskiene, 2015). The organization is seeking advantage from the investment in information technology by saving the costs in services as well as by increasing the speed and achieving high quality of services (Klovienė and Gimzauskiene, 2015).

8.6. Conclusion

In the above sectioned we discussed in detail how accounting is advanced through the ages, modern techniques used in accounting and how they affect the business operations. Throughout our history accounting was considered very important factor in economic and financial operations. The methodology of accounting has been advancing throughout the ages. In the past accounting was very difficult and required a lot of work and manpower. There were a large number of records of all the transactions, personnel, entities and operations and all of them were handwritten and stored in storage rooms. Such a large number of records required a lot of resources for the company and there were greater chances of humane error in storing and retrieving records. Also, there was a greater risk of theft or stealing of records. The advancement of technologies made a great improvement in all fields especially in accounting, now a days large number of data is stored inside servers and can be retrieved very quickly and efficiently, for security purpose large number of firms have developed protocols so that data is secured. Computing devices have also reduced traveling and infrastructures costs, in the past in order to transfer record from one place to another people have to use transportations and they have to deal this in person, now a day internet has made lives a lot easier, data can travel through internet all over the world. Now a days with a centralized system all the businesses are very advanced and can be modularized very efficiently. All the operations are carried out in respective branches with authorization of main branch like centralized banking system.

There are many tools that are introduced for businesses and for accounting as well. The most important one is internet and E-business, accountants use intranet to manage operations within the company and use internet to deal with customers and clients. Second tool is data process. Clients or business can input their data according to their needs and computer will store it and will display it in desirable forms. Third tool is cloud computing, even in the field of IT data storage was always a very important concern, previously large amount of data was stored inside the company and for that company had to build a massive storage room for all those computers and hardware. This was a very costly process, now with cloud computing the top companies of the world like Google, Microsoft have created cloud system though which all the data can be stored in servers which are at someplace secure. Company doesn't have to worry about the storage and space as cloud platforms provide it all, business can buy their space on cloud and can store data their and it is very secure. Data is retrieved from the cloud though very advanced and secure algorithms. The one most important tool is AI. Previously lot of professionals and business analysts spend a lot of time doing analysis on the financial operations and predict the outcome but that also has been replaced by AI as AI does it all, company has to provide machine a large amount of dataset, by using that dataset machines learn about the operations and do a very effective predictions and forecast.

9 Conclusion

From our detailed analysis and study, we have made a list of conclusions. These conclusions will give a good insight in accounting and finances and how to achieve financial stability.

Financial stability is very important for an organization to survive and even grow. Financially instable organizations collapse very quickly and cause a lot of damage to financial and non-financial institutions, as we have seen in the past that financial crisis from one country caused a great deal of damage to not only that country but other countries as well leading to global crisis which affects every country. Financial stability is all about maintaining stable environment for a business and organization, company's financial operations must be so sound that it will ensure that incoming cash is greater than outgoing cash, total liabilities never exceed their assets and they must be so stable that they are able to absorb shocks in case of imbalance or some loss. The main factors that ensure financial stability are in large amount but we will discuss them briefly starting with very sound macroeconomic activities and policies, public policies, market discipline, transparency in operations and transactions, trust and reliability, accounting and accounting standards, financial statements and modern tools used in accounting and financial operations. Failure in these methods may lead to crisis and cause the companies to become insolvent.

Accounting and accounting standards play a lot of roles in financial stability, the most important standard as described by IRS is transparency, meaning implementing transparency in all of the financial operations and transactions, this may introduce a little risk as you are exposing your business plans to competitors but it will attract many investors also because information is very reliable and transparent. There are many criteria for effective accounting standards which will ensure financial stability like we must use principle-based accounting approach as it ensures creativity and intuitiveness, usage of relevant and reliable figures meaning all the transactions and operations must be reliable and accurate, a very efficient identification and analysis of risk, financial statements must be very accurate and reliable.

Unable to fulfill the above-mentioned criteria the companies will go bankrupt and may become a target of instability, because in facing this situation company will go bankrupt it will be unable to pay its creditors, all those investors that invested in this company will face great loss even if they receive some of their debts by liquidation still, they have suffered a loss and will lose their trust in that organization. Also, for the insolvent company it will take a lot of time for them to get back on their feet and gain trust again as nobody will want to invest more in this company, so we can see that bankruptcy and insolvency not only affects only one organization but a large number of creditors and investors also. Investors and shareholder will lose their confidence if they have invested a large amount of money and will have second thoughts next time if they want to invest someplace else, these activities build a large platform for instability.

We have studied how the technologies have affected the accounting and finances. With increase in technology there is exponential increase in businesses as well, which means that any failure in these kinds of businesses will have impact on larger scales. Like everything else failure in any operation may have great consequences, in all above-mentioned accounting standards and other practices, error in any operation whether it is humane, or machine error may cause irreparable damages and may lead to instability also. In the field of IT usage of modern tools must be very effective and error less. We take example of human error, if by some fault user is able to enter wrong figure for transaction than this will cause a great deal of tension in many people, as participants in the transaction will not trust that company anymore and this will affect their relationship. Now from our understanding this is fault from both accountant and machine or algorithm he was using while doing this transaction, machine should be programmed in such a way it should have feedback system and will prevent this failure, second very good example is in the field of AI, if company has provided wrong dataset to the machine or the algorithm designed for predictive analysis is not very efficient, in that case machine will present false predictions and will affect the future operations of the company. All of these factors play vital role in sound financial and accounting operations, and we have seen that accounting plays an important role in financial stability.

References

Acharya, V., and M. Richardson. 2009. Causes of the Financial Crisis. *Critical Review* 21 (2–3): 195–210.

Ainsworth, P., and D. Deines. 2017. *Introduction to Accounting: An Integrated Approach*. New Jersey: John Wiley & Sons.

Akyüz, Y. 2021. External Balance Sheets of Emerging Economies: Low-Yielding Assets, High-Yielding Liabilities. *Review of Keynesian Economics* 9 (2): 232–252.

Allen, W., and G. Wood. 2006. Defining and Achieving Financial Stability. *Journal of Financial Stability* 2 (2): 152–172.

Anon. 2018. Accounting and Auditing. *Fsb.org*. https://www.fsb.org/work-of-the-fsb/market-and-institutional-resilience/accounting-and-auditing/.

Arditti, F. D., and H. Levy. 1980. A Model of the Parallel Team Strategy in Product Development. *The American Economic Review* 70 (5).

Arnold, A. G., Ellis, R. B., and Krishnan, V. S. 2018. Toward Effective Use of the Statement of Cash Flows. *Journal of Business and Behavioral Sciences, 30*(2), 46–62.

Arya, A., J. Fellingham, and D. Schroeder. 2000. Estimating Transactions Given Balance Sheets and an Income Statement. *Issues in Accounting Education* 15 (3): 393–411.

Atena, F., and A. Tiron-Tudor. 2019. Gender as a Dimension of Inequality in Accounting Organizations and Developmental HR Strategies. *Administrative Sciences* 10 (1): 1.

Aziz, A., and G. Lawson. 1989. Cash Flow Reporting and Financial Distress Models: Testing of Hypotheses. *Financial Management* 18 (1): 55.

Balakrishnan, K. P., L. Prakash, and L. Ramesh. 2020. Impact of AI Technology in Accounting and Finance. *The International Journal of Analytical and Experimental Modal Analysis* 12 (5): 629–636.

Baldwin, A., C. Brown, and B. Trinkle. 2006. Opportunities for Artificial Intelligence Development in the Accounting Domain: The Case for Auditing. *Intelligent Systems in Accounting, Finance and Management* 14 (3): 77–86.

Bao, Y., b. Ke, B. Li, Y. Yu, and J. Zhang. 2020. Detecting Accounting Fraud in Publicly Traded U.S. Firms Using a Machine Learning Approach. *Journal of Accounting Research* 58 (1): 199–235.

Barbier, E. 1987. The Concept of Sustainable Economic Development. *Environmental Conservation* 14 (2): 101–110.

Barbier, E. 2007. Frontiers and Sustainable Economic Development. *Environmental and Resource Economics* 37 (1): 271–295.

Bărbuţă-Mişu, N., and M. Madaleno. 2020. Assessment of Bankruptcy Risk of Large Companies: European Countries Evolution Analysis. *Journal of Risk and Financial Management* 13 (3): 58.

Barniv, R., A. Agarwal, and R. Leach. 2002. Predicting Bankruptcy Resolution. *Journal of Business Finance & Accounting* 29 (3&4): 497–520.

Bascand, G. 2019. *Renewing the RBNZ's Approach to Financial Stability*. Reserve Bank of New Zealand. https://www.rbnz.govt.nz/hub/publications/speech/2019/speech2019-06-26

Bauer, K., and H. Jan. 2020. Accounting as a Source of Financial Information on Insolvency in Liquidation Proceedings. *Central European Management Journal* 28 (4): 2–29.

Bertomeu, J. 2020. Machine Learning Improves Accounting: Discussion, Implementation and Research Opportunities. *Review of Accounting Studies* 25 (3): 1135–1155.

Bertomeu, J., E. Cheynel, E. Floyd, and W. Pan. 2020. Using Machine Learning to Detect Misstatements. *Review of Accounting Studies* 26 (2): 468–519.

Bezemer, D. 2010. Understanding Financial Crisis through Accounting Models. *Accounting, Organizations and Society* 35 (7): 676–688.

Bischof, J., C. Laux, and C. Leuz. 2021. Accounting for Financial Stability: Bank Disclosure and Loss Recognition in the Financial Crisis. *Journal of Financial Economics* 141 (3).

BMW. 2020. *Financial Statements of BMW AG*. BMW Group.

Borden, T., A. Akhtar, J. Hadden, and D. Bose. 2020. The Coronavirus Outbreak Has Triggered Unprecedented Mass Layoffs and Furloughs. Here Are the Major Companies that Have Announced They Are Downsizing Their Workforces. *Business Insider*. https://www.businessinsider.com/coronavirus-layoffs-furloughs-hospitality-service-travel-unemployment-2020.

Bragg, S. 2014. *Project Accounting*. United States of America: CPE.

Brundtland, G. 1987. Report of the World Commission on Environment and Development: Our Common Future. United Nations General Assembly document A/42/427.

Burchell, S., C. Clubb, A. Hopwood, J. Hughes, and J. Nahapiet. 1980. The Roles of Accounting in Organizations and Society. *Accounting, Organizations and Society* 5 (1): 5–27.

Bureau of the Fiscal Service. Financial Report of the United States Government – Financial Statements of the United States Government for the Fiscal Years Ended September 30, 2020, and 2019. *Fiscal.treasury.gov*. https://www.fiscal.treasury.gov/reports-statements/financial-report/balance-sheets.html.

Caruana, J., I. Brusca, E. Caperchione, S. Cohen, and F. Manes Rossi. 2019. Exploring the Relevance of Accounting Frameworks in the Pursuit of Financial Sustainability of Public Sector Entities: A Holistic Approach. *Financial Sustainability of Public Sector Entities*: 1–18.

Centre for Inclusive Growth (IPC-IG), Brasilia

Cerullo, M. J., and V. Cerullo. 1999. Using Neural Networks to Predict Financial Reporting Fraud: Part 1. *Computer Fraud & Security* 1999 (5): 14–17.

Cescon, F., A. Costantini, and L. Grassetti. 2018. Strategic Choices and Strategic Management Accounting in Large Manufacturing Firms. *Journal of Management and Governance* 23 (3): 605–636.

CGMA. 2013. *Essential Tools for Management Accountants*. CGMA.

CGMA. 2018. *Creating a Sustainable Future*. CGMA.

Chartered Professional Accountants Canada (CPA). 2016. *The 2030 Agenda for Sustainable Development A Snapshot of the Accountancy Profession's Contribution*. Canada: CPA.

Cho, S., M. Vasarhelyi, T. Sun, and C. Zhang. 2020. Learning from Machine Learning in Accounting and Assurance. *Journal of Emerging Technologies in Accounting* 17 (1): 1–10.

Christauskas, C., and R. Miseviciene. 2012. Cloud–Computing Based Accounting for Small to Medium Sized Business. *Engineering Economics* 23 (1): 14–21.

Chychyla, R., A. Leone, and M. Minutti-Meza. 2019. Complexity of Financial Reporting Standards and Accounting Expertise. *Journal of Accounting and Economics* 67 (1): 226–253.

Cicchiello, A., A. Fellegara, A. Kazemikhasragh, and S. Monferrà. 2021. Gender Diversity on Corporate Boards: How Asian and African Women Contribute on Sustainability Reporting Activity. *Gender in Management: An International Journal* 36 (7): 801–820.

Çolak, M. 2021. A New Multivariate Approach for Assessing Corporate Financial Risk Using Balance Sheets. *Borsa Istanbul Review* 21 (3): 239–255.

Corporate Finance Institute. n.d. *Statement of Cash Flows*. [online] Available at: https://corporatefinanceinstitute.com/resources/knowledge/accounting/statement-of-cash-flows/ [Accessed 28 November 2021].

Daniel, F. 2003. *Institutional Arrangements that Promote Financial Stability*. Technical Report No. 95. Essays on Financial Stability: Bank of Canada.

Danziger, S. 2013. Evaluating the Effects of the Great Recession. *The ANNALS of the American Academy of Political and Social Science* 650 (1): 6–24.

Davila, A., and M. Wouters. 2004. Designing Cost-Competitive Technology Products through Cost Management. *Accounting Horizons* 18 (1): 13–26.

Davila, T., and M. Wouters. 2006. Management Accounting in the Manufacturing Sector: Managing Costs at the Design and Production Stages. In *Handbooks of Management Accounting Research*, C. Chapman, A. Hopwood and M. Shields ed. Elsevier Ltd.

De Walque, G., O. Pierrard, and A. Rouabah. 2010. Financial (In)Stability, Supervision and Liquidity Injections: A Dynamic General Equilibrium Approach. *The Economic Journal* 120 (549): 1234–1261.

Del Pozo-Antúnez, J., H. Molina-Sánchez, A. Ariza-Montes, and F. Fernández-Navarro. 2021. Promoting Work Engagement in the Accounting Profession: A Machine Learning Approach. *Social Indicators Research* 157 (2): 653–670.

Deloitte. 2019. *Women in the Boardroom A Global Perspective. Developing Countries: Approaches and Issues*, Working Paper, No. 94, International Policy

Dhieb, N., H. Ghazzai, H. Besbes, and Y. Massoud. 2020. A Secure AI-Driven Architecture for Automated Insurance Systems: Fraud Detection and Risk Measurement. *IEEE Access* 8: 58546–58558.

Elliott, B., and Elliott, J., 2009. *Financial Accounting and Reporting*. 13th ed. Englewood Cliffs, New Jersey: Prentice Hall.

Financial Stability Board. 2021. *Accounting and Auditing*. Financial Stability Board. https://www.fsb.org/work-of-the-fsb/market-and-institutional-resilience/accounting-and-auditing/

Foundation Software. 2023. Construction Accounting 101: A Basic Guide for Contractors. *Foundation Software*. https://www.foundationsoft.com/learn/construction-accounting-101/.

Gadanecz, B., and K. Jayaram. 2008. Measures of Financial Stability – A Review. In *Proceedings of the IFC Conference on "Measuring financial innovation and its impact"*. Basel: Bank for International Settlements.

Gai, P. 2005. Financial Stability, Monetary Stability and Public Policy. *Bank of England Quarterly Bulletin*.

Ghasemi, M., V. Shafeiepour, M. Aslani, and E. Barvayeh. 2011. The Impact of Information Technology (IT) on Modern Accounting Systems. *Procedia – Social and Behavioral Sciences* 28: 112–116.

Ghosh, C. 2021. New Era of Accounting System Based on Artificial Intelligence (AI)- Triadic- Entry Accounting. *Account and Financial Management Journal* 06 (11): 2566–2570.

Guo, F., and J. K. Gershenson. 2007. Discovering Relationships between Modularity and Cost. *Journal of Intelligent Manufacturing* 18 (1): 143–157.

Handley, M. 2005. Balance Sheets: Tools to Inform Changes in Practice. *The Permanente Journal* 9 (2): 61–62.

Hart, O. 2000. Different Approaches to Bankruptcy. *National Bureau of Economic Research Working Paper Series* (Working Paper 7921).

Hasanaj, P., and B. Kuqi. 2019. Analysis of Financial Statements. *Humanities and Social Science Research* 2 (2): 17.

Hawkins, J. 2003. *BIS Papers Fiscal Issues and Central Banking in Emerging Economies* (20).

Hayes, A. 2021. Using the Variance Equation. *Investopedia.* https://www.investopedia.com/terms/v/variance.asp.

Hertenstein, J., and M. Platt. 1998. Why Product Development Teams need Management Accountants. *Management Accounting* 79 (10): 50–55.

Hertenstein, J., and M. Platt. 2000. Performance Measures and Management Control in New Product Development. *Accounting Horizons* 14 (3): 303–323.

Hillegeist, S., E. Keating, D. Cram, and K. Lundstedt. 2004. Assessing the Probability of Bankruptcy. *Review of Accounting Studies* 9 (1): 5–34.

Hoogervorst, H., and M. Prada. 2015. Working in the Public Interest: The IFRS Foundation and the IASB. *IFRS.*

Hsu, D., 2007. Case Studies in Financial Accounting Software. *E-Leader Prague.*

Husin, M., and M. Ibrahim. 2014. The Role of Accounting Services and Impact on Small Medium Enterprises (SMEs) Performance in Manufacturing Sector from East Coast Region of Malaysia: A Conceptual Paper. *Procedia – Social and Behavioral Sciences* 115: 54–67.

International Federation of Accountants (IFAC). 2011. *Sustainability Framework 2.0.* USA: IFAC.

International Federation of Accountants (IFAC). 2020. New Research Links the Accountancy Profession to Economic Development. *IFAC.* https://www.ifac.org/news-events/2020-11/new-research-links-accountancy-profession-economic-development.

International Institute for Sustainable Development. Sustainable Development. *International Institute for Sustainable Development.* https://www.iisd.org/about-iisd/sustainable-development.

International Standards of Accounting and Reporting. *Financial Inclusion – International Standards of Accounting and Reporting.* Isar.unctad.org. Retrieved 26 February 2022, from https://isar.unctad.org/financial-inclusion/.

Jansen, K. 2001. Thailand, Financial Crisis and Monetary Policy. *Journal of the Asia Pacific Economy* 6 (1): 124–152.

Jauhiainen, T. 2021. How Should Corporate Governance Structures and Mechanisms Be Created to Comprise AI-Based Accounting and Its Auditing in the Future?. Masters, Hanken School of Economics.

Júdice, P., and Q. Zhu. 2021. Bank Balance Sheet Risk Allocation. *Journal of Banking & Finance* 133: 106257.

Karagiorgos, A., A. Gaitanaki, O. Ignatiou, and A. Terzidou. 2020. Role and Contribution of Administrative Accounting to Small and Very Small Businesses. *Journal of Accounting and Taxation* 12 (2): 75–84.

Kearney III, W. 2018. *Case Studies of Financial Accounting Theories and Techniques*. Honours, University of Mississippi.

Klarin, T. 2018. The Concept of Sustainable Development: From its Beginning to the Contemporary Issues. *Zagreb International Review of Economics and Business* 21 (1): 67–94.

Klovienė, L., and Gimzauskiene, E., 2015. The Effect of Information Technology on Accounting System's Conformity with Business Environment: A Case Study in Banking Sector Company. *Procedia Economics and Finance* 32: 1707–1712.

Kornberger, M., D. Pflueger, and J. Mouritsen. 2017. Evaluative infrastructures: Accounting for platform organization. *Accounting, Organizations and Society* 60: 79–95.

Koskivaara, E. 2004. Artificial Neural Networks in Analytical Review Procedures. *Managerial Auditing Journal* 19 (2): 191–223.

KPMG. 2022. *Accounting for Bankruptcies – Handbook*. KPMG. https://frv.kpmg.us/reference-library/2022/handbook-accounting-bankruptcies.html

Kruglinski, J. 2009. Many Doors to Opportunity. *Pennsylvania CPA Journal* 79 (4): 38.

Kulikova, L., A. Garyntsev, and G. Gafieva. 2015. The Balance Sheet as Information Model. *Procedia Economics and Finance* 24: 339–343

Kuttner, M., S. Mayr, C. Mitter, and C. Duller. 2022. Impact of Accounting on Reorganization Success: Empirical Evidence from Bankrupt SMEs. *Journal of Accounting & Organizational Change*.

Lamberton, G., 2000. Accounting for Sustainable Development—A Case Study of City Farm. *Critical Perspectives on Accounting*, 11(5), pp. 583–605.

Laudon, K. and Laudon, J. 2006. *Management Information Systems: Managing the Digital Firm*, 9th ed. Prentice Hall. ISBN-10:0131538411, ISBN-13: 978-0131538412..

Laux, C. 2012. Financial Instruments, Financial Reporting, and Financial Stability. *Accounting and Business Research* 42 (3): 239–260.

Lee, C., and F. Tajudeen. 2020. Usage and Impact of Artificial Intelligence on Accounting: 213 Evidence from Malaysian Organisations. *Asian Journal of Business and Accounting* 13 (1): 213–240.

Li, L., and R. Faff. 2019. Predicting Corporate Bankruptcy: What Matters?. *International Review of Economics & Finance* 62: 1–19.

Li, Y., and Y. Wang. 2018. Machine Learning Methods of Bankruptcy Prediction Using Accounting Ratios. *Open Journal of Business and Management* 06 (01): 1–20.

Liang, P., and G. Zhang. 2018. On the Social Value of Accounting Objectivity in Financial Stability. *The Accounting Review* 94 (1): 229–248.

Lim, F. 2013. Impact of Information Technology on Accounting Systems. *Asia-pacific Journal of Multimedia Services Convergent with Art, Humanities, and Sociology* 3 (2): 93–196.

Lin, J., M. Hwang, and J. Becker. 2003. A Fuzzy Neural Network for Assessing the Risk of Fraudulent Financial Reporting. *Managerial Auditing Journal* 18 (8): 657–665.

Livshits, I., J. MacGee, and M. Tertilt. 2010. Accounting for the Rise in Consumer Bankruptcies. *American Economic Journal: Macroeconomics* 2 (2): 165–193.

Mackenzie, G., and P. Stella. 1996. *Quasi-Fiscal Operations of Public Financial Institutions*. Washington, DC: International Monetary Fund.

Makarenko, I., and A. Plastun. 2017. The Role of Accounting in Sustainable Development. *Accounting and Financial Control* 1 (2): 4–12.

Makrelov, K., C. Arndt, R. Davies, and L. Harris. 2020. Balance Sheet Changes and the Impact of Financial Sector Risk-Taking on Fiscal Multipliers. *Economic Modelling* 87: 322–343.

Malik, A., A. Md Isa, M. Jais, A. Ur Rehman, and M. Ali Khan. 2021. Financial Stability of Asian Nations: Governance Quality and Financial Inclusion. *Borsa Istanbul Review*.

Marshall, T., and S. Lambert. 2018. Cloud-Based Intelligent Accounting Applications: Accounting Task Automation Using IBM Watson Cognitive Computing. *Journal of Emerging Technologies in Accounting* 15 (1): 199–215.

McCulloch, H. 2018. World War I, Gold, and the Great Depression - Alt-M. *Alt-M*. https://www.alt-m.org/2018/08/23/world-war-i-gold-and-the-great-recession/.

Mellemvik, F., N. Monsen, and O. Olson. 1988. Functions of Accounting—A Discussion. *Scandinavian Journal of Management* 4 (3–4): 101–119.

Melnyk, N., D. Trachova, O. Kolesnikova, O. Demchuk, and N. Golub. 2020. Accounting Trends in the Modern World. *Independent Journal of Management & Production* 11 (9): 2403–2416.

Moll, J., and O. Yigitbasioglu. 2019. The Role of Internet-Related Technologies in Shaping the Work of Accountants: New Directions for Accounting Research. *The British Accounting Review* 51 (6): 100833.

Moudud-Ul-Huq, S. 2014. The Role of Artificial Intelligence in the Development of Accounting Systems: A Review. *IUP Journal of Accounting Research & Audit Practice* 13 (2): 7–19.

Naidu, G. P. and Govinda, K. 2018, January. Bankruptcy Prediction Using Neural Networks. In *2018 2nd International Conference on Inventive Systems and Control (ICISC)*, pp. 248–251. IEEE.

Nechita, E. 2019. Analysis of the Relationship between Accounting and Sustainable Development. The Role of Accounting and Accounting Profession on Sustainable Development. *Audit Financiar* 17 (155): 520–536.

Newton, G. 2010. *Bankruptcy and Insolvency Accounting*. Hoboken, N.J.: John Wiley & Sons.

Ng, C., and J. Alarcon. 2020. *Artificial Intelligence in Accounting*. 1st ed. Routledge.

Nixon, B., J. Burns, and M. Jazayeri. 2011. *The Role of Management Accounting in New Product Design and Development Decisions*. CIMA Research Executive Summary Series. London: CIMA.

Pak Wing Fong, T., A. Kin Wan Sze, and E. Ho Cheung Ho. 2022. Do Long-Term Institutional Investors Contribute to Financial Stability? – Evidence from Equity Investment in Hong Kong and International Markets. *Journal of International Financial Markets, Institutions and Money*: 101521.

Parthasarathy, K. 2020. *Enhancing Accounting Education: Critical Thinking in Accounting Curricula in the Era of Ai*.

Pearce, D., and E. Barbier. 2000. *Blueprint for a Sustainable Economy*. London: Earthscan Publications Ltd.

Petkov, R. 2019. Artificial Intelligence (AI) and the Accounting Function—A Revisit and a New Perspective for Developing Framework. *Journal of Emerging Technologies in Accounting* 17 (1): 99–105.

Pippin, S., J. Weber, J. Wong, and J. Bergner. 2016. The Inclusion of Sustainability in the Accounting Curriculum. *The CPA Journal* 86 (6): 44.

Prasanna, C. 2005. *Fundamentals of Financial Management*. Tata McGraw-Hill, ISBN 0070599610, 9780070599611.

PricewaterhouseCoopers PwC. 2021. *Bankruptcies and Liquidations*. PwC.

Rabino, S., and A. Wright. 1993. Accelerated Product Introductions and Emerging Managerial Accounting Perspectives: Implications for Marketing Managers in the Technology Sector. *Journal of Product Innovation Management* 10 (2): 126–135.

Reserve Bank of New Zealand. https://www.rbnz.govt.nz/financial-stability. https://www.rbnz.govt.nz/financial-stability.

Scapens, R., and M. Jazayeri. 2003. ERP Systems and Management Accounting Change: Opportunities or Impacts? A Research Note. *European Accounting Review* 12 (1): 201–233.

Schinasi, G. 2004. Defining Financial Stability. *IMF Working Papers* 04 (187): 1.

Schmidt, J. 2023. *Statement of Cash Flows, Corporate Finance Institute*. Available at: https://corporatefinanceinstitute.com/resources/accounting/statement-of-cash-flows/ [Accessed on November 28, 2021].

Schwarz, C., P. Karakitsos, N. Merriman, and W. Studener. 2015. Why Accounting Matters: A Central Bank Perspective. *Accounting, Economics and Law – A Convivium* 5 (1): 1–42.

Sekkel, R. 2015. Balance Sheets of Financial Intermediaries: Do They Forecast Economic Activity? *International Journal of Forecasting* 31 (2): 263–275.

Seth, A., and A. Ragab. 2012. Macroeconomic Vulnerability in Developing Countries: Approaches and Issues. *International Policy Centre for Inclusive Growth* (Working Paper/94).

Setyawati, I. 2018. The Role of Accounting and Risk Management in Supply Chain Management: A Lesson Learnt from the Indonesian Meat Industry. *International Journal of Supply Chain Management* 7 (5): 428–436.

Siddique, Z., D. W. Rosen, and N. Wang. 1998. On the Applicability of Product Variety Design Concepts to Automotive Platform Commonality. *Volume 3: 10th International Conference on Design Theory and Methodology* 3(10): 1–11.

Sorina-Geanina, S., P. Adriana, and C. Ana-Maria. 2018. The Role of The Accounting Profession in Achieving the Objectives of Sustainable Development. *Annals of the "Constantin Brâncuşi" University of Târgu Jiu, Economy Series* (3): 117–122.

Stancheva-Todorova, E. P. 2018. How Artificial Intelligence is Challenging Accounting Profession. *Journal of International Scientific Publications* 12: 126–141.

Stiglitz, J. 2010. Interpreting the Causes of the Great Recession of 2008. *Financial System and Macroeconomic Resilience: Revisited. Bank for International Settlements.*

Stone, R. 1951. Functions and Criteria of a System of Social Accounting. *Review of Income and Wealth* 1 (1): 1–74.

Summers, B., P. Allsopp, and J. Veale. 2009. The Evolution of Real-Time Gross Settlement: Access, Liquidity and Credit, and Pricing. *Economics* 1 (1): 1–53

Tamplin, T. 2021. Current Cash Debt Coverage Ratio. *Finance Strategists*. https://learn.financestrategists.com/explanation/accounting-ratios/current-cash-debt-coverage-ratio/

UNESCO. 2023. *Education for Sustainable Development, UNESCO.org*. Available at: https://www.unesco.org/en/education-sustainable-development (Accessed: 02 June 2023).

United Nations. 2015. *Resolution Adopted by the General Assembly on 25 September 2015*. Agenda items 15 and 116. United Nation.

Viaene, S., R. Derrig, B. Baesens, and G. Dedene. 2002. A Comparison of State-of-the-Art Classification Techniques for Expert Automobile Insurance Claim Fraud Detection. *Journal of Risk & Insurance* 69 (3): 373–421.

Wang, M. 2017. The Relationship between Firm Characteristics and the Disclosure of Sustainability Reporting. *Sustainability* 9 (4): 624.

Watkins, P., T. Lin, and D. O'Leary. 1992. AI Integration for Enhanced Decision Support. In *Advanced Technologies in Information Systems, University of Southern California*, Vol. 25, pp. 133–133. Southern California: IEEE.

Wu, X. 2021. Research on Accounting Risk Based on AI. *Journal of Physics: Conference Series* 1915: 022052.

Yoon, S. 2020. A Study on the Transformation of Accounting Based on New Technologies: Evidence from Korea. *Sustainability* 12 (20): 8669. https://www.mdpi.com/2071-1050/12/20/8669

Zemankova, A. 2019. Artificial Intelligence in Audit and Accounting: Development, Current Trends, Opportunities and Threats – Literature Review. In *2019 International Conference on Control, Artificial Intelligence, Robotics & Optimization (ICCAIRO)*, pp. 148–154. IEEE.

Zhang, Y., F. Xiong, Y. Xie, X. Fan, and H. Gu. 2020. The Impact of Artificial Intelligence and Blockchain on the Accounting Profession. *IEEE Access* 8: 110461–110477.

Appendix

Lists

Figures

Tables

www.ingramcontent.com/pod-product-compliance
Ingram Content Group UK Ltd.
Pitfield, Milton Keynes, MK11 3LW, UK
UKHW020153290926
15471UKWH00005B/842

9 783631 894255